MICKEY ROGERS
JOANNE TAYLORE-KNOWLES
STEVE TAYLORE-KNOWLES

SPEAK YOUR MIND

STUDENT'S BOOK
+ access to Student's App and Digital Workbook

3

macmillan education

	Outcomes	Vocabulary	Grammar	Speaking
Unit 1 Incredible Lives pp. 7–15	• Discuss possible devices that could help disabled people • Ask and answer questions about your achievements • Describe survival situations	• Technology and disability • Noun suffixes • Character adjectives	• Stative and dynamic verbs • Expressing ability Grammar Reference pp 142–143	• Describe a device to help disabled people • Talk about personal achievements • Talk about survival situation
	Language and Life—Decision Making: Manage a Survival Situation			
Unit 2 The Animal Connection pp. 17–25	• Talk about which are the most intelligent animals • Discuss possible jobs with animals • Make arguments for and against people owning exotic pets	• Animal intelligence • Careers with animals • Animals	• Tag questions • Articles Grammar Reference pp 143–144	• Discuss which animals are most intelligent • Talk about working with animals • Argue for and against keeping wild animals
	Language and Life—Problem Solving: Find Solutions to Help Stray Animals			
Unit 3 Think About It pp. 27–35	• Ask and answer questions about confirmation bias • Discuss the importance of expert systems in your future career • Compare different creative uses for things	• Confirmation bias • Word formation • Phrasal verbs	• Future time clauses (*after, as soon as, before, until, when*) • Present perfect progressive Grammar Reference pp 145–146	• Discuss confirmation bias • Talk about expert systems • Compare different objects
	Language and Life—Design Thinking: Design an App			
Unit 4 Beyond Words pp. 37–45	• Present a subject you know • Ask questions and assess someone's body language • Decide on the best means of communication for different situations	• Communication • Ways to communicate • Emojis	• Infinitives with *to* • Separable and non-separable phrasal verbs Grammar Reference pp 146–147	• Give a presentation • Make statements about yourself • Discuss ways to communicate
	Language and Life—Reason Effectively: Discuss Ideas to Improve Communication Problems			
Unit 5 One Planet pp. 47–55	• Discuss global warming problems • Talk about solutions • Brainstorm products	• Climate change • Taking action • Materials and products	• Review of conditionals • Present and future hopes and wishes Grammar Reference pp 148–149	• Discuss global warming • Discuss environmental solutions • Discuss if measures are practical
	Language and Life—Global Competence: Explain and Discuss Ideas about Environmental Issues			
Unit 6 Moments in Time pp. 57–65	• Compare different generational use of technology • Share your opinions about inventions • Brainstorm quiz questions about people in history	• Change • *–ed* and *–ing* adjectives • Adjective suffixes	• Past perfect • Defining relative clauses Grammar Reference pp 149–150	• Compare lists • Discuss an opinion poll • Create a quiz
	Language and Life—Decision Making: Choose a New UNESCO Site			

Confident Communicator	Pronunciation	Listening/Reading	Thinking Skills	Writing
Start Talking • Start a discussion *Repair It* • Express lack of understanding *Keep Talking* • Justify choices	• Word stress with *–ity*	Read an article about technology and disability • Skill—Predict information Listen to part of a lecture about amazing abilities • Skill—Recognize signposts Listen to a podcast about Juliane Koepcke • Skill—Listen for specific information	• Apply • Evaluate • Analyze	Write a blog post about a survival situation
Unit Review p. 16 **Study Skills**—Effective Time Management				
Keep Talking • Invite agreement *Start Talking* • Hypotheticals *Keep Talking* • Disagree politely	• *The*	Read a blog post about animal intelligence • Skill—Understand examples Listen to a careers talk • Skill—Use key information to predict content Listen to a zoo's presentation • Skill—Listen for key words	• Recall • Analyze • Evaluate	Write an opinion post
Unit Review p. 26 **Follow a Pro**—A Wildlife Photographer ▶ Marine Biologist				
Keep Talking • Give yourself time to think *Start Talking* • Start talking *Keep Talking* • Further suggestions	• say, says, said	Read an article about confirmation bias • Skill—Identify the topic Listen to a radio call-in show about AI • Skill—Listen for attitude Listen to a talk about being creative • Skill—Listen for main ideas	• Analyze • Evaluate • Apply	Write an informal email about being productive
Unit Review p. 36 **Study Skills**—Making a Presentation or Giving a Talk				
Keep Talking • Speak to a group *Keep Talking* • Provide more information *Keep Talking* • Make meaning clearer	• Electronic communication	Read an article about communication • Skill—Read for gist Listen to a podcast • Skill—Listen for specific information Listen to a lecture about communication technology • Skill—Listen for the order of events	• Evaluate • Apply • Predict	Write an informal text message as a formal email
Unit Review p. 46 **Follow a Pro**—A PR Professional ▶ Translator/Interpreter				
Start Talking • Speak for a group *Keep Talking* • Talk about problems and solutions *Keep Talking* • Comment on ideas	• Word stress in verb phrases	Read an online article about climate change • Skill— Identify explanations, definitions, and examples Listen to a radio show about environmental problems • Skill—Listen for main ideas Listen to a class discussion about environmental solutions • Skill—Listen for details	• Summarize • Analyze • Categorize	Write an essay about environmental projects
Unit Review p. 56 **Study Skills**—Improving Reading Speed				
Keep Talking • Circumlocution *Keep Talking* • Interrupting politely *Keep Talking* • Express interest and surprise	• Stress in multisyllable adjectives	Read an article about technological changes • Skill—Scan Listen to some interviews about inventions • Skill—Listen for supporting details Listen to a podcast about a famous person • Skill—Listen for numerical information	• Predict • Evaluate • Question	Write a short biographical essay
Unit Review p. 66 **Follow a Pro**—An Archeologist ▶ Mechanical Engineer				

	Outcomes	Vocabulary	Grammar	Speaking
Unit 7 Looking Back pp. 67–75	• Talk about things that a business should have done differently • Discuss things you should not have bought • Recall events you regret	• Phrasal verbs • *spend, lose, waste* • Collocations	• *Should/shouldn't have* • Past perfect for wishes about the past Grammar Reference pp 151–152	• Talk about what people should have done differently • Talk about things you regret buying • Tell an anecdote
	Language and Life—Interpersonal Communication: Plan and Give a Presentation about a Product			
Unit 8 A New Home? pp. 77–85	• Talk about hypothetical events in history • Role play an interview with an astronaut • Discuss your opinions of space exploration	• Extinction of the dinosaurs • Space • Space program inventions	• Third conditional • Indirect questions Grammar Reference pp 152–153	• Speculate about alternative histories • Role-play an interview • Discuss space exploration
	Language and Life—Reason Effectively: Select a Space Team			
Unit 9 The World of News pp. 87–95	• Give your opinions on fake news, journalists and citizen journalists • Compare real and fake news stories • Role-play a job interview for a news career	• News • News stories • News careers	• *So, such, too, enough* • Modals of deduction Grammar Reference pp 154–155	• Discuss news now • Discuss how you knew a news story was true or fake • Role-play a job interview
	Language and Life—Problem Solving: Discuss Ideas to Improve Newspaper Sales			
Unit 10 Got It? pp. 97–105	• Talk about your talents and abilities • Ask and answer questions for a talent show audition • Share advice on how to succeed in the music industry	• Talents and abilities • Phrasal verbs • Idioms and sayings connected to success	• Reported speech: statements • Reported speech: questions Grammar Reference pp 155–156	• Talk about something someone can do well • Talk about talent show contestants • Discuss the usefulness of advice
	Language and Life—Communication: Hold a Talent Contest			
Unit 11 Money in the Bank pp. 107–116	• Discuss who you would employ if you were a millionaire • Share ideas about what to do with a fortune • Compare your budget with that of a partner	• Money • Money verbs and nouns • Paying for things	• Causatives with *have, get* and *make* • Verbs with gerund, infinitive or both Grammar Reference pp 156–158	• Discuss jobs to do yourself • Talk about how to use a lot of money • Talk about monthly budgets
	Language and Life—Collaborate: Manage a Budget			
Unit 12 Inside Advertising pp. 117–126	• Discuss the advertising of energy drinks • Talk about ads that you like and dislike • Debate the effects of advertising	• From the reading Advertising • Advertising campaigns • Discourse markers	• Passive voice: other tenses • Comparative and superlative adverbs Grammar Reference pp 158–159	• Discuss whether to ban advertisements • Talk about improving ad campaigns • Debate the effects of images in advertising
	Language and Life—Media Literacy: Make a TV Ad			

Confident Communicator	Pronunciation	Listening/Reading	Thinking Skills	Writing
Start Talking • Tell an anecdote *Keep Talking* • Give reasons *Start Talking* • Set the scene	• /s/ and /z/	Read an online article about famous mistakes • Skill—Synthesize Listen to a radio interview about regret • Skill—Listen for reasons Listen to a talk about types of regret • Skill—Listen for main ideas	• Evaluate • Analyze • Apply	Write a blog post about regrets
Unit Review p. 76 **Study Skills**—Structuring Your Writing				
Keep Talking • Express probability *Keep Talking* • Ask polite questions *Keep Talking* • Clarify reasons for opinions	• Consonant clusters with /s/	Read an article about the dinosaurs • Skill—Predict Listen to an interview about life in space • Skill—Listen for specific information Listen to a panel discussion about space • Skill—Listen for main ideas	• Analyze • Question • Recall	Write a blog post about space exploration
Unit Review p. 86 **Follow a Pro**—An Astrobiologist ▶ Astronomer				
Keep Talking • Ask for opinions *Repair It* • Interrupt politely *Keep Talking* • Interview techniques	• /ə/ versus /r/	Read texts about news • Skill—Identifying text types Listen to a lecture about fake news • Skill—Listen for information order Listen to an interview about being a foreign correspondent • Skill—Listen for opinions	• Analyze • Apply • Deduce	Write about a job
Unit Review p. 96 **Study Skills**—Making Notes				
Keep Talking • Your achievements *Keep Talking* • Talk in front of a group *Keep Talking* • Use idioms carefully	• Stress in phrasal verbs	Read a text about great artists • Skill—Recognize fact and opinion Listen to excerpts from a TV talent show • Skill—Identify attitude Listen to a radio call-in show about the music industry • Skill—Listen to take notes	• Question • Analyze • Evaluate	Write an informal email
Unit Review p. 106 **Follow a Pro**—A Talent Scout ▶ Musician				
Start Talking • Talk about imagined future situations *Start Talking* • Collaborate on creative ideas *Keep Talking* • Talk or avoid talking about money	• /tʃ/ versus /ʃ/	Read a job ad, article and business profile about the gig economy • Skill—Read for the main idea Listen to an interview about charity • Skill—Listen for specific information Listen to a radio show about managing money • Skill—Listen for the main idea	• Question • Apply • Recall	Write an email listing key points
Unit Review p. 116 **Study Skills**—Personal Development				
Keep Talking • Take turns in a discussion *Repair It* • Getting back on track *Keep Talking* • Paraphrase	• Filler sounds and words	Read an article about advertising • Skill—Identify missing sentences Listen to an ad • Skill—Listen for inference Listen to an interview about advertising • Skill—Recognize discourse markers	• Evaluate • Symbolize • Induce	Write a 'for' and 'against' essay about retouching images
Unit Review p. 126 **Follow a Pro**—A Digital Copywriter ▶ Video Editor				

Grammar Quiz: What Do You Already Know?

A Complete the paragraph with the simple past, past progressive, or present perfect form of the verbs in parentheses.

Colombian teen Yadis Xiomara Chocó Mina has a clear goal: to help others. She **1** ______________ (work) to improve the lives of young girls since she was nine years old. She **2** ______________ (work) with a group called Plan International Colombia when she first **3** ______________ (start) to mentor young girls in her community. Since then, she **4** ______________ (not stop). A few years ago, while she **5** ______________ (visit) Spain, she **6** ______________ (become) mayor of Madrid for a day as part of International Day of the Girl. Yadis has big plans: someday she wants to be Colombia's minister of education.

B Complete the email message with the correct quantifiers from the box.

a few	a little	a lot of	any	enough	too much

New Message

Hi Anna,

I'm home preparing for Ricardo's graduation party. I've finished most of the preparations, but I could use **1** ______________ help. There are going to be **2** ______________ people here—I think about 45 of his friends are coming. We have 40 chairs, but it's not **3** ______________. Can you bring **4** ______________ chairs—maybe three or four? I know we have **5** ______________ food, so there will be leftovers for the guests to take home. So, please don't bring **6** ______________ more food. There is nowhere to put it!

See you soon,
Bev

C Choose the correct option.

1 **Can** / **Would** you like to join us?
2 I'm sure Oscar **will** / **may** be here.
3 **Will** / **May** I put my jacket here?
4 **Could** / **May** you please take a seat?
5 Lena **might** / **would** be late for the wedding.
6 They probably **won't** / **might not** be there.

D Complete the sentences with the correct form of the verb in parentheses.

1 If you ______________ (eat) a lot of sugar, you gain weight.
2 If I (have) more time, I would exercise more.
3 You will enjoy these brain puzzles if you ______________ (try) them.
4 If I ______________ (get) tired at the library, I usually take a short nap.
5 I probably ______________ (not go) to the hospital if I had a bad cold.
6 You ______________ (not feel) better if you don't take this medicine.

E Find one error in each sentence. Then rewrite the sentences correctly.

1 Maggie has belonged to a gym since 15 years.
____

2 Rafael hasn't graduated from high school already.
____

3 A lot cans and plastic are recycled these days.
____

4 People use to buy a lot of music CDs in the 1990s.
____

5 Jae is the more adventurous person in my family.
____

6 Students need to introduce themself in class.
____

Go to the Grammar Review on pages 140–141.

UNIT 1 Incredible Lives

WHAT DO YOU ALREADY KNOW?

1 Think about your family: what characteristics do you share with them and which are unique to you? Write the words.

2 IN PAIRS Share and compare your ideas. If possible, add more words about yourself or your partner.

Shared characteristics

Unique characteristics

VIDEO

DISCUSS & SHARE

3 IN GROUPS Watch the video and answer the question.

BYM What influences a person's character: family values or life experience?

In this unit, you will ...

- discuss possible devices that could help the lives of others, ask and answer questions about your achievements, and describe survival situations.
- use thinking skills: apply, evaluate, and analyze.
- read about technology for an accessible world.
- use strategies to start a discussion, use language to say you do not understand to repair a conversation, and justify reasons in a discussion.
- use decision-making skills to choose items and write a survival list.
- learn skills for effective time management.

LESSON 1 Life-Changing Technology

READING

A READING SKILL—Predict information **Look at the picture. What do you think the article is going to be about?**

B 1.01 **Read the article. Then answer the questions.**

Technology Creating an Accessible World

Through the use of technology, we are changing the world that is accessible to us. People such as Hugh Herr, co-director of the MIT Center for Extreme Bionics, are responsible for these changes. After losing both of his legs in a mountain climbing accident, Hugh Herr designed and developed new bionic legs. These new legs have a number of features that were previously **impossible**. The legs can be made longer or shorter. The feet can change depending on the surface of the mountain. It is even possible to attach different climbing equipment. All of these advances mean that Hugh Herr can **achieve** climbs that no one else has ever been able to do before. The MIT Center for Extreme Bionics is currently working on a digital nervous system which will connect the brain with a computer that can control artificial arms and legs.

Another area in which connections with computers are having a huge effect is communication. Facebook is currently working on a "silent speech" project: computers that can **recognize** what people are thinking so they can type messages with their brain. This system can help people who are **disabled** because of **disease** or injury. It can also help **able-bodied** people who want a faster way to type their ideas. Early tests in similar systems have used a person's thoughts to **select** letters and then write words. However, systems will get much faster. The aim of the silent speech project is for thoughts to be **turned into** text at a speed of 100 words per minute. How would you use technology to access a whole new world?

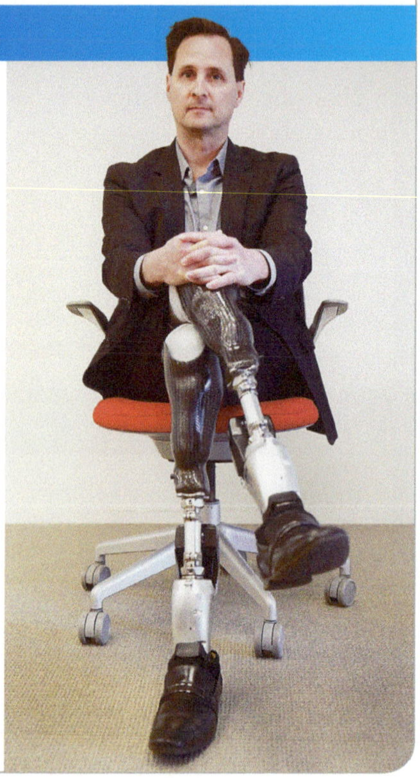

GLOSSARY

artificial (adj): made by people and used instead of something natural
accessible (adj): when a place or object can be easily used by all.

1 What technology did Hugh Herr develop? ______
2 What is special about that technology? ______
3 How else can systems that connect people to computers help us? ______
4 What advantages of these systems are mentioned in the text? ______

______

C THINKING SKILL—Apply **Explain how technology improves your ability to work, travel, socialize, and study.**

VOCABULARY

A **Match the words in bold in READING B with the definitions (1–8).**

1 ______ (phr v): made one thing become another
2 ______ (adj): unable to use part of your body in the way most other people can
3 ______ (adj): not possible
4 ______ (v): chooses
5 ______ (v): know what you are seeing because you have seen it before
6 ______ (adj): able to use your body in the way most other people can
7 ______ (v): be successful, usually after hard work
8 ______ (n): illness

GRAMMAR stative and dynamic verbs

A Complete the sentences from the text in READING A.

1 Through the use of technology, we ______________ the world that is accessible to us.
2 These new legs ______________ a number of features that were previously impossible.
3 Another area in which connections with computers ______________ a huge effect is communication.
4 Computers that can recognize what people ______________ so they can type messages with their brain.

B Read the sentences in A and choose the correct options.

1 Stative verbs, e.g., *know*, *have*, and *like*, describe actions / states.
2 Dynamic verbs, e.g., *write*, *walk*, and *use*, describe actions / states.
3 Stative / Dynamic verbs are not usually used in progressive tenses.
4 Some verbs, e.g., *be*, *have*, and *think*, can be used both ways with the same / a different meaning.

For more practice, go to page 142.

C Check (✓) the correct sentences. Both sentences may be correct.

1 ☐ Do you know how disabled people use technology?
☐ Are you knowing anything about technology and disability?
2 ☐ I'm not understanding how the technology will help people.
☐ I don't understand what you're saying.
3 ☐ What do you think we can do to improve people's lives?
☐ What were you thinking about before this lesson began?
4 ☐ Do you have any problems that technology could solve?
☐ Are you having any problems with what I'm saying?

D IN PAIRS Ask and answer the questions.

1 What careers do you know that involve working with disabled people?
2 Which of those careers do you think would be most suitable for you?

MAKE IT REAL

Some people might use verbs such as *like* and *love* with progressive tenses, e.g., *Are you liking your new apartment? Yes, I'm loving it!* This makes the statement more intense. Remember, though, that some people don't think it's correct.

SPEAKING

A IN PAIRS Decide which of these pieces of technology you think would make the most difference in people's lives. Say why.

- a device that knows what you are thinking about and says the words aloud
- a device that knows what you are looking at and recreates the image on a computer screen

B Think of another device that would help the lives of others. Draw a simple picture or write a short explanation. Tell the class about your device. Use the Confident Communicator box to help you.

CONFIDENT COMMUNICATOR
START TALKING

To start a discussion, use *What do you think about …*
What do you think about a device to help people with reading?

VOCABULARY noun suffixes

A Complete the table with words from the box and nouns formed from the words.

achieve	develop	impossible	responsible
argue	hard	kind	sad
available	ill	possible	

Verb + *–ment*	Adjective + *–ness*	Adjective ending in *–able/–ible* + *–ity*
entertain–entertainment	*happy–happiness*	*able–ability*

B IN PAIRS Ask and answer the questions.

1 What do you think your greatest achievement is?
2 What was the last argument you had? What happened?

LISTENING

A 1.02 You are going to listen to part of a lecture. Look at the pictures and say why you think these two people might be mentioned in the lecture. Listen and check.

Wolfgang Amadeus Mozart (1756–1791)

Daniel Tammet (1979–)

B 1.02 LISTENING SKILL—Recognize signposts Listen again and complete the sentences.

1 Over the ________________ few lectures, we looked at …
2 To ________________ with, people with perfect pitch can …
3 As you ________________ know, Mozart could play …
4 Moving ________________ to language learning, we all have …

C 1.02 Listen again and complete the notes with the relevant numbers.

1 People with perfect pitch: 1 in ____________
2 Mozart played violin and keyboard, age ____________
3 Mozart wrote symphony, age ____________
4 Daniel Tammet speaks ____________ languages.
5 David Tammet learned Icelandic in ____________ week.

D THINKING SKILL—Evaluate Consider how Daniel Tammet was able to learn Icelandic so quickly.

GRAMMAR expressing ability

A Match the sentences (1–5) with the correct explanations of the language of ability (a–c). You will use some explanations more than once.

1 People with perfect pitch **can** hear a musical note and tell you exactly what it is. ______
2 Mozart **could** play the violin and the keyboard at the age of five. ______
3 And he **managed to** write his first symphony at the age of eight. ______
4 And many of us **have succeeded in** learning one or two foreign languages. ______
5 Some people **are able to** learn languages amazingly quickly. ______

a a general ability in the present
b a general ability in the past
c an ability that has been achieved despite difficulty

For more practice, go to page 142.

B Choose the correct options.

1 Some people … speak more than one language.
a don't succeed in **b** aren't able to **c** don't manage
2 How many languages … now?
a can you speak **b** could you speak **c** did you manage to speak
3 After a lot of practice, I finally … to learn how to play the piano.
a succeeded **b** could **c** managed
4 I … ride a bike by the time I was six.
a managed **b** can **c** could
5 Even though my brother has perfect pitch, he … becoming a professional musician.
a couldn't **b** wasn't able to **c** didn't succeed in

C IN PAIRS Tell your partner one thing you managed to do this week.

PRONUNCIATION word stress with *–ity*

A 1.03 Underline the stressed syllable in each word. Listen, check, and practice.

1 able ability
2 available availability

SPEAKING

A Think of a time when you did something that was hard, e.g., passed an exam, learned a new skill, etc. Make notes about any details you remember.

B IN PAIRS Ask and answer the questions about your achievements. Use the Confident Communicator box to help you.

1 Do you have an achievement you are proud of?
2 How did you manage to do it?
3 What did you do in the beginning? How did you feel?
4 What did you manage to do that helped you?
5 How did that help you? What were you able to do then?
6 What happened in the end?

CONFIDENT COMMUNICATOR
REPAIR IT

When you don't understand something, use the following phrases to repair the conversation:
Sorry, what was that?
I'm sorry—I didn't understand what you said.
What do you mean by personal achievements?

VOCABULARY character adjectives

A Find and underline the negative character adjective. Use a dictionary if necessary.

brave	confident	curious	independent	reliable
calm	creative	generous	selfish	

MAKE IT YOURS

Do these adjectives describe you? What other words could you use to describe your character?

B Write an adjective from the box for each description.

1 Danielle never thinks about other people's feelings. ____________
2 Lauren isn't afraid of anything. She likes dangerous situations! ____________
3 Kyle never seems to be nervous. He really believes in himself. ____________
4 Juan Carlos will happily give you money if you need some. ____________
5 Madison always wants to know more about things and asks lots of questions. ____________
6 Joshua doesn't like asking for help and wants to do things himself. ____________
7 Sophie never gets angry or worried. She always seems to be relaxed. ____________
8 Chelsea always does what she says she will. She won't disappoint you. ____________

LISTENING

A Look at B. Before you listen, predict what kind of information you need to write.

B 1.04 LISTENING SKILL—Listen for specific information
Listen to a podcast. Then complete the notes with a number, word, or short phrase.

Juliane Koepcke

1 Born: ____________
2 Crash happened when she was: ____________
3 Height of plane: ____________
4 Saved by: ____________
5 Food: ____________
6 In rain forest for: ____________
7 Later, became: ____________
8 *When I Fell From the Sky* published in: ____________

C 1.04 THINKING SKILL—Analyze Listen again and explain why you think Juliane followed a stream.

WRITING a blog post

A Read the blog post and choose *True* or *False*.

AN AMAZING STORY

Hi, guys! I want to share with you an amazing story of survival. Some of you might know about it already. In 2018, 12 teenagers and their football coach went into caves in Thailand. It started to rain and they couldn't get out because of the water. They were in there for nine days without any food or light. They drank water from the cave walls! Divers managed to find them after a long search, but they still had a problem. The water made it very hard to get the boys out, and most of them couldn't swim. And it was the start of the rainy season, so they didn't have a lot of time. Finally, the divers succeeded in getting all the boys out, but it wasn't easy.

I hate the idea of being stuck in a dark cave! I'd be very scared. You need to be calm and independent to survive a situation like that. I think the boys were really brave, and so were the divers who rescued them. They had to be creative to find a solution to the problem, but they did it. If you are curious, search online and read the whole story.

The writer …

1	speaks directly to the readers to create a friendly style.	True / False
2	gives his or her personal reaction and then describes what happened.	True / False
3	explains what problems different people faced.	True / False
4	imagines himself or herself in the survival situation.	True / False
5	gives his or her opinion of the people in the situation.	True / False
6	tells readers to write their own blog posts.	True / False

B Choose the correct spelling.

1 **a** surviveal **b** survival
2 **a** achievement **b** achievment
3 **a** possibileity **b** possibility
4 **a** amazement **b** amazment
5 **a** amazeing **b** amazing

C Make notes about a story of survival. You can use the story in LISTENING B, the story in WRITING A, or another story of survival you know about.

1 When did this happen? ______
2 Who was involved? ______
3 What happened first? ______
4 Then what happened? ______
5 What happened in the end? ______
6 What's your reaction? ______
7 What do you think of the people involved? ______

D Write a blog post about a story of survival.

SPEAKING

A Choose one of these survival situations. Make notes.

a hurricane

an earthquake

a flood

How I would feel:

______

______

What I would do:

______

______

B IN PAIRS **Tell your partner about the survival situation you have chosen. Then ask and answer the questions. Use the Confident Communicator box to help you.**

1 What personal qualities does it take to survive in a hard situation?
2 Do you think you have those personal qualities?

CONFIDENT COMMUNICATOR
KEEP TALKING

To justify reasons in a discussion, it helps to describe your feelings and explain your choices:
In a hurricane / an earthquake / a flood, I would feel nervous and frightened.
I'd hate to be in a hurricane / an earthquake / a flood because it would be very frightening.

Language and Life

Decision Making – Survival Situation

A 1.05 **Read the description. Then answer the questions.**

Surviving in the Desert

It is 9 o'clock in the morning on a warm July day. You and your three colleagues were on a short flight to a conference in Southern California when your plane developed mechanical problems. The plane was forced off course by a few miles. Finally, the mechanical problems got worse, the pilot lost control of the plane, and you all crash-landed in the desert. You and your three colleagues find yourselves quite far from the plane. Although you keep looking, unfortunately it seems that the pilot is missing. You and your colleagues are on your own.

The nearest town, which you saw from the window when you flew over it half an hour ago, is about 30 kilometers away. That is an extremely long walk, and you know that it will be very difficult. None of you can get any signal at all on your cell phones, and without signal, none of the apps work. Daytime temperatures in this area can reach 40°C, and at night, they can fall below 0°C. It is already starting to get very warm, and you know that soon you will be in danger. One of your colleagues remembers reading an article about the desert, and he says it is better to move around during the evening, because it is less hot. He says that between late afternoon and sunset is the best time to move.

In different parts of the desert around you, you see a variety of different things, including a map, an empty lighter, and a few items of clothing. You discuss ideas with your colleagues and as you talk, you realize that you need to come up with a plan if you are going to manage to survive. Suddenly, there is a smell of smoke in the air. You look towards the plane and you see that it is beginning to catch fire. You know that this means that there is not much time to decide what to do because the fuel in the plane's tanks could explode. What do you do?

1 How would you feel in a situation like this? ______

2 What skills do you think you would need in a situation like this? ______

______

3 What are the main problems you and your group face? ______

______

B IN GROUPS **Look at the items you have recovered from the crash. Decide how important each one is to you. Number them from 1 (most important) to 8 (least important). How might you use each item? Make sure everyone in your group agrees.**

☐ lighter

☐ clothes

☐ map of the area

☐ chocolate bars

☐ mirror

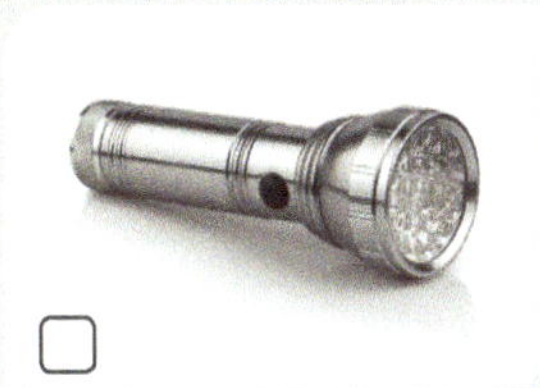

☐ flashlight

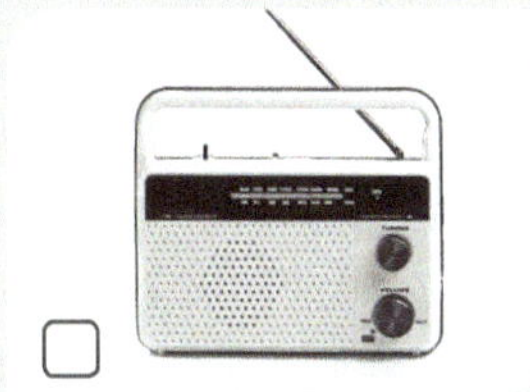

☐ radio

☐ container of water

C Write your top four items from B. Explain to the class what they are and why you have chosen them instead of the other items. Take turns to explain an item so that each person in your group gets to speak. Leave the scores for each item until later.

Top 4 items:

1 ____________________ Score: _____ **3** ____________________ Score: _____

2 ____________________ Score: _____ **4** ____________________ Score: _____

D Complete each sentence with an object from B. Then calculate the scores for your choices in C.

The best survival strategy is to stay where you are. Each pilot files a flight plan before taking off, and so rescuers will follow that when the flight doesn't arrive at your destination. The worst strategy is to set off to try to reach the town. You would be unlikely to get there before becoming exhausted. Therefore, the **1** ____________________ is not very useful: 0 points. The **2** ____________________ is also unlikely to be much help, because you can only receive a signal, not send one: 0 points. The **3** ____________________ will be useful when the temperature drops at night: 5 points. The **4** ____________________ will make a spark and can be used to start a fire: 10 points. The **5** ____________________ will provide you with some energy and are easy to digest: 10 points. The **6** ____________________ is useful for signaling at night: 10 points. The **7** ____________________ is essential for when you get thirsty: 15 points. The **8** ____________________ is also extremely important. You can use it to reflect the sun to signal to any rescuers: 15 points.

E Add the scores of each of your top four items and record your total score.

Total Score	
45–65	Congratulations! You've got great survival skills. You are finally rescued when you are able to signal a plane overhead. Perhaps your adventures have given you a taste for the great outdoors!
35–45	Good job. It wasn't easy, but you succeeded in getting the attention of the rescuers. Think twice before going out into the wilderness again.
Less than 35	Uh-oh. It looks like the desert was the winner this time. You need to think clearly and stay calm if you're going to come out on top next time!

F Discuss the questions.

1. What approach did you use to decide which items to choose?
2. In what other situations might you use this approach?

MAKE IT DIGITAL

Go online and find other stories of survival. How did those people survive and what did they use?

VOCABULARY review

SCORE: / 10

A Complete the sentences with words from the box. There are three words you don't need.

able-bodied brave calm creative curious disabled reliable selfish

1 If you are ________________, you are good at making things or coming up with new ideas.
2 If you are ________________, you are unable to use part of your body.
3 If you are ________________, you don't care about other people.
4 If you are ________________, you have courage and you are not afraid.
5 If you are ________________, you want to know more about a subject.

B Complete the sentences with nouns.

1 Jack took a lot of days off work last year because of ________________ (ill).
2 I like working here because there are opportunities for professional ________________ (develop).
3 Is there any ________________ (possible) that you're wrong about this issue?
4 I had an ________________ (argue) with the janitor because I couldn't get into the building in my wheelchair.
5 My greatest ________________ (achieve) is learning to climb again after my accident.

GRAMMAR review

SCORE: / 10

A Choose the correct words and phrases.

The *Jascon-4*, a small boat, went down in heavy seas near Nigeria on May 26, 2013. No one **1** thought / was thinking that there were any survivors. However, one man, Harrison Odjegba Okene, the ship's cook, managed **2** surviving / to survive. At a depth of 30 meters, it was totally dark and he **3** can't / couldn't see a thing. He **4** knew / was knowing that he needed to find a safe space. Time **5** ran / was running out, but luckily, he succeeded **6** to find / in finding a pocket of air in the engineer's office. It **7** can / is able be dangerous in cold water, but he was able **8** make / to make a small platform from a mattress that kept his upper body out of the water. He was there for three days. Finally, he **9** can / could hear a noise. It was the divers who **10** searched / were searching for the boat. He was rescued, but he said he would never go to sea again!

16–20 correct: You can describe people's characters and form nouns with suffixes.
You can use stative and dynamic verbs and express ability.
0–15 correct: Look again at the Vocabulary and Grammar sections in the unit.

TOTAL SCORE: / 20

WHAT DO YOU KNOW NOW? Look back at page 7 and add the words you know now to the boxes.

STUDY SKILLS — EFFECTIVE TIME MANAGEMENT

Take the quiz about effective time management. Go to Study Skills on page 127 to find the answers. Then learn more about effective time management.

1 Which two of the following are useful time management strategies?
a regularly checking your email **b** prioritizing what is important **c** making a detailed study plan

2 Rewarding yourself at the end of a study session will not help your motivation.
a True **b** False

3 Which of the following is likely to prevent effective time management?
a clarifying how you currently use your time **b** discussing challenges and solutions with other students **c** being surrounded by distractions

4 Effective time management skills are only really useful in academic settings.
a True **b** False

UNIT 2

The Animal Connection

WHAT DO YOU ALREADY KNOW?

1 Think about animals you know and their characteristics. Write the names of the animals.

2 IN PAIRS Share and compare your ideas. Add more words to your list.

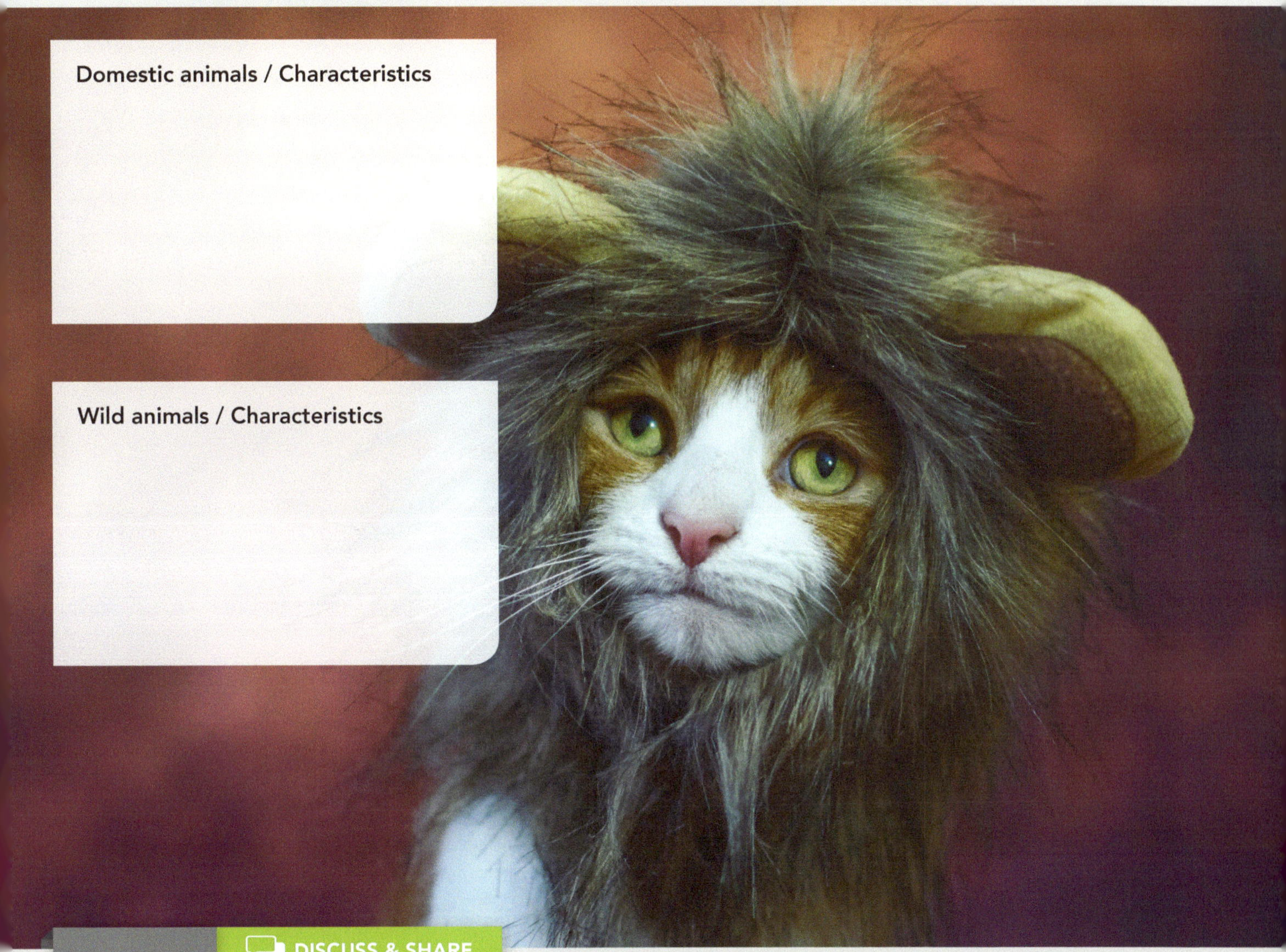

Domestic animals / Characteristics

Wild animals / Characteristics

DISCUSS & SHARE

VIDEO

3 IN GROUPS Watch the video and answer the question.

GYM Are you a dog person or a cat person?

In this unit, you will ...

- talk about intelligent animals, discuss possible jobs with animals, and make arguments for and against owning exotic pets.
- use thinking skills: recall, analyze, and evaluate.
- read about animals and the mirror test for intelligence.
- use strategies and language to move on to your next point, start a conversation about hypothetical situations, and disagree politely.
- use problem-solving skills to find solutions to help stray animals.
- follow a wildlife photographer to learn about this job and the skills needed for this industry.

READING

A **Apart from humans, which animals do you think are intelligent?**

B 2.01 **Read the blog post. Then choose *True* or *False*.**

The Mirror Test

Animals are interesting, aren't they? They can be **cute**, they can be fast, and they can be strong. But are they **intelligent**?

That isn't an easy question to answer. Animals all live in different habitats and their **behavior** is right for that situation. We need a standard way to test an animal's behavior. The mirror test, developed in 1970 by Dr. Gordon Gallup Jr., gives us that.

You recognize your own reflection in a mirror, don't you? But does an animal know that it's looking at itself when it looks in a mirror, or does it think it's a different animal? If an animal passes the mirror test, there's a good chance it is intelligent. We give the animal medicine so it goes to sleep. Then, we put a colored mark on the animal's body where it can't see it in a normal way, such as on its forehead or on its ear. When the animal wakes up and sees itself in a mirror, we watch how it behaves.

Animals that pass the mirror test see the mark and touch it or try to remove it. So far, the species that have passed the test are great apes (chimpanzees, bonobos, and orangutans), elephants, dolphins, orcas, and Eurasian magpies. Some people say, though, that the test only works with animals that mainly use **sight** to explore the world, and it may not be a fair test of other animals, such as dogs, who use **smell** or sound more than sight and fail the test.

GLOSSARY

habitat (n): place where an animal naturally lives

1 An animal's environment changes how it acts. True / False
2 The mirror test is done while the animal is asleep. True / False
3 In the mirror test, the animal puts color on its body using the mirror. True / False
4 Animals pass the mirror test if they know they are looking at themselves. True / False

C **READING SKILL—Understand examples** **Find and write examples from the text in B.**

1 a good place to put a mark on an animal for the mirror test ________________
2 an animal that passes the mirror test ________________
3 an animal that fails the mirror test ________________

D **THINKING SKILL—Recall** **Without reading the text again, describe how the mirror test works.**

VOCABULARY

A **Complete the definitions (1–5) with the words in bold in READING B.**

1 The sense of ________________ is very important to animals that hunt with their eyes, such as cats.
2 The sense of ________________ is very important to animals that use their noses a lot, such as bears.
3 An ________________ person is good at understanding difficult ideas.
4 An animal's ________________ is the way it acts and the things it does.
5 People often think that baby animals, such as kittens and puppies, are ________________.

GRAMMAR tag questions

A Read the tag questions and choose the correct options.

Animals are interesting, aren't they?

You recognize your own reflection in a mirror, don't you?

1 To form a tag question with the verb *be*, we use the verb **be** / **do** and an appropriate pronoun.
2 To form a tag question with other verbs, we use the verb **be** / **do** and an appropriate pronoun.
3 To form a tag question with a modal, **use the verb be** / **repeat the modal**.
4 When the verb in the main part of the sentence is positive, the verb in the tag is **negative** / **positive**.

For more practice, go to page 143.

B Complete the tag questions.

1 You're James, ______________________?
2 It's cold today, ______________________?
3 Jack's a really smart dog, ______________________?
4 Horses are very intelligent, ______________________?
5 Dolphins can be taught tricks, ______________________?
6 Your mom works with animals, ______________________?

MAKE IT REAL

In informal situations, some people might use *right* at the end of a sentence instead of using a tag question, e.g., *You're a vet,* ***right?***

SPEAKING

A Put the animals in order of intelligence from 1 (most intelligent) to 5 (least intelligent).

 ____

 ____

 ____

 ____

 ____

B IN PAIRS Tell each other what order you have put the animals in. Explain your reasons. Use the Confident Communicator box to help you.

A: Parrots can talk, can't they? I think that means they're smart.

B: Maybe, but dolphins are smarter, aren't they? They can learn lots of tricks.

CONFIDENT COMMUNICATOR
KEEP TALKING

Use the following phrases to move on to your next point for discussion.

What about *horses? Do you think they're intelligent?*

Let's move on to *rabbits. Are they intelligent?*

Next, let's think about *parrots. They're intelligent, aren't they?*

Working With Animals

VOCABULARY careers with animals

A Check (✓) the careers you need a degree to do.

☐ dog handler

☐ vet/veterinarian

☐ zookeeper

☐ wildlife photographer

☐ breeder

☐ marine biologist

☐ horse trainer

☐ zoologist

B IN PAIRS Decide which career(s) from A would be most appropriate for Holly.

Holly is 18 and is considering a career with animals. She loves small animals and has always had a number of pets. She has good exam results, but she would rather take a practical course than an academic course.

LISTENING

A What do you think this person is doing?

B 2.02 LISTENING SKILLS—Use key information to predict content. Listen to Part 1 of a talk. Then check what topics you expect to hear in the rest of the talk.

- ☐ academic qualifications
- ☐ salary
- ☐ work experience
- ☐ personal qualities

C 2.03 Listen to Part 2 of the talk. Then complete the sentences.

1 A marine biologist is someone who studies animals that live ________________.
2 Some marine biologists do ________________ in the summer months.
3 To be a marine biologist, you'll need a ________________ in biology or marine biology.
4 The person who gets venom from a snake is known as a ________________.
5 Venom is used to make antivenom for when a snake ________________.

D THINKING SKILL—Analyze Decide what kind of person would make a good snake milker. Say whether you think you would be good at that job.

GRAMMAR articles

A Match the sentence beginnings (1–3) with the ends (a–c).

A marine biologist is someone who studies animals that live in the sea.
A snake milker takes venom from a snake. The venom is very useful.

1 We use the indefinite article (*a*, *an*) _____
2 We use the definite article (*the*) _____
3 We use no article _____

a with singular countable nouns, with plural countable nouns when we are being specific, and when there is only one of something (*the sun, the sky, etc.*).
b with plural countable nouns and uncountable nouns when we are talking generally.
c with singular countable nouns when we are not being specific or when we mention something for the first time.

For more practice, go to page 144.

B Complete the sentences with *a*, *an*, or *the*. If no article is needed, put an *X*.

When **1** __________ director needs **2** __________ animal for **3** __________ movie, they turn to **4** __________ animal trainer. **5** __________ animal trainer then provides **6** __________ trained animal to do whatever **7** __________ director wants them to do. But what does it take to become **8** __________ animal trainer?
Of course, you need to enjoy working with **9** __________ animals. More than that, though, you have to be interested in **10** __________ animal behavior. You should also be in shape and able to work outdoors.

C IN PAIRS Say if you think you would be a good animal trainer.

PRONUNCIATION *the*

A 2.04 Listen to the sentences. What do you notice about the pronunciation of *the*?

I have to take my dog to the vet.
My dog has to stay in the animal hospital.

B Practice the sentence: I like to see the animals at the zoo.

SPEAKING

A Read the questions and make notes.

1 If you were going to work with animals, what kind of animals would you like to work with (small, large, marine, etc.)? __________
2 What kind of place (lab, outdoors, etc.) would you like to work in? __________
3 How closely would you like to work with animals? __________

B IN PAIRS Talk about your answers to the questions in A. Discuss what careers with animals each of you might enjoy. Use the Confident Communicator box to help you.

CONFIDENT COMMUNICATOR
START TALKING

To start a conversation about hypothetical situations, use the following phrases:
If I were going to work with animals, I would like to work with small animals, such as cats and dogs.
The animals I'd like to work with are marine animals.

VOCABULARY animals

A Name the animals. Then check (✓) the ones you think are endangered.

☐ crocodile ☐ dolphin ☐ hippo ☐ polar bear ☐ porcupine
☐ puma ☐ shark ☐ tiger ☐ turtle ☐ whale

1  ________
2  ________
3  ________
4  ________
5  ________
6  ________
7  ________
8  ________
9  ________
10  ________

B IN PAIRS Compare your answers. Say why you think some of the animals are endangered.

LISTENING

A Have you visited a zoo? What was it like?

B 2.05 LISTENING SKILL—Listen for key words
Look at the word cloud. Listen to a presentation and circle words and phrases you hear.

C 2.05 Listen again and choose the correct options.

1 The zoo tries to make ...
a the zoo environment as natural as possible. b animals behave in different ways.
2 The zoo wants to educate people about ...
a the work the zookeepers do with the animals. b the problems some animals face in the wild.
3 The zoo's breeding program ...
a provides animals for other zoos. b aims to help endangered species in the wild.

D THINKING SKILL—Evaluate What arguments can you think of against zoos? Choose the most persuasive points.

WRITING an opinion post

A Read the arguments for and against supporting zoos. Then answer the questions in your notebook.

Should we support zoos in the work that they do?

Zoos do a lot of good work. First of all, they educate the public. This inspires the next generation of zookeepers, vets, and environmentalists. In addition, zoos help to protect endangered species through the breeding work they do. Last, zoos are involved in environmental programs of different kinds around the world. We need to support our zoos.

Alessa, Lima, Peru

Zoos are cruel and unnecessary. To start with, animals in captivity are bored and cannot behave naturally. Many animals find being on display very stressful. What's more, some animals die younger in zoos than they would in the wild. Last but not least, zoos care more about baby animals, which attract paying visitors. We should not support zoos.

Jacob, New York, US

1 What are the main arguments given in favor of zoos?
2 What are the main arguments given against zoos?

B Write words and phrases from A that have the same meaning as these words and phrases.

first: **1** ____________, **2** ____________
also: **3** ____________, **4** ____________
finally: **5** ____________, **6** ____________

C You are going to write a post for the website on the following statement. Make notes to answer the questions.

We should close all zoos and release the animals into the wild.

1 Are you going to argue for or against this statement? ____________
2 What is your main argument? ____________
3 What other arguments do you want to mention? ____________

D Write an opinion post for the website arguing either for or against the statement. Use the phrases from B to structure your post.

SPEAKING

A Think of arguments for and against allowing people to own exotic pets, such as tigers, chimpanzees, snakes, etc. Make notes.

Main arguments for:

____

Main arguments against:

____

B IN PAIRS Do you think people should be allowed to keep wild animals as pets? Why or why not?

C Tell the rest of the class what you talked about. How many of you are for and how many of you are against the idea? Use the Confident Communicator box to help you.

CONFIDENT COMMUNICATOR
KEEP TALKING

To disagree with someone politely, use *Yes, but …*
I think people should have the right to own exotic pets if they want to.
Yes, but *what about the animals? Don't they have rights, too?*

Language and Life

Problem Solving – Strays

A 2.06 **Read the article. Then answer the questions.**

The Trouble With Strays

Puppies are cute, aren't they? And kittens are adorable. But those puppies and kittens grow up to be adult dogs and cats. Often the demands of being a pet owner just get to be too much for people and the cats and dogs end up on the street as strays. Sometimes it's the responsibility of looking after an adult animal that causes problems, and sometimes there are financial reasons. It's a growing problem. In the city of Detroit in the US, it is estimated that there are 50,000 stray dogs. The World Health Organization estimates that there are about 200 million stray dogs worldwide.

This situation causes a number of problems. First of all, the lives of stray animals are hard and stressful. Every day is a struggle to find enough to eat and a safe place to sleep. That means the animals are often in poor condition and get injured or die young. In addition to that, stray animals cause a number of problems for city residents. They can run into the road and cause traffic accidents. Stray animals can also carry diseases. They can pass these diseases on to people or to domestic pets. Last, packs of dogs can be dangerous and may attack people.

However, there may be a solution to the problem. One country that has reduced the number of stray dogs is the UK. In 2016, a new law was introduced. All dogs must be microchipped. This means that a small chip—the size of a grain of rice—is inserted under the dog's skin. It's a quick and painless procedure. Microchips contain a unique code that is connected to a national database. When the chip is scanned, it shows the owner's address. If your dog does not have a chip, you can receive a fine of up to £500. Microchipping is useful if your dog is lost or stolen, and it also encourages people to take more responsibility for their pets. According to the Dogs Trust's *Stray Dogs Survey Report*, in 2018, the number of stray animals in the UK was at its lowest level in 21 years—so this is a step in the right direction.

1 What are the causes of the stray animal problem? ______

2 What problems do stray animals cause for city residents? ______

3 How did the UK solve this problem? ______

B **IN GROUPS Talk about the situation in your own city or area. Check (✓) the main problems with animals and add details and ideas of your own.**

Main animal problems in our city/area

☐ stray dogs
packs of dogs in some neighborhoods

☐ stray cats

☐ unwanted pets

☐ other problems

C **Read and assess the opinions. Do you think they are good suggestions? Why or why not?**

Amy2001	*We need more shelters. We should take the animals off the streets.*
CityGirl	*We should make sure the animals can't breed. And then release them back onto the streets.*
Ed_99	*We need to educate people more and stop the problem where it begins, in people's homes.*

A: Having more shelters is a good idea.

B: I agree, but maybe that's a short-term solution.

D **Brainstorm solutions for your city or area. Try to estimate the costs.**

Possible solutions for our city/area

Our estimated costs

E **Present your solutions to the class. Vote to choose the best ideas at a realistic cost.**

F **Discuss the questions.**

1. How did the costs of the solutions affect your choice?
2. What other factors did you consider when choosing solutions?
3. Why is it important to consider many factors when solving a problem?
4. What problems have you solved recently? How did you solve them?

MAKE IT DIGITAL

Find websites where people debate ideas. Read some of the posts and see what phrases they use for starting, for introducing further points, and for concluding.

VOCABULARY review

SCORE: / 10

A Complete the sentences with words from the box. There are two words you don't need.

apes	breeders	handlers	polar bears	species	wildlife
behavior	cute	hippos	sight	whales	zoologists

My job as a **1** ________________ phot ographer takes me all over the world. My main interest is in recording endangered **2** ________________ before they disappear. I've taken shots of **3** ________________ in the Arctic. That was dangerous because they aren't at all **4** ________________, cuddly creatures! They're real killers. I've also photographed **5** ________________ out at sea and I've taken shots of lions, **6** ________________, and zebras in Africa. My next project is to record the amazing **7** ________________ of the Asian jungles. I'd like to record their natural **8** ________________, as well as collect data that **9** ________________ will find useful. They have a good sense of hearing and a good sense of **10** ________________, particularly at night, so it won't be easy to find them!

GRAMMAR review

SCORE: / 10

A Check (✓) the correct tag questions. Rewrite the incorrect question tags.

1 ☐ Tigers are amazing animals, **aren't they?** ________________
2 ☐ You majored in marine biology, **don't you?** ________________
3 ☐ Gorillas will soon disappear in the wild, **will they?** ________________
4 ☐ We don't do enough to protect endangered species, **are we?** ________________
5 ☐ It's important to learn about nature in schools, isn't it? ________________

B Add five articles (*a*, *an*, *the*) to the text.

One of the most intelligent animals is the octopus. Octopuses can solve puzzles and can even open jar to get food. And when they solve puzzle, they can remember how to do it if they see puzzle again. Scientists estimate that octopus is about as intelligent as three-year-old child.

16–20 correct: You can talk about animals and people who work with animals. You can use tag questions and articles.
0–15 correct: Look again at the Vocabulary and Grammar sections in the unit.

TOTAL SCORE: / 20

WHAT DO YOU KNOW NOW? Look back at page 17 and add the words you know now to the boxes.

FOLLOW A PRO — ANIMALS

Take the quiz about animals. Go to **Follow A Pro** on page 128 to find the answers. Then learn more about working with animals.

1 Where is the largest zoo in Mexico?
a Mexico City **b** Guadalajara **c** Puebla

2 How long is veterinary school in the US?
a one year **b** two years **c** four years

3 Approximately how many polar bears are there in the wild?
a 4,000 **b** 12,000 **c** 26,000

4 Which animal is the hippo most closely related to?
a whale **b** horse **c** dog

UNIT 3

Think About It

WHAT DO YOU ALREADY KNOW?

1 Think about words you know connected to thinking or skills. Write the words.

2 IN PAIRS Share and compare your ideas. Add more words to your lists.

Thinking/Skills

DISCUSS & SHARE

VIDEO

3 IN GROUPS Watch the video and answer the question.

SYM When do you think better: in the morning or in the evening?

In this unit, you will …

- ask and answer questions about confirmation bias, discuss the importance of expert systems in your future career, and compare different creative uses for things.
- use thinking skills: analyze, evaluate, and apply.
- read about confirmation bias.
- use strategies and language to give yourself time to think, start a conversation, and ask for further suggestions.
- use design-thinking skills to design a new social media app.
- learn tips to create a presentation or give a talk.

LESSON 1 How We Think

READING

A **Do you think the world is generally getting better or getting worse? Why do you think that?**

B **3.01 READING SKILL—Identify the topic** **Read the article. Then choose the best definition.**

a confirmation bias (*n*): the mistake we make when we don't think carefully enough about a subject and think that our first idea is correct

b confirmation bias (*n*): the thinking habit that means we accept evidence that supports the opinion we already have and don't accept other evidence

CONFIRMATION BIAS

Scientists believe that the average person receives about 34 gigabytes of information and sees or hears 100,500 words every day. That's a lot of information, and no one can possibly **concentrate on** all of it. We choose what we **pay attention to** and what we think is important. That creates a problem: confirmation bias. We like to be right, and so we listen to **evidence** that supports what we already believe and we **ignore** evidence that goes against what we believe. For example, if you believe that the world is generally getting worse, you will see only evidence to support your opinion when you hear the news. You will pay attention to stories about rising crime and environmental problems. And you will ignore evidence that suggests people around the world are getting richer, becoming healthier, and living longer.

Confirmation bias means we see what we want to see. It can create problems. For instance, a business may try a new strategy. The managers will notice positive results, such as increased sales, before they notice negative ones, such as increased costs. That could be expensive for the business. Social media and other websites can make confirmation bias worse. Groups of online friends often agree with each other. They easily share information and news stories that support their opinions. They **rarely** hear the other side of the argument and miss **relevant** information. Some people are worried that this kind of "social media bubble" is bad for society.

Is there anything you can do to question your own confirmation bias? You can **make an effort** to listen to people with different views. You can visit websites that present a different opinion from yours. As soon as you do that, you will learn something about how other people think.

C **Write short answers to the questions.**

1 What is the cause of confirmation bias? ______

2 Why might confirmation bias cause problems for a business? ______

3 Why can social media make confirmation bias worse? ______

4 What can you do to prevent confirmation bias? ______

D **THINKING SKILL—Analyze** **Explain other ways in which confirmation bias could be a problem.**

VOCABULARY

A **Complete the sentences with the words and phrases in bold in READING B.**

1 If you ______ the lecturer, you will understand the topic better.

2 People ______ listen carefully to other people's opinions—in fact, they almost never do!

3 Please don't ______ me! Listen to what I'm saying.

4 What ______ do you have that supports your opinion?

5 I know learning to play an instrument is hard, but if you ______, you'll improve.

6 I like to collect all the ______ information before I make an important decision.

7 I can't ______ my work with all this noise!

GRAMMAR future time clauses (*after, as soon as, before, until, when*)

A Choose the correct option.

1 You will see only evidence to support your opinion when … the news.
a you hear **b** you will hear

2 The managers will notice positive results before … negative ones.
a they notice **b** they will notice

B Choose the correct options.

1 We use / don't use the future tense in a time clause.
2 We use the simple present / simple past in the time clause.

For more practice, go to page 144.

C Complete the sentences.

1 I ______________ (call) you as soon as I ______________ (get) home.
2 From now on, I ______________ (not share) a story on social media until I ______________ (check) it.
3 I think the problem ______________ (get) worse before it ______________ (get) better.
4 ______________ (you / meet) me at the airport when I ______________ (arrive)?
5 After I ______________ (watch) the movie, I ______________ (tell) you whether I like it or not.

D IN PAIRS Ask and answer the questions.

1 What will you do when this lesson ends?
2 What will you do as soon as you get home tonight?

MAKE IT REAL

We also use time clauses with *the minute* or *the instant*, meaning "immediately," e.g., *Call me **the minute** you get there.*

SPEAKING

A Make notes. You do not need to write complete sentences.

1 Do you and your online friends always agree about things or do you sometimes disagree? What do you disagree about?

____

2 In what ways do you think confirmation bias is a problem?

____

3 Now that you've read about confirmation bias, will you do anything different when you are online?

____

B IN PAIRS Ask and answer the questions in A. Use the Confident Communicator box to help you.

CONFIDENT COMMUNICATOR
KEEP TALKING

Use the following phrases to give yourself time to think when asked a question.
That's a good question.
Let me think about that for a minute.

Artificial Intelligence

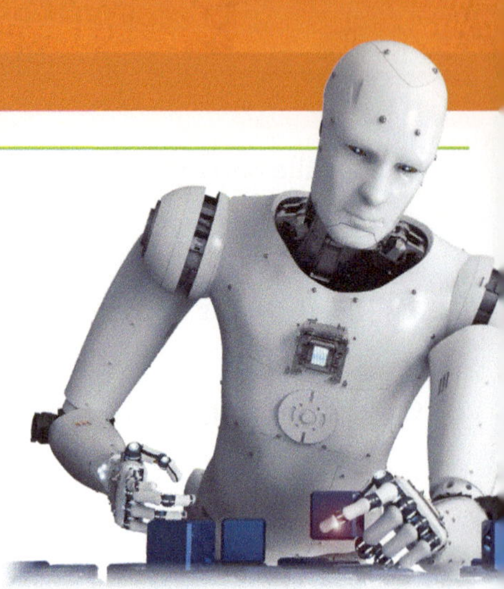

LISTENING

A Do you think machines will be able to think in the future?

B 3.02 LISTENING SKILL—Listen for attitude Listen to a radio call-in show. Match the callers (1–4) to the statements (a–d).

1 Julia: ______ a This person is confident that AI makes the world safer.
2 Rafael: ______ b This person is afraid that AI will change the economy.
3 Megan: ______ c This person is doubtful that machines will ever be intelligent.
4 Victor: ______ d This person is worried that AI might get out of control.

C 3.02 Listen to the call-in show again. Then complete the sentences.

1 Julia says that machines are just ______________ when they play games such as chess.
2 Julia says that humans are good at thinking because they have been doing it for ______________.
3 Rafael says that humans make mistakes because they get ______________.
4 Megan says that ______________ how some computer systems work and that's dangerous.
5 Victor says that machines may do ______________ of American jobs in the future.
6 Victor says that people who work ______________ may lose their jobs.

D THINKING SKILLS—Evaluate Consider and describe other ways we use AI today.

VOCABULARY word formation

A Complete the table with the different forms of the words. Check your ideas in pairs.

Verb	Adjective	Noun (abstract)	Noun (person)
create	1 ______	5 ______ 6 ______	11 ______
power	2 ______ 3 ______	power	
solve	solvable	7 ______	solver
think		8 ______	thinker
	4 ______	danger	
employ	employable	9 ______ 10 ______	12 ______ 13 ______

B IN PAIRS Discuss the questions.

1 As computers get more powerful, is there a danger to employment from AI?
2 Will computers ever be powerful enough to understand emotions?

PRONUNCIATION *say, says, said*

A 3.03 How do we say each of the words in bold? Listen, check, and practice.

1 Some people **say** that AI is a danger.
2 My mom **says** that she'll never lose her job to a robot.
3 My dad **said** the same thing and then lost his job!

GRAMMAR present perfect progressive

A Read the sentences from LISTENING B and complete the explanation.

Scientists have been researching artificial intelligence since the 1950s.
Humans have been thinking and solving problems for 200,000 years.
I've been thinking about AI a lot recently.

We form the present perfect progressive with *has/have* + ______________ + ______________.

B **Read the sentences in A again and choose the correct option.**

1 We use the present perfect progressive to talk about …
  a an activity that started in the past and is still in progress now.
  b an experience at a particular time in the past.
2 We also use the present perfect progressive to talk about …
  a the result of a recent continuing action.
  b an experience at any time in the past.
3 To talk about a finished action in the past that has results in the present, we use …
  a the present perfect.
  b the present perfect progressive.
4 When we mention the point the action began, we use **for** / **since**.
5 When we mention the duration of the action, we use **for** / **since**.

For more practice, go to page 145.

C **Complete the sentences.**

Expert Systems

An expert system is a computer program that uses AI to solve problems. People in various professions have **1** ____________ using expert systems **2** ____________ a number of years. An expert system uses a database of knowledge together with rules for using that knowledge. Scientists **3** ____________ been using them **4** ____________ 1965, when the first expert system was developed. Many health professionals, such as doctors and nurses, use expert systems. Health professionals **5** ____________ been recording our health data **6** ____________ the day we were born. Perhaps your doctor **7** ____________ been using one **8** ____________ some time to help decide what is wrong with his or her patients. Expert systems are just one of the ways in which AI **9** ____________ been helping people in the workplace. Where else do you think expert systems are used?

D **IN PAIRS** **Ask and answer the questions.**

1 How have people been using AI recently?
2 What have you been doing in another class / at work recently?
3 How long have you been living where you live now?

SPEAKING

A **Think about your chosen career and answer the questions.**

1 Are expert systems used in your chosen career now? In what ways?
2 Do you think expert systems will be used more in your chosen career in the future? In what ways?
3 Do you think your chosen career is in danger from expert systems or AI? Why or why not?

B **IN PAIRS** **Ask and answer the questions in A.**

A: I'm planning to be a lawyer in future. I think that lawyers have been using expert systems for years to research past cases.

B: Do you think that lawyers will use expert systems more in the future?

CONFIDENT COMMUNICATOR

START TALKING

To start your conversation, use the following phrases:
I'm planning to be a doctor.
I'm hoping to work as an engineer.
I want to work in accounting.

Get Creative

VOCABULARY phrasal verbs

A Match the phrasal verbs in bold (1–6) to the definitions (a–f).

1 How do you **come up with** all your amazing ideas? ____
2 You should never **give up** if you want to achieve your dreams. ____
3 Why don't you **look up** the word in an online dictionary? ____
4 Don't **make up** excuses! I know you broke my phone! ____
5 You can **rely on** this smartphone. It'll never break down or stop working. ____
6 I might **take up** a new sport to try to get in shape. ____

a stop making an effort
b find information in a book or online
c write or say something that isn't true
d think of, create
e start doing a regular activity, a hobby, etc.
f trust someone or something to do what they should do

MAKE IT YOURS

There are many different ways to describe how you have ideas. How could you describe the way you have ideas?

B IN PAIRS Choose the answers that are true for you. Talk to your partner about your choices.

1 I find it easy / hard to come up with ideas.
2 I often / sometimes / never give up if I find things hard.
3 I often / sometimes / never look things up to check information.
4 I often / sometimes / never make things up and I always / don't always tell the truth.
5 I often / sometimes / never rely on other people.
6 I often / sometimes / never take up a new activity.

LISTENING

A Discuss when it is important or useful to think creatively.

B 3.04 Listen to Part 1 of a talk and choose *True* or *False*.

1 Some people always find it easy to be creative. True / False
2 Some people will never be creative. True / False
3 Knowledge stops you from being creative. True / False
4 Feeling like a new learner helps creativity. True / False

C 3.05 LISTENING SKILL—Listen for main ideas Listen to Part 2 of the talk. Make notes about the three creative exercises the speaker describes.

Exercise 1: ____________________
Exercise 2: ____________________
Exercise 3: ____________________

GLOSSARY

fictional (adj): invented for a book, play, or movie

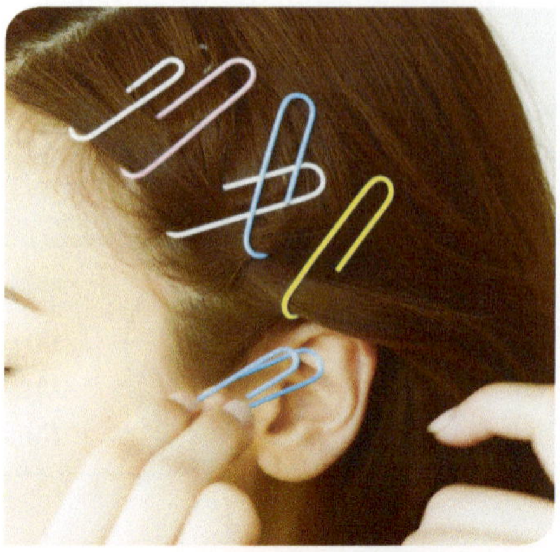

D THINKING SKILL—Apply Record as many different ways to use a paper clip as you can. You have three minutes.

WRITING an informal email

A Read the email. Then answer the questions.

New Message

To: Cc Bcc

Subject:

a Hi Alex.

Sorry I didn't reply to you sooner. **b** I've been working a lot, but it isn't so bad now.

We had a talk at work about being productive, and **c** I thought you would be interested in it. The speaker said we can all be productive, and he gave us a few tips.

d First of all, it's a good idea to have a to-do list. It really helps you to keep going when you just feel like giving up! And it also helps you to focus on what you're doing.

e The second thing he mentioned is the 2-Minute Rule. When you can't start something, choose a task that will take two minutes. Everyone has two minutes to do something. And when you start, it's easy to continue!

f Hope you find this useful.

g Regards,

h Grace

Send

1. What reason does Grace give for not writing?
2. What did Grace do at work?
3. How does a to-do list help?
4. How does the 2-Minute Rule help?

B Match the descriptions (1–8) with the correct parts of the email in A (a–h).

1. the second main point _____
2. a closing expression such as *Love*, *Best wishes*, etc. _____
3. a piece of personal news _____
4. a general description of the rest of the email _____
5. the writer's first name _____
6. a short wish or hope _____
7. a greeting with *Hi* or *Dear* _____
8. the first main point _____

C Write an email to a friend. Describe the talk in LISTENING B. Use the email in A as a model.

SPEAKING

A Write one more object in each list. Make sure that the objects you add are different from the ones already listed.

List A	List B
a pineapple	a guitar
a fork	a ladder
a cell phone	a clock
______________	______________

B IN PAIRS At random, choose one thing from List A and one thing from List B. How are those two things the same? Discuss and make a list of as many ways as you can.

A: We've got a cell phone and a guitar. They can both play music. Anything else?

B: You use both of them with your fingers!

CONFIDENT COMMUNICATOR

KEEP TALKING

To ask for further suggestions, use the following expressions:

What else do they have in common?

Are there any other ways that they're the same?

What other ideas do you have?

Language and Life

Design Thinking – An App

A 3.06 **Read the article. Then answer the questions.**

The Trouble With Social Media

Social media companies have been feeling worried recently. People have realized that there are a few problems connected to social media. One is the problem of confirmation bias. Our online friends make comments and share posts that we already agree with. We accept them as true and we never see any evidence of other opinions. This can mean that we share and like false stories more easily because they match what we already believe.

There are other problems, too. Some people spend too much time on social media. They update their status many times a day and their phones show notifications of other people's posts. This often means they waste time, or they ignore their real-life family and friends. They might also become anxious about how many shares or likes their posts get. Other people experience cyberbullying, where people make up comments about them. That can have an effect on people's lives and their health.

Another issue is our digital footprint. Every time we post, share, or comment, we leave a digital record. It often follows us for a very long time. When you apply for a job or when you meet someone new, they might check your social media. What will they see? Are you sure that you want them to see everything you've posted?

Finally, people share a lot of information on social media. They share their location, when they're on vacation, and what they do every day. That can leave the person vulnerable to crime or other problems.

Many people agree that we need to find ways to help people be safer on social media and to think more about the information they see and share.

1 What five problems with social media are mentioned? ______

2 Have you or anyone you know ever had those problems with social media? ______

B You work for a company. Read the email from your manager. What does she want you to do?

New Message

Subject: app idea

Hi all,

We see a gap in the market for an app to help people deal with problems created by social media. It might fact-check stories in the media. Or it might help delete your social footprint. It could be anything, really. See if you can come up with a few ideas and we'll meet to discuss them.

Regards,

Rose

Send

C **On your own, think of an app to suggest to your manager. Make a short note of what your app does.**

an app that immediately checks the facts in any story you see online

My suggested app: ____________________

D **IN GROUPS You are going to use a method called starbursting. Read the description. Have you used starbursting or a similar technique before?**

Starbursting is a way of brainstorming good questions to ask about a suggestion. In the middle of a star, you write the suggestion. On the points of the star are the words *What, Who, Where, When, How,* and *Why*. You use these to come up with questions to ask about the suggestion. For example, you might ask: "Who will use this app?" By asking and answering the questions, you provide more detail on the suggestion and highlight key considerations.

E **IN GROUPS Write your app from C in the middle of the star. Use the starbursting method to write questions to ask about the app. Then ask and answer the questions for each person's app.**

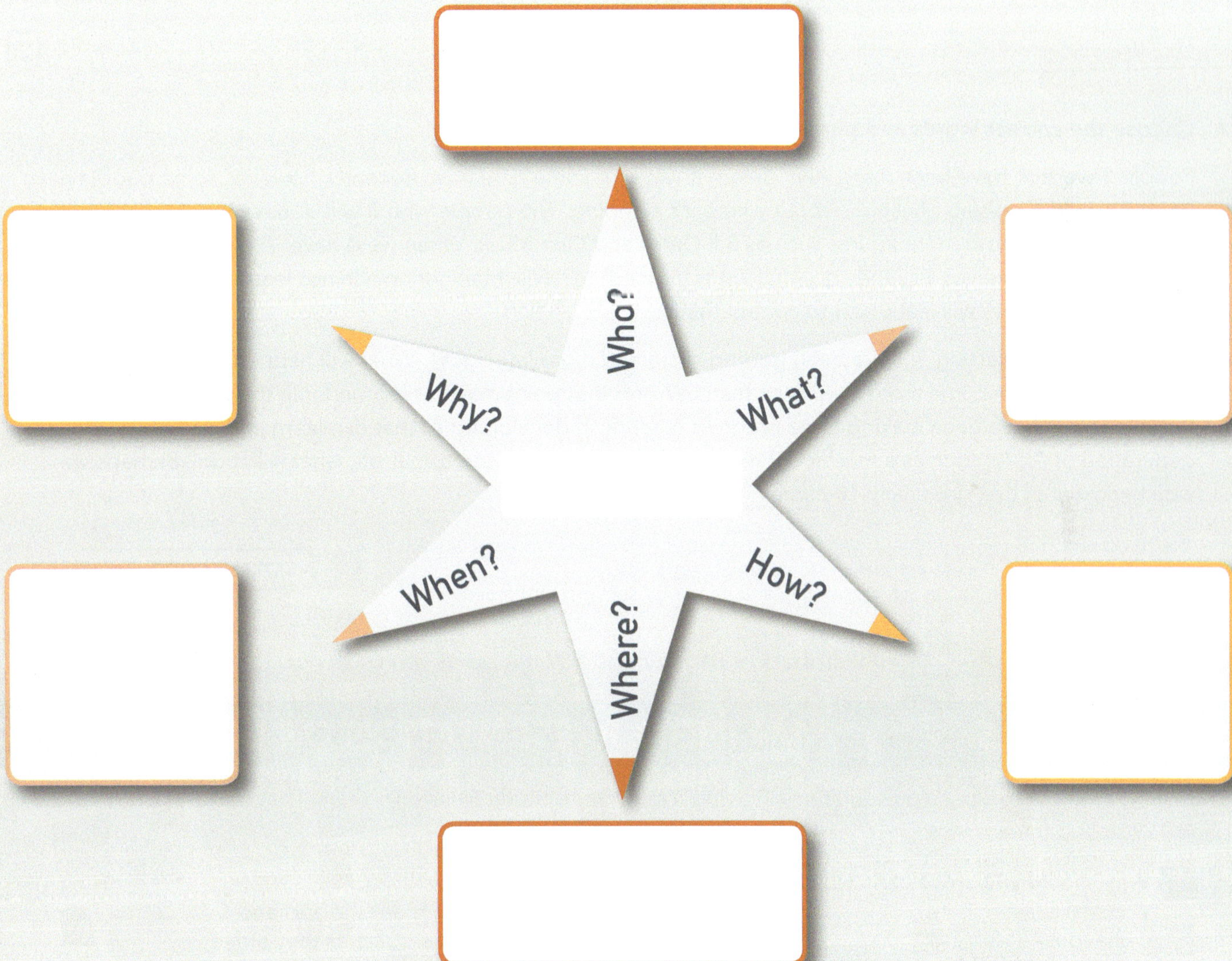

F **Compare the different apps from each group and choose which you like the best. Tell the class about the apps and about the answers to the questions in E.**

G **Discuss the questions.**

1. How useful did you find the starbursting method?
2. What key issues did the process highlight?
3. In what other situations do you think starbursting would help?

MAKE IT DIGITAL

Research the most popular apps in your country on different online app sites. Why do you think they are popular?

VOCABULARY review

SCORE: / 10

A Complete the sentences.

1 I'll create a fantastic design for your website. You can rely __________ me!
2 I wonder how great writers make __________ such wonderful stories.
3 I find it hard to concentrate __________ my work with all this noise!
4 When did you take __________ running in your spare time?
5 You'll remember more if you pay attention __________ what the speaker is saying.

B Complete the sentences using forms of the words in parentheses.

1 After brainstorming ideas, we finally found a __________ (solve) to the problem.
2 Many people have lost their jobs recently and __________ (employ) is a big problem.
3 It takes a lot of __________ (create) to produce beautiful works of art.
4 Do you think AI will be __________ (danger) in the future?
5 Computers are becoming more and more __________ (power) every year.

GRAMMAR review

SCORE: / 10

A Choose the correct words and phrases.

People **1 were / have been** using AI in different ways for some time now. Recently, however, some people have been **2 raised / raising** questions about where it's all going. The people who **3 will / have been** asking these questions include important figures such as Bill Gates and Elon Musk. When we **4 have / will have** machines that can think for themselves, will they do what we want them to? Will intelligent machines learn right from wrong before we **5 learn / will learn** how to control them?

Machines **6 have getting / have been getting** more and more intelligent. What will happen when our machines **7 become / will become** more intelligent than us? And that point may not be too far in the future. Researchers **8 has made / have been making** huge progress recently in developing AI that can learn and can design the next generation of AI. As soon as a machine **9 realizes / will realize** we can turn it off, what will it do? Perhaps we won't know until that day finally **10 comes / will come**.

16–20 correct: You can use phrasal verbs and form word derivatives. You can use future time clauses and the present perfect progressive.
0–15 correct: Look again at the Vocabulary and Grammar sections in the unit.

TOTAL SCORE: / 20

WHAT DO YOU KNOW NOW? Look back at page 27 and add the words you know now to the box.

STUDY SKILLS MAKING A PRESENTATION OR GIVING A TALK

Take the quiz about making a presentation or giving a talk. Go to **Study Skills** on page 129 to find the answers. Then learn more about the topic.

1 Why should you arrive early when you are giving a talk?
a to make last-minute changes to your talk
b to have time for tea or coffee
c to meet the audience members as they arrive

2 When you are giving a talk, where should you look?
a at one person in the audience
b into the eyes of a few different people
c at your notes

3 It's best if your slides don't contain a lot of text.
a True
b False

4 What should you wear when you are giving a talk?
a professional-looking clothing that you have worn before
b comfortable old clothing that you would wear to relax in
c fashionable new clothing that you would wear to a special event

UNIT 4

Beyond Words

WHAT DO YOU ALREADY KNOW?

1 Think about words you know about communication. Write the words.

2 IN PAIRS Share and compare your ideas. Add more words to your lists.

Personal communication

Digital communication

VIDEO

DISCUSS & SHARE

3 IN GROUPS Watch the video and answer the question.
SYM Would you rather call someone or text them?

In this unit, you will ...

- present a subject you know, ask questions and assess someone's body language, and decide on the best means of communication for different situations.
- use thinking skills: evaluate, apply, and predict.
- read about how to be a good communicator.
- learn strategies to use eye contact, use language to ask for more information, and to make your meaning clearer.
- use reasoning skills to discuss the pros and cons of a company proposal.
- follow a PR professional to learn about this job and the skills needed for this industry.

READING

A **Do you think you are a good communicator? Why or why not?**

B 4.01 READING SKILL—Read for gist **Read the article quickly. Then choose the best summary.**

Being a Good Communicator

Many of us find it hard to communicate. You may know what you want to say but not know how. What makes a good communicator? You might think a good communicator is someone who can speak well and explain his or her ideas. You might think a good communicator can **persuade** people to do what he or she wants. However, there's a lot more to communication than expressing yourself well. Communication is an important skill in our personal, academic, and professional lives. And it's easy to learn a few simple communication techniques.

The first is active listening. Good communicators listen carefully to understand the other person's thoughts. They repeat ideas back to the other person to show they understand. They also encourage the person to say more by asking relevant questions. For example, a good communicator might say: "I hear you saying that you're unhappy with your major. How, exactly?"

Good communicators are **honest**. In an argument with a friend, you don't help communication when you pretend that everything is fine. Good communicators talk honestly about how they feel.

Finally, good communicators make a personal **connection** with people. They try to find something they **have in common** with the person they are speaking to. That helps them to understand what the other person wants from a situation. Or they might try to put themselves in the other person's position and ask: "If I were him or her, what would I want to hear?"

Using these techniques will help to improve your relationships with other people at home, at school, and at work.

1 Communication is a way of getting other people to agree with you. You do this by asking them questions and talking about your feelings.

2 You can become a better communicator by listening carefully, telling the truth, and building relationships with people.

C **Read the article in B again and choose the correct options.**

1 What point is the writer making in the first paragraph?
- **a** It isn't right to try to change other people's opinions.
- **b** Communication isn't just about explaining things well.

2 According to the writer, active listening is a way of …
- **a** understanding someone's opinion.
- **b** getting people to understand you.

3 According to the writer, good communicators …
- **a** pretend they feel the same way as the other person.
- **b** tell the truth about their emotions.

4 It can help you understand what people want when you …
- **a** look for things that are true for both of you.
- **b** help them understand a situation correctly.

D THINKING SKILL—Evaluate **Decide what other things make someone a good communicator.**

VOCABULARY

A **Complete the sentences using the words in bold in READING B.**

1 You need to explain your ideas clearly to ______________ other people to do what you want.
2 I find it easy to communicate with you because we ______________ a lot ______________.
3 I have a very strong ______________ with my twin brother and I know what he's thinking.
4 Be ______________. You don't like my new hairstyle, do you?

GRAMMAR infinitives with *to*

A Match the sentences (1–4) to the correct explanations (a–d).

1 Many of us find it hard to communicate. ____
2 You may know what you want to say but not know how. ____
3 You might think a good communicator can persuade people to do what he or she wants. ____
4 … listen carefully to understand the other person's thoughts. ____

We use the infinitive with *to* …
a to express a purpose
b after some verbs (*advise, tell, warn, persuade*, etc.) + direct object
c after some verbs (*agree, like, prefer, want*, etc.)
d after some adjectives (*easy, happy, hard, ready*, etc.)

For more practice, go to page 146.

B Circle one more example of each use in READING B.

1 to express a purpose
2 after a verb + direct object
3 after a verb
4 after an adjective

C Complete the sentences with the correct forms of the words from the box.

agree	appear	communicate	learn
make	see	understand	

Good Public Speakers
All public speakers try **1** ____________ their message to their audience. Good ones plan their presentation carefully **2** ____________ sure their message is clear. They know that it's hard **3** ____________ a complicated speech, so they make it as simple as they can. Then, they start **4** ____________ the material. Many practice in front of a mirror **5** ____________ how confident they appear. Appearing confident is very important in getting your audience **6** ____________ with your ideas. Everyone gets nervous, but successful speakers try not **7** ____________ nervous to the audience.

MAKE IT DIGITAL
People in many careers need to give presentations. Watch expert presenters online and learn from them. Look for opportunities to give short presentations in class.

D IN PAIRS Have you ever given a presentation?

SPEAKING

A Think of a subject you know something about. It could be an academic subject, a famous person, a kind of music, etc. Make notes for a short presentation to a small group.

Subject: ____________________
Main points: ____________________

B IN GROUPS Take turns giving a short presentation (2–3 minutes) on your chosen subject. Use the Confident Communicator box to help you.

CONFIDENT COMMUNICATOR
KEEP TALKING
To be a good communicator, make eye contact with the person or people you are talking to. When you are talking to a group of people, try to make eye contact with each of them equally.

What Do You Really Mean?

VOCABULARY ways to communicate

A Complete the sentences with words from the box.

distance	position	speed	touch
tone	space	volume	

1 Your ______________ of voice is the way you say something and it shows how you feel.
2 Some people talk at a fast ______________, which can be hard to understand.
3 How much personal ______________ do you need when you are talking to someone?
4 The ______________ of your voice is how loud or quiet it is.
5 The ______________ from New York to London is 5,567 kilometers.
6 The ______________ of your arms can mean you are friendly or it can mean you feel uncomfortable.
7 In some countries, ______________ is a part of communication and people often put their hands on each other's arms.

B IN PAIRS Think about your country compared to other countries. Choose and then talk about your choices with a partner.

	Strongly agree	Agree	Neither agree nor disagree	Disagree	Strongly disagree
1 People talk at high speed and high volume.	☐	☐	☐	☐	☐
2 People need a lot of personal space.	☐	☐	☐	☐	☐
3 Touch is a part of communication.	☐	☐	☐	☐	☐

LISTENING

A Look at the picture. What do you think they are talking about? What does their body language tell you?

B 4.02 LISTENING SKILL—Listen for specific information Listen to Part 1 of an interview and label the diagram and key.

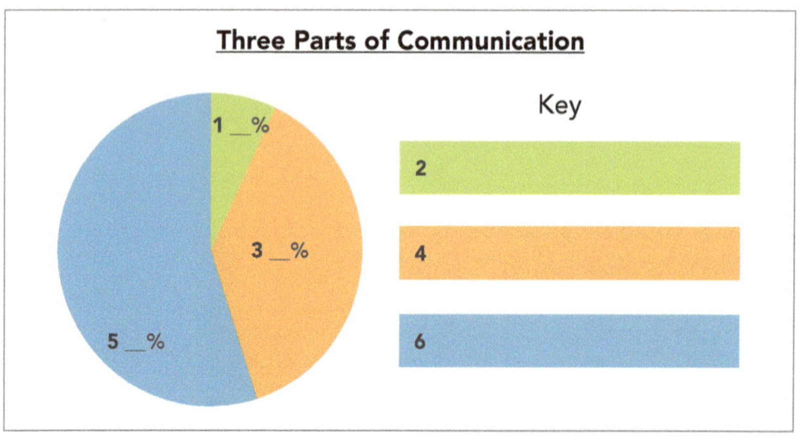

C 4.03 Read the sentences and predict what the missing words or short phrases could be. Then listen to Part 2 and complete the sentences.

1 It's easy to misunderstand when communicating ______________ because there's no tone of voice.
2 People in Romania want almost twice as much personal space as people in ______________.
3 We often have our arms ______________ when we are interested in another person's opinion.
4 You need to be careful when someone's body language means ______________ of their words.

GLOSSARY
verbal (adj): connected to words

D THINKING SKILLS—Apply How close you would stand to (a) a stranger, (b) someone you know, and (c) a close friend? Record your answer on the diagram and compare with a partner.

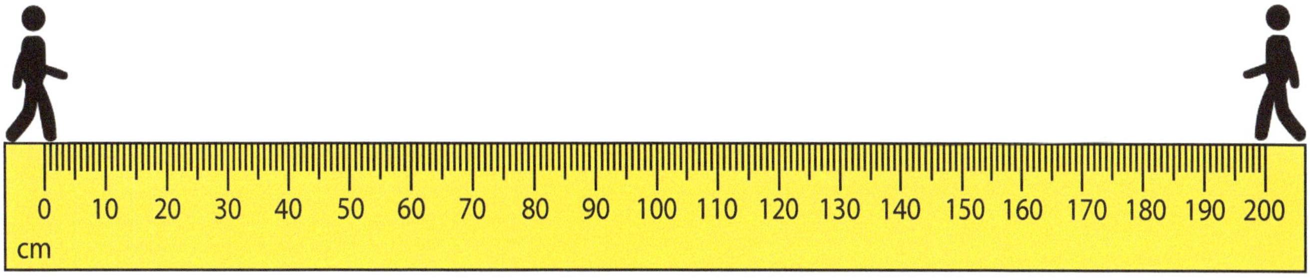

GRAMMAR separable and non-separable phrasal verbs

A Check (✓) the correct sentences.

1 ☐ I looked up "body language" online.
☐ I looked "body language" up online.
☐ I looked it up online.
☐ I looked up it online.

2 ☐ You can rely on Ruby to give a good talk.
☐ You can rely Ruby on to give a good talk.
☐ You can rely on her to give a good talk.
☐ You can rely her on to give a good talk.

B Choose the correct options.

With separable phrasal verbs, you **1** can / can't put a noun between the verb and the particle. With non-separable phrasal verbs, you **2** can / can't. With separable phrasal verbs, we **3** always / never separate the verb and the particle when the object is a pronoun (*you*, *it*, *them*, etc.). Phrasal verbs with a particle plus a preposition (e.g., *come up with*) are **4** always / never separable.

For more practice, go to page 147.

C Choose the correct options. Both may be correct.

1 Her body language told me she was making the story up / making up the story.
2 Her body language told me she was making it up / making up it.
3 I told Matt you would call back him / call him back.
4 You should take up psychology / take psychology up to learn more about body language.
5 I ran into Alice / ran Alice into outside class yesterday and we had a good chat.

D IN PAIRS Do you know when someone is making a story up? Discuss.

SPEAKING

A Write three statements about yourself. Two of the statements should be true and one should be false. Don't tell anyone which one is false.

I once went to New York. I'm thinking of taking the violin up. I have a cat named Dog.

B IN PAIRS Follow the instructions. Use the Confident Communicator box to help you.

Find someone in class who doesn't know you very well. Ask each other questions about your statements. As your partner talks, watch his or her body language carefully. Can you tell which statement is false?

CONFIDENT COMMUNICATOR
KEEP TALKING

To ask someone to provide more information, use the following phrases:
Tell me more about taking up the violin.
What happened when you went to New York?
What else can you tell me about your cat?

From Words to Pictures

LISTENING

A **Discuss how communication has changed in your lifetime.**

B 4.04 LISTENING SKILL—Listen for the order of events **Listen to a lecture. Write an event which took place in each of the years listed below.**

1971	1973	1992	1999	2007	2009	2011
______	______	______	______	______	______	______

C 4.04 **Listen again and answer the questions.**

1 How many emails are sent each day? ______
2 What percentage of people have a cell phone? ______
3 How many emojis are there today? ______
4 How many apps are there for the iPhone? ______
5 How many messages are sent through WhatsApp each day? ______
6 How many people use Snapchat? ______

D THINKING SKILL—Predict **Calculate how many messages of different kinds (emails, text messages, etc.) you send each year. Compare with a partner.**

PRONUNCIATION electronic communication

A 4.05 **How do you say each of the phrases in italics? Discuss with a partner. Then listen and check.**

Go to www.macmillan.com
My email is lisa_jackson3@emailtoday.org
Under the picture, it says #selfie and #mybestlook
My email is carrie-smith@fly.org

MAKE IT YOURS

Think about other types of electronic communication you use. How do you say the phrases associated with those types of communication?

B **Practice saying the sentences in A.**

VOCABULARY emojis

A **Write a word or phrase from the box under each emoji.**

clap	point	punch	shake hands	smile	thumbs up	wave

1 ______

2 ______

3 ______

4 ______

5 ______

6 ______

7 ______

B IN PAIRS **Do you use emojis? Why or why not? Discuss.**

WRITING text message and email

A Read the text message. Match each informal phrase (1–8) with a more formal phrase (a–h).

[1] Hi Pedro. [2] Come to my party next Friday. [3] It's at the Sunrise Café, 7pm. [4] It's for my 21st birthday. [5] Hope you can be there. [6] Don't worry about a present. 🙂 [7] Can you come? [8] ♥ Alexa

1 ______ 5 ______

2 ______ 6 ______

3 ______ 7 ______

4 ______ 8 ______

a The party is taking place at the Sunrise Café at 7 p.m.
b Please let me know if you are able to attend.
c I would like to invite you to my party next Friday.
d The event is to celebrate my 21st birthday.
e Best wishes,
f I hope you will be able to come.
g Dear Pedro,
h Please don't feel you need to bring a gift.

B Read the email and underline two sentences that are informal. Rewrite the sentences more formally.

New Message

Dear Amelie,

Come to my house-warming party. I have just moved into a new apartment and I thought it would be a good chance to get to know everyone in the office. The party is taking place on the 15th after work. I hope you will be able to come. Don't bring any gifts.

Please let me know if you are able to come so that I know how many people to expect.

Sincerely,
Millie

Send

1 ______________________________

2 ______________________________

C Read the information. Then write an email to a colleague you don't know very well inviting him or her to the event.

Event: a party to celebrate my birthday
Time and place: my home, 4th, 8:30 p.m.
Comments: no gifts, I need to know who's coming

D Swap emails with a partner. Check for the correct spelling and punctuation and the right level of formality.

SPEAKING

A Which is the best way to communicate in each situation?

	Text message	Email	Phone call
1 telling a friend some bad news	☐	☐	☐
2 congratulating a friend on success	☐	☐	☐
3 wishing your grandparents a happy anniversary	☐	☐	☐

B IN PAIRS Why would you use different means of communication in different situations? Discuss.

CONFIDENT COMMUNICATOR
KEEP TALKING

To make your meaning clearer, use the following phrases:
I mean, you can't give someone bad news in a text message.
In other words, you need to speak to someone in person when it's serious.

Language and Life

Reason Effectively – An International Company

A 4.06 **Read the article. Then answer the questions.**

Communication Problems

Businesses and other organizations succeed when the people communicate well with each other. There needs to be a free flow of information and instructions. Unfortunately, communication often goes wrong.

One reason for communication problems is that in large, multinational corporations, people often come from different cultures and speak different languages. They may use a common language to communicate, often English, but that doesn't remove the possibility of misunderstandings. People from some cultures, such as the US and Western Europe, may think it's important to clearly express their ideas and say how they feel. They might not see a problem in correcting a colleague or criticizing an idea. However, this can make people from some *other* cultures feel very uncomfortable. Similar problems can happen when people are from the same culture but have different life experiences.

Another reason for problems is communication technology. Many of us work from home at least some of the time these days. We communicate with colleagues through software such as Skype or Google Hangouts, and it doesn't always work perfectly. When we don't completely understand something and we are not able to check our understanding, it can lead to problems.

You might be surprised to hear that another possible reason for communication problems is friendships at work. Normally, we think of friends as people we communicate well with. However, mixing personal and professional communication isn't a good idea. It makes some people feel uncomfortable and it can start arguments.

Many organizations work hard to improve communication, for example, organizing diversity training sessions for employees. Another idea is a no-email day. One day a week, no one sends emails. Instead, they speak to people on the phone or meet in person. Small changes like that can make a big difference.

1 Why might there be misunderstandings in a multinational corporation?

____

2 Why can there be misunderstandings between people from the same culture?

____

3 How can communication technology cause communication problems?

____

4 Why does the writer say "You might be surprised"?

____

5 What happens on a no-email day?

____

6 What difference do you think a no-email day has on the people in a company?

____

B **Read and evaluate the information. Think about what you need to do. What are your next steps?**

You work for a large corporation with offices in different countries. Managers have noticed some communication problems recently. They feel that people from different countries seem to misunderstand each other, although they all speak English well. They are looking for ideas to improve everyone's communication skills and they have asked you and your team for suggestions.

C IN GROUPS **Analyze each of the ideas and identify the pros and cons. Add more ideas of your own. Use the phrases to discuss your thoughts.**

One good thing about diversity training is …

Overseas visits are useful because …

One problem with language training is ….

1. Diversity training

Advantages:____________________

Disadvantages:____________________

2. Overseas visits

Advantages:____________________

Disadvantages:____________________

3. Language training

Advantages:____________________

Disadvantages:____________________

4. Other idea

____

____

D **Decide which ideas you are going to suggest. Choose one or two.**

E **Tell the class which ideas you have chosen. Explain how you made your choice.**

F **Discuss the questions.**

1 What reasoning skills did you use to form an opinion and select an idea?

2 In what other situations do you think this process would be useful?

MAKE IT DIGITAL

Go to your college or company's website. Do they have a diversity and inclusion policy? Do they offer any training for this?

VOCABULARY review

SCORE: / 10

A Complete the sentences with words from the box.

common	express	shake	thumbs	volume
connection	persuade	smile	tone	wave

All human cultures have at least two things in **1** ______________. First of all, we all use language to **2** ______________ ourselves. Exactly how we speak may change. We may speak at a higher **3** ______________ when we are excited or use a different **4** ______________ of voice when we are angry. We may speak in a certain way when we want to **5** ______________ somebody to do something. But all of us use words to try to make a **6** ______________ to other people every day. Second, we all communicate non-verbally through gestures. Interestingly, a **7** ______________ up gesture generally means something good in Western countries, but it isn't a polite gesture in West Africa. People in many countries **8** ______________ hands when they meet, but the strength used might be different. And in some countries people just **9** ______________ at each other to say hello. There are even differences in how often people **10** ______________ to show they are happy!

GRAMMAR review

SCORE: / 10

A Use the prompts to write sentences in your notebook.

1 It is hard / persuade people / do / what you want them / do.
2 It's important / try / relax / if you want your audience / agree with you.
3 I always advise public speakers / not speak too fast.
4 Speak to people in person / avoid communication problems and / see their body language.
5 I prefer / speak to small groups because it's possible / see if they're listening.

B Check (✓) the correct responses. Rewrite the incorrect responses in your notebook.

1 "When did you take up karate?" ☐ "I took it up about a year ago."
2 "How did you come up with the idea for your app?" ☐ "I came it up with when I was at work."
3 "Is your story based on real life?" ☐ "No. I just made up it."
4 "Do you use your smartphone every day?" ☐ "Oh, yes! I rely it on for everything!"
5 "What does *irrelevant* mean?" ☐ "Why don't you look up it in the dictionary?"

16–20 correct: You can talk about communication and gestures. You can use infinitives with *to* and separable and non-separable phrasal verbs.
0–15 correct: Look again at the Vocabulary and Grammar sections in the unit.

TOTAL SCORE: / 20

WHAT DO YOU KNOW NOW? Look back at page 37 and add the words you know now to the boxes.

FOLLOW A PRO COMMUNICATION

Take the quiz about communication. Go to **Follow A Pro** on page 130 to find the answers. Then learn more about working in communication.

1 Where do companies spend the most money on advertising?
a television **b** newspapers **c** the internet

2 What percentage of the world's population can access the internet?
a 30%–35% **b** 55%–60% **c** 85%–90%

3 When was writing invented?
a 3,000 BCE **b** 500 BCE **c** 500 CE

4 When was the first radio program broadcast?
a 1906 **b** 1922 **c** 1935

UNIT 5 One Planet

WHAT DO YOU ALREADY KNOW?

1 Think about the words you know for weather. Write the words.

2 IN PAIRS Share and compare your ideas. Add more words to your lists.

Weather

Severe weather

DISCUSS & SHARE

VIDEO

3 IN GROUPS Watch the video and answer the question.

SYM Do you think the changes in severe weather are natural or caused by people?

In this unit, you will ...

- discuss global warming problems, talk about solutions, and brainstorm products.
- use thinking skills: summarize, analyze, and categorize.
- read about climate change.
- use strategies to start speaking for a group, talk about problems and solutions, and comment on ideas.
- use global-competence skills to explain your ideas about environmental projects.
- learn strategies to improve reading speed.

VOCABULARY

A Match the words in the box with the definitions.

climate degree forest fire melt trap weather

1 ____________________: a unit to measure temperature
2 ____________________: to keep something like air or gas in one place
3 ____________________: conditions in the atmosphere like temperature, rain, clouds, etc.
4 ____________________: a large area of trees burning
5 ____________________: the type of weather that a country or region has
6 ____________________: to change a solid material to a liquid

MAKE IT YOURS

Do these words used to describe climate change describe the changes where you live?

B IN PAIRS Test your partner. Take turns reading definitions from A and saying the correct word.

READING

A 5.01 IN PAIRS Choose *True* or *False*. Then read the article to check your answers.

1 Global warming and climate change are the same thing. True / False
2 Global warming is caused by the greenhouse effect. True / False
3 If the Earth's temperature rises just a little, there won't be any problems. True / False
4 If the polar ice caps melt, the seas will rise. True / False
5 If we do nothing, some coastal cities may disappear. True / False

FAQs About Climate Change

Followers

1 Are climate change and global warming the same thing?
Global warming refers to the general rise in the Earth's temperatures that has happened since the beginning of the Industrial Revolution. Climate change refers to all of the changes in weather and climate that are caused by global warming, such as hotter summers, more severe storms, and more forest fires.

2 What causes global warming?
Global warming began with the Industrial Revolution when we started using fossil fuels—carbon-based fuels like oil and gas—but most global warming has happened since the 1970s. When we burn fossil fuels, they produce carbon dioxide. The carbon dioxide in the atmosphere traps heat and holds it near the Earth. Other types of gases, like methane, also trap heat near the Earth. This is called the greenhouse effect.

3 Does it really matter if the Earth is only a few degrees warmer than it was?
It is true that the Earth is only about 0.99°C warmer than it was in the mid-20th century, but if temperatures go up even a small amount, big changes take place. Sea levels rise and more severe weather events happen. The United Nations predicts that if temperatures rise more than 1.5°C, the effect on our lives will be extreme. If we didn't burn so many fossil fuels, the effects of global warming wouldn't be so serious.

4 What are the effects of global warming and climate change?
Unless we stop global warming, the polar ice caps will melt and sea levels will rise. This will affect Arctic and Antarctic species like polar bears and penguins, and it will mean more floods in coastal cities. Some areas will have hotter summers with long droughts and terrible fires. Other areas will have colder winters with bad ice and snowstorms. There will be more severe weather events like tornadoes and hurricanes.

If we don't do anything about global warming, there will be terrible consequences. Some coastal cities like Miami, Osaka, and parts of Rio de Janeiro may disappear. Many species of animals may also disappear, and this will change the Earth's ecosystems. One thing is certain: our planet will not be the same place it is today.

GLOSSARY

drought (n): a long period of time when there is little or no rain and plants die

B **READING SKILL—Identify explanations, definitions, and examples** **Find and underline the following things in the text in A.**

1 definitions of global warming and climate change (Question 1)
2 three examples of changes caused by global warming (Question 1)
3 an explanation of what fossil fuels are (Question 2)
4 an explanation of what the greenhouse effect is (Question 2)
5 two examples of severe weather events (Question 4)

C **THINKING SKILL—Summarize** **Explain why scientists say that today's climate change and global warming are primarily caused by human activity.**

GRAMMAR review of conditionals

A **Match the conditionals (1–3) to the verb forms (a–c) to complete the rules.**

If temperatures go up even a small amount, big changes take place.
If that happens, the effect on our lives will be extreme.
Unless we stop global warming, the polar ice caps will melt.
If we didn't burn so many fossil fuels, global warming wouldn't happen so quickly.

1 (zero conditional) *If/Unless* + simple present verb, _____	**a** + *will/won't* + base verb
2 (first conditional) *If/Unless* + simple present verb, _____	**b** + *would/wouldn't* + base verb
3 (second conditional) *If/Unless* + simple past verb, _____	**c** + simple present verb

For more practice, go to page 148.

B **Label the sentences *zero, first,* or *second* according to the rules in A.**

1 If we stopped using fossil fuels, there would be less carbon dioxide. ______________
2 If sea levels rise, some cities will be in danger. ______________
3 Ice melts if the temperature goes above 0°C. ______________
4 If you watch a program about global warming, how do you feel? ______________
5 If you buy a new car, will you buy an electric one? ______________
6 If you could change one thing in your town or city, what would it be? ______________

C **IN PAIRS** **Discuss questions 4, 5, and 6 in B.**

SPEAKING

A **IN PAIRS** **Discuss which of the effects of global warming are affecting your country. Make some suggestions about what will happen and possible solutions. Make notes in your notebooks.**

- Rising sea levels
- Drought
- Severe rainstorms
- Hurricanes
- Tornadoes
- Severe winters

If sea levels continue to rise, we will probably lose three of our major coastal cities.

There are already more droughts in the center of the country, and they will get worse. This will affect our food supply because ...

If we changed to electric cars, we would produce less pollution.

B **IN GROUPS** **Work with another pair. Compare your ideas from A. Do you all agree? Use the Confident Communicator box to help you.**

A: We think that if sea levels rise, we'll lose ..., ..., and ... .
B: We agree about ... and ... . We might not lose ... because it's higher.

CONFIDENT COMMUNICATOR
START TALKING

To start the conversation when speaking for a group, use the following phrases:
We think ... / We believe ... / As we understand it, ... / As far as we know, ... / Our view is ... / We decided ...

VOCABULARY taking action

A Complete the sentences with words and phrases from the box.

create laws	pay a fine	reduce
don't allow	provide	require

Air and water pollution: Make companies that produce pollution **1** ____________.
Have lower taxes for people and companies that use clean energy.
Trash: 2 ____________ free recycling services. **3** ____________ the use of plastic.
Make people pay for plastic bags in stores and grocery stores. Make products that
4 ____________ less packaging.
Overfishing: Limit fishing of certain types of fish. **5** ____________ certain types of fishing nets.
Endangered species: 6 ____________ to protect species that are disappearing.

PRONUNCIATION word stress in verb phrases

A 5.02 Listen to the phrases and underline the stressed word in each phrase. What type of word is stressed?

verb + noun

1 reduce pollution
2 provide recycling
3 create laws

verb + adjective/adverb + noun

4 pay for plastic bags
5 require less packaging
6 use clean energy

B IN PAIRS Practice reading the sentences with stress on the correct words.

1 They should create a law that requires less packaging.
2 The city should provide recycling and support businesses that use clean energy.

LISTENING

A Discuss the questions as a class.

Do you think young people in your country are very concerned about environmental problems? Why or why not?

B 5.03 LISTENING SKILL—Listen for main ideas Listen to four short radio interviews. Which four environmental problems do the speakers talk about?

C 5.03 Choose the correct options. Then listen again and check.

1 The first person thinks the main cause of global warming is companies using …
  a fossil fuels. **b** taxes. **c** clean energy.
2 According to the second person, … of the people in the world don't have clean water to drink.
  a thousands **b** millions **c** billions
3 The third speaker is worried about trash, especially …
  a glass. **b** plastic. **c** metal.
4 The fourth speaker says that overfishing could destroy her country's …
  a oceans. **b** ecosystems. **c** economy.
5 The host says that he hopes … are taking environmental problems seriously.
  a governments **b** all countries **c** young people

D IN GROUPS THINKING SKILL—Analyze Prioritize the environmental issues mentioned in B. Which two are the most important?

GRAMMAR present and future hopes and wishes

A Write whether the sentences refer to the present (*P*) or the future (*F*).

1 I hope our generation is taking environmental problems seriously. ______
2 I hope our generation makes a lot of changes to help save the planet! ______
3 I hope all cities will provide free recycling soon. ______
4 I wish fossil fuels didn't exist! ______
5 I wish every country had stronger laws against water pollution. ______
6 I wish my government would make fishing companies reduce certain types of fishing. ______

B Match the structures (1–4) with the functions (a–d).

1 *wish* + *would* or *could* ______
2 *hope* + simple present, present progressive, or *can* ______
3 *hope* + *will*, *can*, or simple present ______
4 *wish* + simple past ______

a something that you want and expect to be true in the present
b something that you want and expect to happen in the future
c something that you would like to be true in the present but isn't
d something that you would like to happen in the future but probably won't

For more practice, go to page 148.

C Complete the conversations with the correct forms of the words in parentheses.

A: I hope it **1** ______________ (not rain) this weekend!
B: Let's see … My phone says it will be clear on the weekend. I hope that it **2** ______________ (be) correct!
A: I wish I **3** ______________ (have) more time to do volunteer work.
B: Me, too. I hope I **4** ______________ (can) do some volunteer work next semester.
A: I wish my brother **5** ______________ (help) me with my ecology project, but he says he can't.
B: I wish I **6** ______________ (not have) so much work because I would help you with it.
A: I hope the government **7** ______________ (create) a new soda tax law.
B: Yeah. I wish they **8** ______________ (create) a tax on plastic bottles, too!

D IN PAIRS Change the underlined information in C to make new conversations with your own ideas.

SPEAKING

A Think about the answers to these questions. Make notes.

1 Which environmental issues are most important in your country? Why?
2 What do you wish your country would do about these issues?
3 What do you hope your generation will do about environmental problems in the future?

A: I think global warming is the most important issue for us because we have two coasts.
B: I agree. If the seas rise, we'll lose some of our cities, and also, we'll have a lot of hurricanes and other bad storms. I wish we had stronger air pollution laws.
C: I hope young people will help educate the public about the problem of global warming.

B IN GROUPS Discuss your answers to the questions in A. Do most of you have similar ideas? Use the Confident Communicator box to help you.

CONFIDENT COMMUNICATOR
KEEP TALKING

To talk about problems and solutions, use the following phrases:
Problems
One problem/issue is …
The biggest/main problem/issue is…
… is a big/major/serious problem.
Solutions
If we had stronger laws, we wouldn't have so much pollution.
What if we had stronger pollution laws?
I think we need / should have stronger pollution laws.

LISTENING

A Match the environmental solutions (1–8) with the photos (a–h).

a

b

c

d

e

f

g

h

1 plant pots made from tires ____
2 recycled paper flip-flops ____
3 super trees ____
4 recycled plastic houses ____
5 fog catchers ____
6 school desks made from recycled materials ____
7 living walls ____
8 green roofs ____

B 5.04 LISTENING SKILL—Listen for details **Listen to a class discussion. Under the photos a–h in A, write the name of the country where each environmental solution is taking place.**

C 5.04 THINKING SKILL—Categorize **Listen again and decide who should do each of the eight projects. Categorize the projects as *private companies, the government,* or *either*. Give reasons for your opinions.**

I think the government would have to … because it would be very expensive.

MAKE IT REAL

Informal ways to say strange or unusual: *weird, bizarre, wild*

VOCABULARY materials and products

A Match the descriptions with words from the box.

coconut	flip-flop	net	pot	roof	rubber	steel	tire

1 a material with spaces made of string, rope, or metal wire: ____________
2 the part of a wheel that is filled with air: ____________
3 a container used to cook or to plant flowers or other plants: ____________
4 the fruit of a kind of palm tree: ____________
5 a strong metal made of iron and carbon: ____________
6 the top of a house or other building: ____________
7 a type of sandal with a V-shaped strap: ____________
8 a flexible material similar to plastic that comes from a tree: ____________

B IN PAIRS **Think of other things that can be made from recycled materials. Discuss.**

WRITING

A **Read the essay. Does the writer have a generally positive or generally negative opinion of his country's actions on the environment? Tell a partner.**

My country has changed a lot since I was a small child. Twenty years ago, air pollution was terrible in big cities, and water pollution was very bad, too. The government has given tax breaks to industries that moved to new locations, and they have created strong anti-pollution laws. Companies that pollute the air or water have to pay big fines. My city has built new parks and other green spaces, and it has created new pollution laws for vehicles.

The results from the changes have been positive, but I wish we would do more to help with problems like deforestation and global warming. If universities offered programs to train people in rural areas to do different jobs, they wouldn't have to cut down trees to get money. Also, my city gives people free trees to plant in their yards. There will be a lot more trees if all of the cities do that. Another thing that helps with the problem of air pollution and global warming in general is roof gardens. If companies put gardens on their roofs, the plants would put oxygen into the air and take out carbon dioxide. I believe that my country is doing some good things for the environment, and I hope we will do many more things in the near future.

B **IN PAIRS Find and underline actions and their results in the second paragraph of the text in A. Say which is the action and which is the result in each case.**

If universities offered programs to train people in rural areas to do different jobs (action), they wouldn't have to cut down trees to get money (result).

C **Think about environmental projects in your country. Make a list of actions your government or companies have taken and the results for the environment. Make another list of actions you recommend and the results.**

Action	*Result*
Reduced taxes for companies that move to new locations	*Less air pollution in big cities*
Recommended action	*Result*
Plant more trees in the cities	*More oxygen in the air*

D **Use your notes from C to write a short essay similar to the one in A.**

SPEAKING

A **IN PAIRS Brainstorm new ideas for programs or products to help the environment in your country.**

B **IN GROUPS Discuss which ideas are practical. Use the Confident Communicator box to help you.**

A: The government could create a law that requires all buildings to have living walls.
B: If they did that, it would be too expensive for a lot of people.
A: That's true. What if just big companies had to do it?
C: I think that's an awesome idea! It wouldn't be too hard, and it would help with air pollution.

CONFIDENT COMMUNICATOR
KEEP TALKING

To comment on good or unusual ideas, use the following phrases:
Good ideas: *What a cool / awesome / brilliant idea!*
Unusual ideas: *That's a (very) weird / bizarre / different / strange idea!*

Language and Life

Global Competence – Environmental Issues

A 5.05 **Read the blog. What is the blogger's main point?**

a Governments should do more to help the environment.
b Individual people and communities can only help the environment in very small ways.
c Individual people and communities can help the environment a lot.

Evan the Eco Guy—Micro-Ecology

How often have you heard or said this about a problem: "Why don't *they* do something?" Who is *they*? In the case of environmental problems, *they* probably refers to the government or to the world in general. But what if we stopped saying *they* and started saying *we*? There are many things that we, the people, can do to reduce global warming and to help the environment in general.

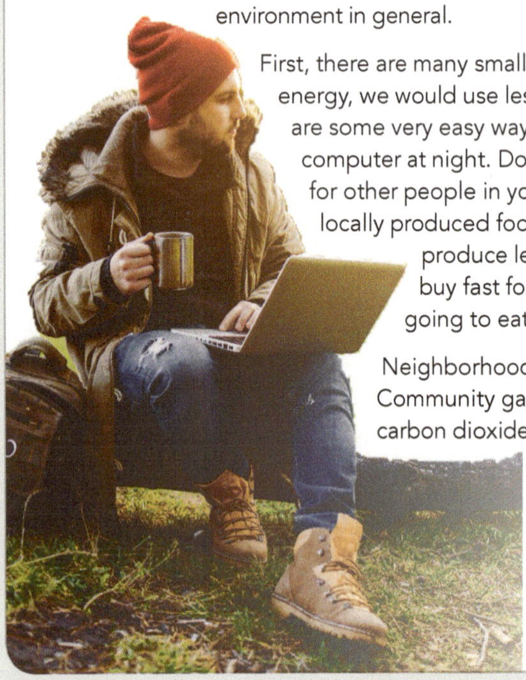

First, there are many small things that individual people and families can do. If we all tried to save energy, we would use less oil and gas, and there would be less carbon in the atmosphere. There are some very easy ways to save energy. Turn off lights when you are not in a room. Turn off your computer at night. Do several errands when you go out in your car, and offer to do errands for other people in your family. Share rides to school or work with family or friends. Try to buy locally produced food and other products. There are also many things that we can all do to produce less trash. Use reusable shopping bags for all types of shopping. When you buy fast food, don't take too many napkins, and don't take plastic forks if you are going to eat the food at home.

Neighborhoods and communities can also do many things to help the environment. Community gardens help in several ways. First, plants put oxygen into the air and use carbon dioxide. Second, if people eat food from local gardens, they are not eating food that was transported by trucks or planes. Third, flowers attract insects and birds that pollinate plants. Communities can also set up neighborhood websites to share rides, recycle things like clothes or toys, or organize volunteers to pick up trash in local parks and recycle it. If we did a little more as individuals and communities, we could have a very positive effect on our environment.

B IN PAIRS **Answer the questions about the blog in A.**

1 According to the blogger, who does the word *they* usually refer to?
2 What would happen if everyone did a few small things to save energy?
3 How do you think sharing rides and doing errands for other people can help save energy?
4 Why do you think buying local products helps the environment?
5 How many reasons does the writer give for having community gardens?
6 How can people use neighborhood websites?

C **Look at some ideas for individual environmental projects. Check (✓) the *Yes* column for the ones that you already do or think you would do. For the ones that you would not do, write the number of the reason in the *No* column.**

	Yes	No	Reason Not to Do It
Use a carpool to go to work or school.			1 I don't think it works.
Plant trees or flowers.			
Use my own coffee cup or water bottle.			2 It's expensive.
Combine errands with friends and neighbors.			3 It takes too much time or effort.
Use my own shopping bags.			4 I don't know how/where to do it.
Use energy-efficient light bulbs.			
Take shorter showers.			5 I won't remember to do it.
Have a vegetarian day once a week.			6 I don't want to do it.
Save gift wrapping and use it for other gifts.			7 It isn't possible in my area.
Buy locally produced food and products.			

D **IN GROUPS** **Discuss your answers to C. Encourage your classmates to take action and try some of the ideas.**

A: It's easy to buy local products. For example, you can shop at the farmer's market.

B: We should take shorter showers. Why? Because it saves water, and it also takes less time!

C: It doesn't matter if you don't know how. If you look online, you can find out how to …

D: It's really important to … because …

E **With your group, think of more ideas to take action and help the environment. Make a list of ideas.**

____

____

____

____

____

F **Share your ideas with the class and discuss whether you think they would work in your community. Agree on the top three ideas.**

A: I think a community garden is a great idea.

B: Me too. We could sell the vegetables we grow.

C: I'm not sure. You would need lots of volunteers.

G **Discuss the questions.**

1. Was it easy or difficult to encourage people to try your ideas? Why or why not?
2. How can we encourage people to change their every day habits?
3. What global impact would there be if we made these changes?

MAKE IT DIGITAL

Go online to find out what town or neighborhood programs already exist in your community and volunteer to help. If there are no initiatives, use social media to organize one.

VOCABULARY review

SCORE: / 10

A Complete the sentences with words from the box.

fines	melts	provide	rubber	traps
fog	nets	reduce	steel	weather

1 We need to ____________ our use of fossil fuels.
2 ____________ is a cloud close to the ground.
3 We're having bad ____________ this week—a lot of storms.
4 Cities ____________ many services, such as trash collection and electricity.
5 The greenhouse effect happens when carbon dioxide ____________ heat in the atmosphere.
6 Companies that pollute should have to pay ____________.
7 ____________ are often used to catch large numbers of fish.
8 If the ice in the Arctic and Antarctic ____________, sea levels will rise to dangerous levels.
9 ____________ is a natural material used to make things like tires and flip-flops.
10 ____________ is a type of very strong metal.

GRAMMAR review

SCORE: / 10

A Complete the blog entry with the correct forms of the verbs in parentheses.

Earth Citizen

I hope everyone **1** ____________ (read) this. If we **2** ____________ (not do) something about climate change in the near future, it **3** ____________ (be) too late. Years ago, scientists told us that if we didn't stop using so much fossil fuel, there **4** ____________ (be) terrible consequences. It isn't too late yet. If we used less fossil fuel, there **5** ____________ (be) less carbon in the atmosphere. Climate change would happen more slowly if we **6** ____________ (create) stronger laws, but unless we **7** ____________ (act) soon, we **8** ____________ (not have) our beautiful planet anymore! I wish everyone **9** ____________ (understand) the importance of this problem, and I wish world leaders **10** ____________ (work) together in the future to save our planet.

16–20 correct: You can talk about environmental issues and offer solutions. You can use conditionals for present and future hopes and wishes.
0–15 correct: Look again at the Vocabulary and Grammar sections in the unit.

TOTAL SCORE: / 20

WHAT DO YOU KNOW NOW? Look back at page 47 and add the words you know now to the boxes.

STUDY SKILLS IMPROVING READING SPEED

Take the quiz about improving reading speed. Go to **Study Skills** on page 131 to find the answers. Then learn more about improving reading speed.

1 It is always important to read things quickly.
a True **b** False

2 Reading aloud is always beneficial for reading.
a True **b** False

3 Which two of the following are active reading strategies?
a scanning **b** questioning **c** skimming **d** predicting

4 Moving your finger down the page as you read can help you read faster.
a True **b** False

UNIT 6

Moments in Time

WHAT DO YOU ALREADY KNOW?

1 Think about events, inventions, and people in history. Write the words.

2 IN PAIRS Share and compare your ideas. Add more words to your lists.

The past

DISCUSS & SHARE

VIDEO

3 IN GROUPS Watch the video and answer the question.

Do you wait for inspiration or do you do your work step by step?

In this unit, you will ...

- compare different generational use of technology, share your opinions about inventions, write quiz questions about people in history.
- use thinking skills: predict, evaluate, and question.
- read about technological change.
- use strategies to keep a conversation going when you do not know a word, interrupt politely, and express interest and surprise.
- use decision-making skills to make judgments about UNESCO sites.
- follow an archaeologist to learn about this job and the skills needed for this industry.

READING

A 6.01 **READING SKILL—Scan** **Check (✓) the commercial technology events that you think happened before 1900. Then scan the first paragraph of the magazine article to check your answers.**

- ☐ the first electric taxis
- ☐ the first commercial flight
- ☐ the first commercial telephone company
- ☐ the first movie theater
- ☐ the first locomotive passenger train
- ☐ the first radio station

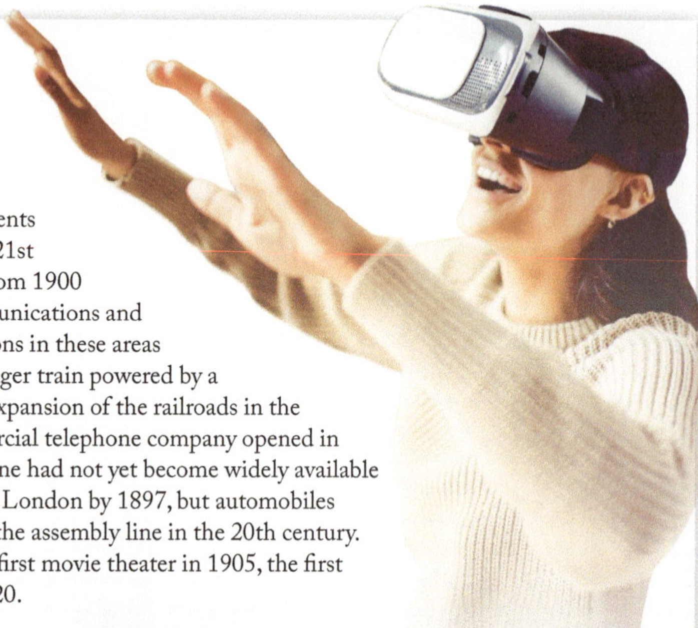

In Just 20 Years...

By the end of the 19th century, the Industrial Revolution had changed the world forever, and technology has continued to make many improvements since then. The first two decades of both the 20th and the 21st centuries brought life-changing progress in technology. From 1900 to 1920, there were enormous changes, especially in communications and transportation. Of course, there had already been innovations in these areas when the 20th century began. For example, the first passenger train powered by a locomotive had started in 1825 in England, but the huge expansion of the railroads in the US and Europe came in the 20th century. The first commercial telephone company opened in 1878, but at the beginning of the 20th century, the telephone had not yet become widely available to the public. Most surprisingly, there were electric taxis in London by 1897, but automobiles became available to ordinary people with the invention of the assembly line in the 20th century. The first two decades of the 20th century also brought the first movie theater in 1905, the first commercial flight in 1914, and the first radio station in 1920.

In the first two decades of the 21st century, progress in information technology was particularly important. This "Digital Revolution" included two of the most important developments in communications since the telephone — smartphones and the creation of social media platforms. The first social media network was Friendster in 2002, and the first modern smartphone was the iPhone in 2007. Entertainment technology also changed enormously from the close of the 20th century to the first decades of the 21st century. Some of the major 21st-century inventions so far have been wireless headsets in 2002, YouTube and internet radio in 2005, e-readers in 2007, and virtual reality headsets in 2016. It is hard to imagine where digital technology will take us by the end of the 21st century!

B **IN PAIRS** **Read the article. Then answer the questions.**

1. What two types of revolution does the article mention? When did they happen?
2. How many centuries are mentioned in the article?
3. What types of technology are mentioned in the first paragraph?
4. What were two important developments in communications in the 21st century?
5. How did entertainment technology change in the 21st century?
6. Did most of the progress in IT mentioned in the article happen in the first or the second decade of the 21st century?

GLOSSARY

innovation (n): a new idea, method, or object
assembly line (n): a system for making things in a factory in which each worker or machine adds one part
decade (n): 10 years

C **IN GROUPS THINKING SKILL—Predict** **The writer says it's hard to imagine where digital technology will take us by the end of the 21st century. Predict what technology you think will exist by the end of this century.**

A: I think people will have ... *B: I don't think so, but I think ... / Maybe there will be ...*

VOCABULARY

A Scan the article in READING A and write a word with a similar meaning for each of these words.

1 close (n): ______________________ [para. 1]
2 progress (n): ______________________ [para. 1]
3 huge (adj): ______________________ [para. 1]
4 especially (adv): ______________________ [para. 2]
5 invention (n): ______________________ [para. 2]
6 important (adj): ______________________ [para. 2]

GRAMMAR past perfect

A Label the underlined times or events *1* or *2* to indicate which happened first.

1 By the end of the 19th century, the Industrial Revolution had changed the world forever …

2 Of course, there had already been innovations in these fields when the 20th century began.

3 …, but at the beginning of the 20th century, the telephone had not yet become widely available to the public.

B Choose the correct options.

1 Use the **simple past** / **past perfect** to talk about an action that happened before another action in the past.
2 Use the **simple past** / **past perfect** to talk about an action that happened after another action in the past.
3 Form the past perfect with *have* / *had* + a past participle.

For more practice, go to page 149.

C Complete the paragraph with the simple past or past perfect forms of the verbs in parentheses.

I was born in 1980, so I've seen a lot of changes in technology in my life. When I **1** ______________ (start) college in 1998, I **2** ______________ (use) a computer, but I **3** ______________ (not send) an email because I didn't have internet. I **4** ______________ (get) internet service at home in 2000, and by 2002, when I **5** ______________ (graduate) from college, I **6** ______________ (learn) to use email, and I **7** ______________ even ______________ (join) the Friendster social media network! I **8** ______________ (think) I was very modern! 🙄

D Think about technology the year you became a teenager. Write three things you had already done and three things you hadn't done yet at that time. Share your sentences with a group or a partner. Who used more technology as a preteen?

I had already learned to use the internet.
I hadn't bought a tablet yet.

SPEAKING

A IN PAIRS Make a list of as many things as you can think of that people in the 21st century frequently do online, such as make plane reservations, buy things, or ask for advice about problems. Use the Confident Communicator box to help you.

B Make a list of things you think your parents had and had not done online by 2000.

C IN GROUPS Compare your lists. Whose parents had already done a lot of things online by 2000? Which things have they now done online that they hadn't done in 2000?

CONFIDENT COMMUNICATOR
KEEP TALKING

To continue the conversation when you don't know a word, use the following phrases to communicate what you mean:
I can't think of the exact word, but It's similar to … / It's a kind of …
What's the word I'm thinking of? It means …

LISTENING

A IN PAIRS Look at these 21st-century inventions. Match each picture (a–f) to a category (1–6), according to your opinions.

a car that drives itself

a waterproof notepad for the shower

a hammock for feet

a light that creates a bike lane

a camera that takes 360° photos

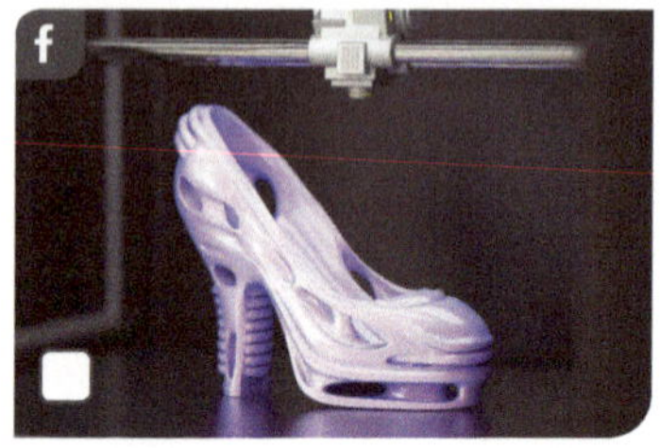

a printer that makes 3-D objects

1 the most unusual invention _____
2 the most amusing invention _____
3 the most exciting invention _____
4 the most worrying invention _____
5 the most useful invention _____
6 the most useless invention _____

B 6.02 Listen to the street interviews. Check (✓) the things in A that the speakers mention. Make notes of words the speakers use to describe each invention.

C 6.02 IN PAIRS LISTENING SKILL—Listen for supporting details Listen again. Then answer the questions.

1 Why is the first man worried about 3-D printers? ______________________________

2 Why is the first woman excited about 360° cameras? ______________________________

3 How does the second man feel about many 21st-century inventions? ______________________________

4 What is the second woman worried about with driverless cars? ______________________________

D IN GROUPS THINKING SKILL—Evaluate Assess the opinions of the people who were interviewed in B. Do you agree or disagree with their opinions? Discuss.

VOCABULARY *–ed* and *–ing* adjectives

A Read the examples from LISTENING B. Then choose the correct options to complete the rules.

A: I'm pretty worried about some of the recent inventions.
B: To me, the invention that is the most worrying so far is the 3-D printer.
A: I'm really amused by some of the things that have been invented.
B: Yes, I guess some inventions are more amusing than useful.

1 Adjectives like *worried* and *worrying* are formed from nouns / verbs.
2 Adjectives with *–ing* are used to describe something or someone / a feeling about something or someone.
3 Adjectives with *–ed* are used to describe something or someone / a feeling about something or someone.

B **Choose the correct adjective forms.**

I'm not sure about driverless cars. Personally, I think driving is **1** **amazed / amazing**, so I would be **2** **disappointed / disappointing** if I couldn't do it anymore. I understand that there are many people who would like to have a driverless car. How **3** **relaxed / relaxing** to sit in your car and read or sleep! I definitely get **4** **bored / boring** driving in traffic, and it would be very **5** **entertained / entertaining** to watch a video or play a game on your phone while your car drives, but we need to be patient and wait until the technology is more advanced.

MAKE IT YOURS

Some people think technology is amazing. Others are terrified. How do the different types of technology around you make you feel?

GRAMMAR defining relative clauses

A **Underline the word or phrase that each relative pronoun in bold refers to.**

1. I'm on a street **where** lots of young people hang out on Saturday evenings. ____________
2. If there's a time **when** people can make most of their own products, ... ____________
3. There are some inventors **who** are creating some pretty amusing things! ____________
4. ... to me, the invention **that** is the most worrying so far is the 3-D printer. ____________
5. The 21st-century device **which** does everything is the phone. ____________

B **Now label the sentences in A** ***person***, ***place***, ***time***, **or** ***object*** **according to what the relative pronoun refers to. Then choose the correct option in the rule.**

You can use *that / when* instead of *who* or *which*.

For more practice, go to page 150.

C **Complete the sentences with relative pronouns. Then think of a response to each sentence.**

1. Give an example of a time ____________ you bought something that you were disappointed with.
2. Name the main places ____________ you shop, apart from online.
3. Give examples of some recent innovations ____________ you have used lately.
4. Think of a person ____________ has been very important in the first decades of the 21st century.

D IN PAIRS **Share your responses in C with your partner.**

SPEAKING

A **Answer the questionnaire.**

Opinion Poll on 21st-Century Innovations and Inventions

1. What recent invention or innovation is the most exciting to you?
2. Are there any modern inventions that you find confusing and hard to use?
3. Was there a time when you were disappointed by a new product?
4. Is there an inventor or innovator who is a role model to you?
5. What possible future inventions are you interested in or excited about?

B IN GROUPS **Share your opinions about the poll in A.**

CONFIDENT COMMUNICATOR
KEEP TALKING

To interrupt someone politely, use these phrases:
Excuse me, can/may I interrupt?
Just a second. Can I ask you a question?
Sorry, can you repeat that?

LISTENING

A Match the people in the pictures (a–d) with the things they did (1–4).

a 
Michel Krieger

b 
Mario Molina

c 
Dr. Christiaan Barnard

d 
Mary Anderson

1 identified the danger of chlorofluorocarbons in the atmosphere. _____
2 performed the first heart transplant. _____
3 co-founded Instagram. _____
4 invented windshield wipers. _____

GLOSSARY

transplant (n): a medical operation to take an organ from one person's body and put it into another person's body
cardiac surgeon (n): a doctor who operates on human hearts
defect (n): a fault or problem in something
pneumonia (n): a serious illness of the lungs and respiratory system

B 6.03 THINKING SKILL—Question Predict the types of information in the podcast about a famous person. Write questions to ask about that information. Then listen and write the answers to your questions.

Questions	Answers
1 What was his name?	______________
2 ______________	______________
3 ______________	______________
4 ______________	______________

C 6.03 LISTENING SKILL—Listen for numerical information Listen again and write information about each number in your notebook.

1 1922 2 1967 3 54 4 18 5 7,000

D IN PAIRS Compare your notes in C. Explain in your own words the importance of each number.

VOCABULARY adjective suffixes

A Add the suffixes *–ful*, *–less*, *–able*, and *–ible* to form adjectives from LISTENING B. Then check your work with a partner. Some words can go in more than one column.

B	–ful	–less	–able	–ible
1 success–	*successful*			
2 cap–				
3 hope–				
4 incred–				
5 thank–				

B **Match the adjectives in A with the definitions below.**

1 ______________________: grateful or happy about something
2 ______________________: unlikely that a situation will succeed or improve
3 ______________________: achieving the result you want
4 ______________________: believing that something good will happen
5 ______________________: very, very good
6 ______________________: able to do something

PRONUNCIATION stress in multisyllable adjectives

A 6.04 **Listen and underline the stressed syllable in each word.**

hopeful capable thankful successful preventable incredible

WRITING

A **Read the short biographical essay. What was unusual about Valentina Tereshkova?**

Valentina Tereshkova

a In 1960, the idea of humans in space was still a dream. By the end of 1961, the dream had become reality with Soviet cosmonaut Yuri Gagarin. In that decade, science and space travel were dominated by men. **b** However, on June 16, 1963, cosmonaut Valentina Tereshkova became the first woman to travel into space.

c Valentina Tereshkova was born in 1937 in a small town about 277 km. from Moscow. In 1954, she started working at a textile factory, and around that time, she learned to parachute. Because of her parachuting experience, in 1962 she was chosen to train as a cosmonaut. On her space flight in 1963, Tereshkova orbited the Earth 48 times in a little less than three days. When she returned to Earth, Tereshkova parachuted over 6,000 meters from her spacecraft to Earth! **d** As the first woman in space, Valentina Tereshkova was a pioneer for women in space travel and for professional women in general.

B **Read the tips for writing a biography. Match the underlined parts (a–d) of the text in A to the tips (1–4).**

1 Choose a specific angle, e.g., the first to do something, and present it in your introduction. _____
2 Write an interesting first sentence to introduce the topic. _____
3 Restate your angle in the conclusion of your essay. _____
4 Give basic biographical facts about the person's life. Include some interesting details. _____

C **Make notes to prepare to write a short biographical essay. Use the tips in B as a guide.**

D **Write your biography. Then share it with a partner. Help each other with ideas for improvements.**

SPEAKING

A IN PAIRS **Match the historical facts (a–d) with the people (1–4).**

1 Roger Bannister (UK) _____
2 Junko Tabei (Japan) _____
3 Gabriela Mistral (Chile) _____
4 Leonardo da Vinci (Italy) _____

a the first woman who climbed Mt. Everest
b the first person who ran a mile in less than four minutes
c the first to understand the circulation of blood in the body
d the first Latin American author to win the Nobel Prize for Literature

B IN PAIRS **Write a quiz similar to the one in A. Your quiz should have four to six items.**

CONFIDENT COMMUNICATOR
KEEP TALKING

Use these phrases to express interest:
Really? *Oh, I didn't know that.* *That's interesting.* *Huh.*
Use these phrases to express surprise:
Seriously?! *That's so cool!*

Language and Life

Decison Making – UNESCO Sites

A 6.05 **Read the information about UNESCO sites. Then choose *True* or *False*.**

UNESCO: Preserving Our Heritage

The main role of the United Nations Educational, Scientific, and Cultural Organization (UNESCO) is to encourage international collaboration, and to promote global security and peace. One way that UNESCO achieves this is through the preservation of sites of great cultural or national importance. This develops respect for those sites among the citizens of those countries. It also educates tourists about those sites and encourages them to discover the beauty of that country's culture.

Tourists can find out more about all of the UNESCO's sites by going to the World Heritage List, which can be found on the official UNESCO website. Currently, there are almost 1,100 sites on this list, including national parks, forests, islands, temples, and houses. Some of the sites are very well-known, like the Great Wall in China and Machu Picchu in Peru, but there are many sites that are well-known only within the countries where they are located. It is possible to use the World Heritage List as a way to find out more about your own country, or to inspire future vacations.

To be included on the World Heritage List, a site needs to be considered of universal importance. UNESCO has created a set of criteria to select World Heritage sites. These criteria examine the site's cultural importance, as well as its natural beauty. There are a total of ten criteria that UNESCO considers in the site selection process, and a site has to have at least one of them to be selected. Some of the criteria are:

1 Be an example of an important cultural tradition of the past or present
2 Be an example of amazing human creativity
3 Be an example of a culture's use of land or sea that is positive for the environment
4 Have incredible natural beauty
5 Represent an important period in the Earth's history
6 Represent great achievements in technology, architecture, the arts, town planning, or landscape design

Khajuraho Temple, Madhya Pradesh, a UNESCO World Heritage site

1	One purpose of UNESCO is to educate people about different cultures.	True / False
2	All UNESCO sites are buildings.	True / False
3	All UNESCO sites are very famous.	True / False
4	A site has to have most of the criteria to be chosen by UNESCO.	True / False
5	Human creativity is important to UNESCO.	True / False
6	Ecology and the environment are factors in UNESCO selections.	True / False

B **IN PAIRS** **Read about a recent UNESCO selection. Decide which of the criteria in A you think UNESCO applied to this site.**

Chiribiquete National Park, Colombia—The Maloca of the Jaguar

The Chiribiquete National Park is the largest protected area in Colombia. The flat, table-top mountains are an unusual geological feature, and they give the park its dramatic beauty. There are rock shelters at the base of the mountains that have over 75,000 paintings dating from 20,000 BCE to the present. The paintings represent the powerful jaguar, and this is a sacred region for indigenous communities.

C **IN PAIRS** **You are going to choose a site in your country to propose as a UNESCO World Heritage Site. Follow the steps to help you make a good decision.**

Making Decisions with Criteria and Weight

1 Rate the six UNESCO criteria in column 1 from 1 to 3 points—3 being very important to you and 1 being the least important to you.
2 Think of a site or region in your country that might qualify for UNESCO. Add it to the table in column 2.
3 Rate your site from 1 to 3 for each of the six criteria (3—completely matches the criterion; 1—does not match the criterion very well).
4 Multiply each criterion by the rating. Add up the total points for each option.

1 UNESCO Criteria (1–3 points)	2 Site/Region: ________ (rating 1–3)	3 Weighting (criterion x rating)
1: _____ pt(s).		
2: _____ pt(s).		
3: _____ pt(s).		
4: _____ pt(s).		
5: _____ pt(s).		
6: _____ pt(s).		
		Total weighting score: ________

D **IN GROUPS** **Present your UNESCO proposal to your group. Compare and evaluate weighting scores and decide which proposal is best for a UNESCO site. Present your proposal to the class.**

E **Discuss the questions.**

1 Do you think this is a useful way to help make decisions? Why or why not?
2 In what other situations might you use this ranking and rating system?

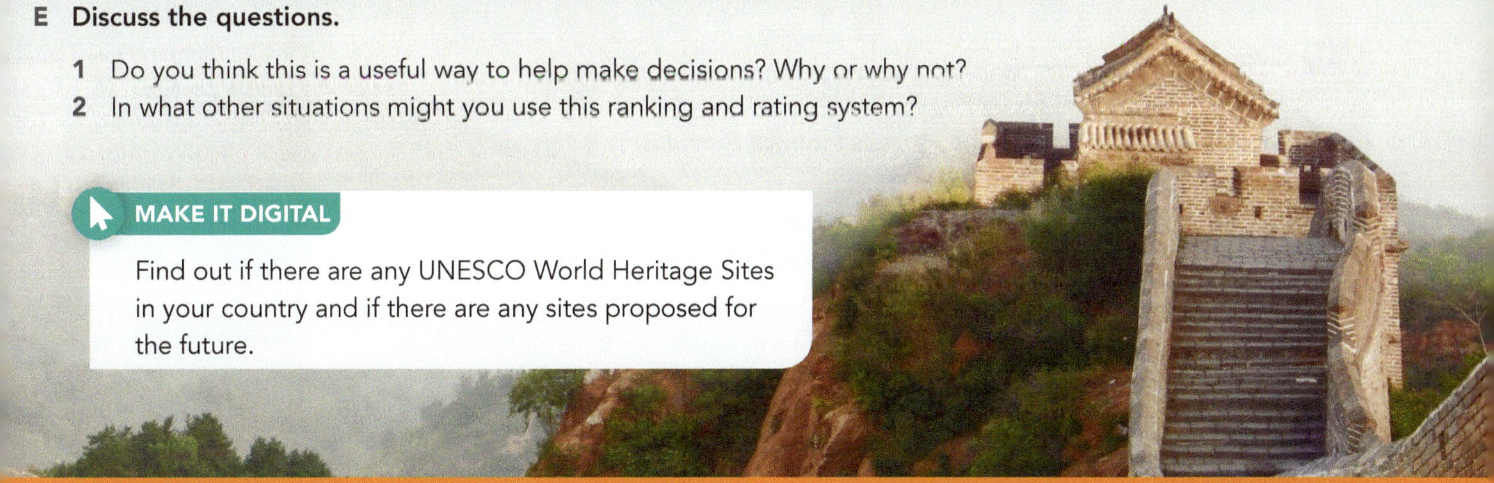

MAKE IT DIGITAL

Find out if there are any UNESCO World Heritage Sites in your country and if there are any sites proposed for the future.

VOCABULARY review

SCORE: / 10

A Choose the correct words.

I'm **1 thankless / thankful** that there are so many **2 capable / hopeful** people who invent useful things! Some are famous and **3 successful / entertaining** people like Bill Gates, but many are not famous at all. There are people who work at companies all over the world to give us **4 amazing / amazed** things like 3-D cameras and driverless cars. It's very **5 entertained / entertaining** to play video games or watch online videos, and someone had to invent that technology. However, being an inventor can be **6 boring / bored** because an inventor has to focus on very small details, and it takes a long time to invent something. Inventors are **7 disappointed / disappointing** when their inventions don't work very well, but sometimes an invention becomes a **8 capable / huge** success. A **9 huge / particularly** important invention in recent years was HD (high-definition) TV. This was an enormous **10 improvement / creation** in TV technology.

GRAMMAR review

SCORE: / 10

A Complete the sentences with the simple past or past perfect forms of the verbs in parentheses.

1. My dad ____________ (not have) a smartphone before I ____________ (give) him one for his birthday.
2. After I ____________ (save) enough money, I ____________ (buy) a small car.
3. When my dad ____________ (buy) his first car, he ____________ never ____________ (drive) a car!
4. At the beginning of the 21st century, many people ____________ (not use) the internet.
5. No one ____________ (hear) the term *social media* when the first social media network ____________ (begin) in 2002.

B Complete the sentences with *who, that, where, when,* and *which.*

1. Driverless cars are an innovation ____________ may change the transportation industry.
2. Tech companies are places ____________ there are a lot of creative people!
3. An AI specialist is a person ____________ works in artificial intelligence technology.
4. My dad was born in a decade ____________ a lot of important technology was invented.
5. There are millions of people in the world ____________ use the internet every day.

16–20 correct: You can talk about events in history and changes in the modern world. You can use defining relative clauses and adjective suffixes.
0–15 correct: Look again at the Vocabulary and Grammar sections in the unit.

TOTAL SCORE: / 20

WHAT DO YOU KNOW NOW? Look back at page 57 and add the words you know now to the box.

FOLLOW A PRO ANCIENT CIVILIZATIONS

Take the quiz about ancient civilizations. Go to **Follow A Pro** on page 132 to find the answers. Then learn more about archeologists.

1 Cleopatra was ...
a Greek. **b** Egyptian. **c** Roman.

2 According to a Roman legend, Rome's founder, Romulus, was raised by a ...
a Greek woman. **b** goddess. **c** wolf.

3 The oldest civilization in the Americas was the ...
a Olmec in Mexico. **b** Caral Supe in Peru. **c** Cherokee in the US.

4 One of the first medical centers was in ...
a Persia (Iran), in the 6th century. **b** Athens, Greece, in the 12th century. **c** London, England, in the 16th century.

UNIT 7 Looking Back

WHAT DO YOU ALREADY KNOW?

1 Think of words about things people sometimes regret. Write the words.

2 IN PAIRS Share and compare your ideas. Add more words to your lists.

Regrets

DISCUSS & SHARE

VIDEO

3 IN GROUPS Watch the video and answer the question.

SYM Do you think it's good to have regrets, or is it better to focus on the future?

In this unit, you will ...

- talk about things that a business should have done differently, discuss things you should not have bought, and recall events you regret.
- use thinking skills: evaluate, analyze, and apply.
- read about famous mistakes in history.
- use strategies and language to introduce an anecdote, give reasons for opinions and decisions, and set the scene for a story.
- use interpersonal communication skills to plan and give a presentation.
- learn skills to structure your writing.

READING

A IN GROUPS THINKING SKILL—Evaluate **Assess a description of the "butterfly effect." Do you think the statement is true, partly true, or false? Explain.**

A butterfly moves its wings in Brazil, and it creates a storm in Texas.

B 7.01 **Read the article about famous mistakes. Is either of the mistakes an example of the butterfly effect?**

Famous Mistakes in History

1. Expensive Decision

In the 1982 mega-hit movie *E.T.* there is a scene where the little boy uses candy to convince *E.T.* the extraterrestrial, to follow him. The filmmakers had planned to use M&Ms for this scene, but Mars, Inc. did not give them permission to use their candy. They then asked Hershey for permission to use Reese's Pieces, and Hershey agreed, so it **turned out** that Reese's Pieces candy was used in the movie. Two weeks after the movie opened, sales of Reese's Pieces **went up** by around 65%. Today, a Reese's product is the number one candy in the US! Mars Inc. shouldn't have missed this opportunity!

2. Lost in Space

The Mars Climate Orbiter was a small spacecraft built to orbit Mars and record information about the surface and atmosphere of the planet. It went into space in December 1998, and it disappeared in September 1999. When researchers **looked into** why the Orbiter was lost, they **came across** an important mistake. They **found out** that the system on the spacecraft had used the metric system, while the computers on Earth had used the imperial system. Because of this mistake, the Orbiter went too close to Mars and **burned up**. Someone should have noticed that the two systems used different measurements!

GLOSSARY

metric system (n): a system of measurement that uses meters and kilograms
imperial system (n): a system of measurement that uses yards and pounds
orbit (v): the path of an object moving around a larger object in space
measurement (n): the exact size of something, expressed in numbers of standard units

C READING SKILL—Synthesize **Match the descriptions below to the famous mistakes in B. Write the numbers.**

1 a mistake caused by different people using different systems ____
2 a mistake that was very lucky for a competitor ____

VOCABULARY phrasal verbs

A Match the phrasal verbs in bold in READING B to the definitions (1–6). Write the base form of each phrasal verb.

1 ______________: to investigate an event or situation
2 ______________: to have a certain result
3 ______________: to discover information
4 ______________: to meet someone or discover something by chance
5 ______________: to be destroyed by fire or heat
6 ______________: to increase

B **Choose the correct phrasal verbs.**

When companies have poor sales, they have to **1** come across / look into the reasons why a product doesn't sell. When they do research, they sometimes **2** find out / turn out that the problem is with the marketing, but sometimes it **3** finds out / turns out that the problem is the product itself. The company may have to stop developing that product and develop a new product. This is not always a problem. Sometimes a series of mistakes can result in new products that make the company's sales **4** look into / go up a lot.

GRAMMAR *should/shouldn't have*

A **Choose the correct options.**

Someone should have noticed that the two systems used different measurements!
Mars Inc. shouldn't have missed this opportunity!

1 *Should have* and *shouldn't have* are used to express …
- **a** recommendations for the past.
- **b** recommendations for the present.
- **c** recommendations for the future.

2 *Should have* and *shouldn't have* are followed by the … form of a verb.
- **a** base form.
- **b** simple past.
- **c** past participle.

For more practice, go to page 151.

B **Complete the responses using *should have* or *shouldn't have* and the correct form of the verb in parentheses.**

1 A British couple asked a lottery official to check their lottery ticket numbers. The official checked the numbers and told the couple that they had not won any money. The official tore the ticket in two pieces and threw it away. However, the couple later received a message to keep their ticket. They got the torn ticket from the lottery official, and it turned out that they had won 57.9 million euros!

The official *should have checked* (check) the numbers more carefully. / The official *shouldn't have thrown away* (throw away) the ticket.

2 In 1999, a company called Excite had the opportunity to buy Google. The heads of Google wanted one million dollars, but then they changed the price to $750,000. Excite thought it was too expensive and turned down the offer. Today, Google is worth billions of dollars.

Excite ____________ (buy) Google. / Excite ____________ (turn down) the offer.

3 J. K. Rowling's first book, *Harry Potter and the Philosopher's Stone*, was turned down by 12 publishers before it was published by Bloomsbury. One reason why Bloomsbury decided to publish the book was that the chief executive officer's eight-year-old daughter read part of the book and loved it.

The 12 publishers ____________ (turn down) the book. / The 12 publishers ____________ (accept) the book.

C **IN PAIRS** **Take turns reading the responses in B. Do you have similar opinions?**

SPEAKING

A **Think of a mistake that a person or a company made and consider what they should have done differently. Use the questions as a guide and make notes.**

1 Who was the person or what was the company?
2 What mistakes did the person or company make?
3 What should they have done differently?
4 How did the situation turn out?

B **IN GROUPS** **Tell your group what happened. Say what you think the person or company should have done differently. Discuss other possible options with your group. Use the Confident Communicator box to help you.**

CONFIDENT COMMUNICATOR
START TALKING

To introduce an anecdote or a short true story, use these phrases:
Here's something that happened to (person/company) in (date).
Listen to this. In (date), (name) made a really bad decision.

Why Did I Buy That?

VOCABULARY *spend, lose, waste*

A Write *spend, lose,* or *waste*.

1 ____________ : to have less money because of mistake
2 ____________ : to use money or time to get something
3 ____________ : to use money or time in a careless way

B Choose the correct words.

1 Many people **waste** / **lose** a lot of money buying unnecessary things.
2 Making a financial plan can help you **waste** / **spend** your money carefully.
3 If you buy lottery tickets, you are probably just **wasting** / **spending** your money.
4 Many people **lost** / **wasted** a lot of money when stock prices fell.
5 My uncle started a small company, but it failed. He **spent** / **lost** all of his money.

LISTENING

A IN PAIRS Which of these things do you think people often regret buying? Discuss.

1 vacation homes

2 a desktop computer

3 exercise equipment

4 collectible objects

5 a new car

6 a swimming pool or a hot tub

B 7.02 Listen to the radio interviews. Check (✓) the items in A they discuss.

GLOSSARY

regret (v): to feel sorry or sad about something that happened
regret (n): a feeling of sadness about something that happened

MAKE IT YOURS

What things do your family and friends regret spending money on? How do you feel about the ways you spend money?

C 7.02 LISTENING SKILL—Listen for reasons Listen to the panel discussion again. Answer the questions.

1 For what two reasons does Steve regret getting a swimming pool? ____________
2 According to Monica, what are the problems with vacation homes? ____________
____
3 Why does Omar regret buying a desktop computer? ____________
4 Why does Sarah say she wishes she hadn't spent money on dolls? ____________

D IN GROUPS THINKING SKILL—Analyze After listening to the panel discussion, what can you infer about people's reasons for buying things that they later regret? Why do so many people waste money on those things?

PRONUNCIATION /s/ and /z/

A 7.03 Do the letters in bold make an /s/ sound or a /z/ sound? Listen and check. Then practice saying the words.

lose   waste   tools   use   exercise   house   desktop   objects

GRAMMAR past perfect for wishes about the past

A Choose the correct options.

1 "We really wish we had never bought that vacation home!" means ...
a "We bought a vacation home."
b "We didn't buy a vacation home."

2 "I really wish I had saved that money instead" means ...
a "I saved money."
b "I didn't save money."

3 The correct form of the verb for a wish about the past is *had* (*not/never*) + ...
a past participle.
b base form.

For more practice, go to page 152.

B Write what the person probably wishes in each situation. You may want to write more than one sentence.

1 Justin bought a motorcycle two years ago. Since then, he has had three accidents and a lot of hospital bills.
a He wishes he hadn't *bought the motorcycle.*
b He wishes he had *been more careful.*

2 Karen sold her house and moved to another town. It's expensive there, and she is paying more for rent than she was paying for her mortgage loan.
a Karen wishes she had ______________________.
b Karen wishes she hadn't ______________________.

3 Paul got a good job offer, so he quit college and took the job. Now he is worried that he won't be able to move forward in his career.
a Paul wishes he had ______________________.
b Paul wishes he hadn't ______________________.

4 Leo is 45, and he is losing his hair. He saw an ad on TV for a machine that makes hair grow. It was expensive, but he ordered it immediately because he didn't want to waste any time. He didn't read any reviews of the product. He has been using the machine for several months, but the machine doesn't work.
a Leo wishes he had ______________________.
b Leo wishes he hadn't ______________________.

C IN PAIRS Read your sentences from B. Did you have similar ideas? Discuss.

SPEAKING

A Think of two or three things you wish you hadn't bought. Use the cues to make notes about each thing.

Object or service bought: ______________________
Reason(s) you bought it: ______________________
Reason(s) why you regret buying it: ______________________

B IN GROUPS Tell your group about the things you regret buying. Use the Confident Communicator box to help you.

CONFIDENT COMMUNICATOR
KEEP TALKING

To give reasons for opinions and decisions, use the following phrases:
One reason why I wish ... is that ...
I should/shouldn't have ... because ...
The problem is/was that ...
I wish I had ... before I ...

Life's Regrets

LISTENING

A THINKING SKILL—Apply As a class, predict five things you think people often regret when they get older.

1 ______
2 ______
3 ______
4 ______
5 ______

B 7.04 Listen to a talk about regrets. Which of your ideas in A does the speaker mention? Did any of the regrets surprise you?

C 7.05 LISTENING SKILL—Listen for main ideas Listen again to three segments of the talk about types of regrets. Then choose the main idea of each segment.

1 Professional Lives
  a People wish they had earned more money.
  b People wish they had not worked so much.

2 Friendships
  a People wish they hadn't lost touch with old friends.
  b People wish they hadn't made old friends angry.

3 Children
  a People wish they had taught their children to do more things.
  b People wish they had had more children.

VOCABULARY collocations

A Match the parts of the verb phrases.

1 turn down ____
2 miss ____
3 get in / stay in / lose ____
4 spend / waste ____
5 break up with ____

a a job / an invitation / an opportunity / a chance
b a boyfriend / girlfriend
c an opportunity / a chance
d touch (with someone)
e time or money

B Complete the paragraph with the correct forms of verb phrases from A.

I'm 84 years old, and I've had a wonderful life, but I have a few regrets. I've **1** ___*missed*___ some ___*chances*___ to do exciting things and make my life even better. I also have a professional regret. I **2** ______ an ______ to go to an excellent art school because I didn't want to move to New York, and I really regret that. I stayed in my small town and lived with my parents. I **3** ______ some ______ (about three years) doing small jobs before I finally went to college. I wish I had gone to college and started my studies earlier. Finally, one of my biggest regrets is that I didn't **4** ______ with my best friend from college, but I'm trying to **5** ______ with her now. I hope I can find her.

MAKE IT REAL

There are many ways to describe the end of a relationship. People can *split up with* or *part ways with* their partners.

WRITING

A **IN PAIRS** **Read the blog entry. Why does the writer have mixed feelings about the messages?**

NO REGRETS? Really?

There are many messages on posters and on the internet that tell us that we should never regret things we think we should or shouldn't have done. **They say that** we should follow our hearts, take chances, and do the things we really want to do. That way, when we are older, we will not think "I wish I had done X," or "I wish I hadn't done Y." **Another argument is that** we should only regret the things we *wanted* to do but didn't do.

I have mixed feelings about these messages. **I think** people sometimes have to take chances in order to reach their goals. **I believe that** people often waste time regretting decisions they made and thinking about what they should have done differently. However, it is unrealistic to think that people can live their whole lives with no regrets. We all have regrets about something.

B **Write the phrases in bold in A in the correct columns in the table.**

Stating Your Opinion	Stating Other People's Opinions
In my opinion, …	Some people say that …
In my experience, …	Other people believe that …
I feel that …	Others feel that …
____________________	____________________
____________________	____________________
____________________	

C **Think about the posters and blog in A. Make notes in your notebook.**

1. What is your opinion of the first poster? Why?
2. What is your opinion of the second poster? Why?
3. What is your opinion of the blog? Do you agree or disagree with the blogger's ideas? Why?

D **Write a blog about your opinion on regrets. Include phrases from B.**

E **IN GROUPS** **Read your blog to your group. What are your group members' opinions about your ideas?**

SPEAKING

A **Make notes to tell an anecdote about a small thing that you regret. Try to think of something funny if possible. You do not have to talk about any regrets that you feel uncomfortable about.**

- What did you do or say?
- What was the result?
- What do you wish you had done differently?
- What did you learn from the experience?

B **IN GROUPS** **Tell your anecdotes. Give your classmates further advice about what they should or shouldn't have done. Use the Confident Communicator box to help you.**

Last week, I was at a restaurant with some friends. We ordered so much food! For dessert, I asked for a "chocolate bomb." It was a huge slice of chocolate cake with a massive serving of chocolate ice cream. I ate all of it, but felt so sick later. I definitely wish I hadn't eaten that dessert! I should have ordered some fruit.

CONFIDENT COMMUNICATOR

START TALKING

To start a story, set the scene.
Place: *I was at / in / on my way to …*
People: *I was alone / with …*
What was happening: *I was / We were … –ing …*

Language and Life

Interpersonal Communication – A Presentation

A 7.06 **Read the case study. Then choose the correct options on the next page.**

Case Study:

The Edsel

INTRODUCTION

In 1957, the Ford Motor Company introduced the Edsel, a car that they were promoting as "the car of the future." However, the Edsel turned out to be one of the greatest mistakes in business history.

BASIC IDEA AND RESEARCH

- In the early 1950s, the US economy was extremely strong, and Ford wanted a new car in the medium-price range. Unfortunately, they did not pay attention to research that showed the US would soon experience a recession.
- Ford did not do enough research to find out what customers really wanted in a car. Instead, they based most of their decisions on the opinions of Ford executives, the people who managed the company.
- The executives spent a lot of money on research to help them decide on the name of the car, but they decided to use the name of Henry Ford's son, Edsel. It turned out that people hated the name.

DESIGN

- Ford wanted to design a car that looked very different from existing cars, but the company did not do research to find out if people liked the design. They didn't show the design to sales people or the public before the car was produced.
- The company wanted to produce a car that many different types of people would buy, so they made 18 different models of the Edsel.
- The Edsel had many new features that hadn't been used in cars before, but those new things did not always work well.

DESIGN

- Ford started promoting the Edsel as "the car of the future" in advertisements a year before the car was produced. There was a lot of excitement about it, and people even waited in line to see it. Unfortunately, many people did not like the new design when they saw it. They decided that it was an ugly, expensive car with a terrible name.

1957 Edsel

1964 Mustang

LESSONS LEARNED

Ford learned from its mistakes with the Edsel. They did excellent research for the Ford Mustang, which they produced in the 1960s. The Ford Mustang became one of the greatest successes in business history. It was exactly the right car for the right customers at the right time, and the Mustang is still a very popular car today.

1 The basic idea for the Edsel was based on ...
   a existing cars. b Ford executives' opinions. c a lot of research.
2 Ford wanted to sell the Edsel to ...
   a young people. b wealthy people. c many types of people.
3 To sell the Edsel, Ford used the idea that it was ...
   a modern and different. b inexpensive. c attractive.
4 People thought the Edsel was _____ it had appeared in the advertisements.
   a better than b not as good as c the same as
5 Ford used _____ process for designing the Mustang.
   a exactly the same b a similar c a completely different

B IN PAIRS Discuss the questions.

1 What should Ford have done differently when it designed, promoted, and produced the Edsel?
2 Why was the Mustang a great success?

C IN GROUPS You are going to work together to plan a presentation about a product that was a failure. Follow the steps. Think about each person's skills and what each person can do to prepare and deliver the presentation. Look at the different points below and decide who in your group should be responsible for each part.

Step 1

Research the product—who likes investigating new facts?

- name and type of product
- company that made it
- target customers
- where it was advertised
- what the advertising promised
- design or quality
- how it was promoted
- the product
- how it was advertised
- what the company and others can learn from this experience

Step 2

Structure the presentation—who likes organizing information in an interesting and logical way?

- Decide the basic structure of the presentation.
- Plan what information there should be in each part.
- Agree on the key point you want to communicate.

Step 3

Give the presentation—who likes talking to groups and communicating their ideas?

- Decide who will say what.
- Discuss how you can engage your audience.
- Give the presentation!

D Discuss the questions.

1 How did you communicate your reasons for choosing each person's responsibility?
2 Did everyone agree with the reasons? Why or why not?
3 In what other situations might you have to communicate with a group of people?

MAKE IT DIGITAL

Before you buy a product, go online and read customer reviews. This can help you decide whether or not to spend money on the product.

VOCABULARY review

SCORE: / 10

A Complete the text with the correct forms of the verbs from the box.

find out	look into	lose touch	spend	turn out
go up	lose	miss	stay in touch	waste

My dad's business wasn't growing, so he **1** ______________ why that was happening, and he **2** ______________ that the main problem was customer service. When the company started, my dad personally **3** ______________ with all of the customers, but as the company grew, he had many other things to do. He said he couldn't **4** ______________ time visiting or talking on the phone to customers. It **5** ______________ that if you don't take care of your customers, you **6** ______________ their business! So he hired some people to help with other parts of the business, and he spoke directly with customers. Now he doesn't **7** ______________ an opportunity to talk to a customer. He **8** ______________ a lot of time each day making phone calls, and he often visits customers. He never **9** ______________ with them! Now my dad's business is growing again! Profits have **10** ______________ and he is happy.

GRAMMAR review

SCORE: / 10

A For each situation, write two sentences: one using *should / shouldn't have* and another using *wish*. Use your notebook.

1 My dad's new cell phone isn't very good. He didn't read any reviews before he bought it.
2 I didn't go to Sam's party last Friday. I heard it was great!
3 Monica didn't help her brother study for his math exam, and he failed it.
4 I moved to another town and lost touch with my old friends.
5 Carol and Steve bought 20 lottery tickets, but they didn't win. They wasted a lot of money!

16–20 correct: You can talk about past mistakes and regrets. You can use *should/shouldn't have* and the past perfect for wishes about the past.
0–15 correct: Look again at the Vocabulary and Grammar sections in the unit.

TOTAL SCORE: / 20

WHAT DO YOU KNOW NOW? Look back at page 67 and add the words you know now to the box.

STUDY SKILLS STRUCTURING YOUR WRITING

Take the quiz about structuring your writing. Go to Study Skills on page 133 to find the answers. Then learn more about structuring your writing.

1 When we use the word *argument* to talk about essay writing, what do we mean?
a a disagreement between the writer and the reader
b the point the writer makes (which also gives the essay its structure)

2 Put the essay outline in order.
_____ main argument
_____ introduction
_____ conclusion
_____ objections to main argument
_____ title

3 Which of the following are linking words?
a although **b** in spite of **c** consequently **d** outline

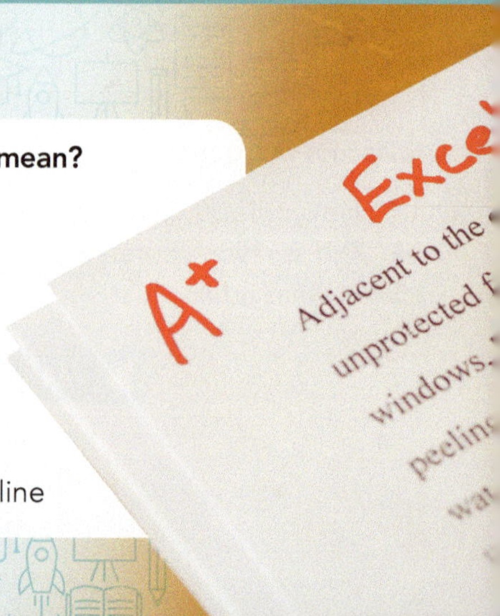

UNIT 8

A New Home?

WHAT DO YOU ALREADY KNOW?

1 Think of words you know about space. Write the words.

2 IN PAIRS Share and compare your ideas. Add more words to your lists.

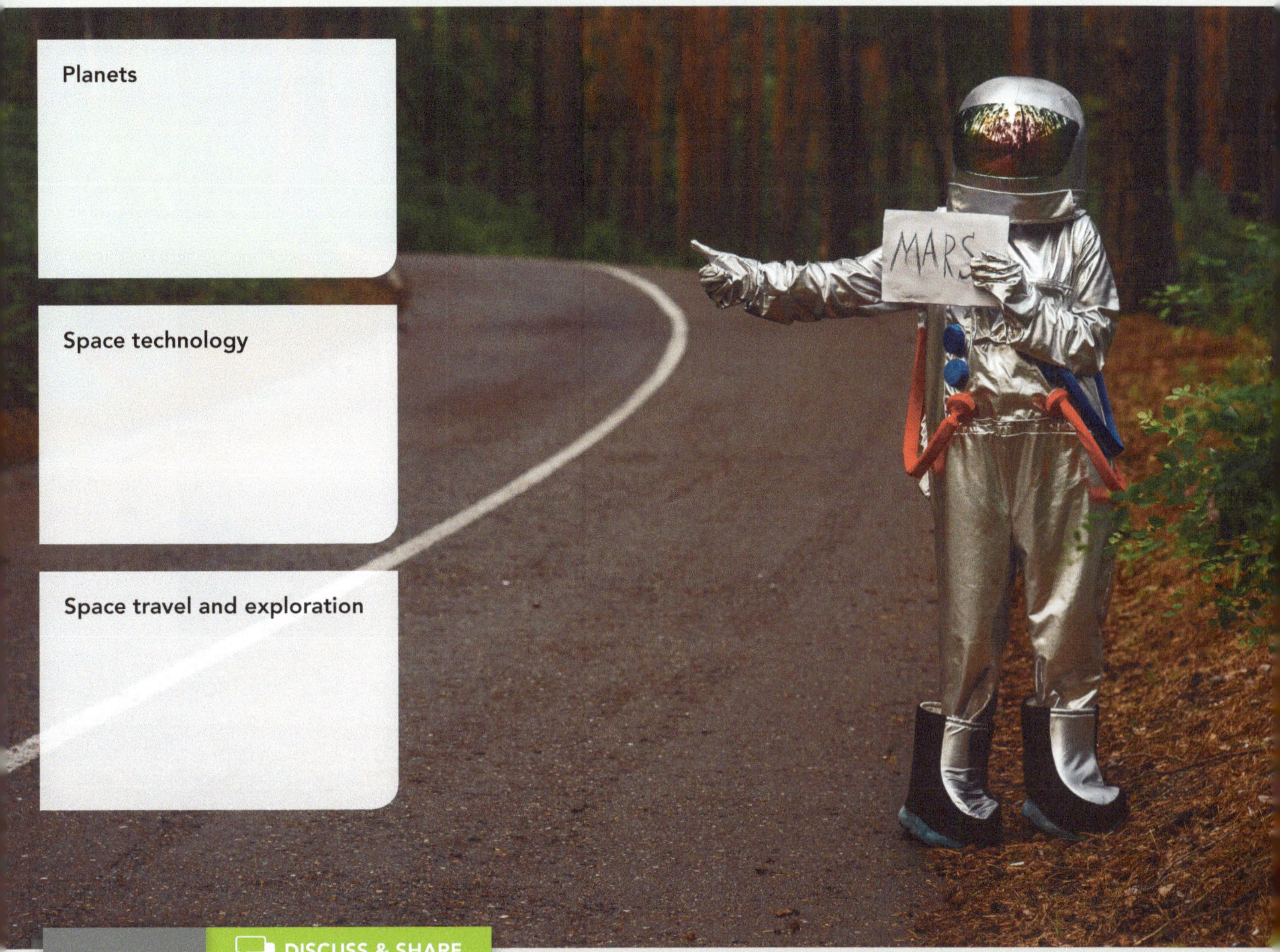

Planets

Space technology

Space travel and exploration

VIDEO

DISCUSS & SHARE

3 IN GROUPS Watch the video and answer the question.

Should we focus on problems on Earth before we explore other planets?

In this unit, you will ...

- talk about hypothetical events in history, role play an interview with an astronaut, and discuss your opinions of space exploration.
- use thinking skills: analyze, question, and recall.
- read about the extinction of the dinosaurs.
- use strategies and language to express possibility or probability, use indirect questions to sound more polite, and clarify reasons for opinions.
- use reasoning skills to make decisions about a space team.
- follow an astrobiologist to learn about this job and the skills needed for this industry.

VOCABULARY

A Match the words to the definitions.

asteroid debris crater tidal wave extinction soot herbivore carnivore

1 ____________: a very large wave
2 ____________: a dirty black substance from a fire
3 ____________: an animal that eats only plants
4 ____________: a mass of rock that moves in space
5 ____________: when a species disappears
6 ____________: a large round hole in the ground
7 ____________: an animal that eats other animals
8 ____________: small pieces left when something is destroyed

READING

A IN PAIRS READING SKILL: Predict Number the events leading up to the extinction of the dinosaurs in the order you think they happened.

☐ Plants died, and the herbivores didn't have food.

☐ Burning debris caused forest fires.

☐ Soot blocked the sunlight.

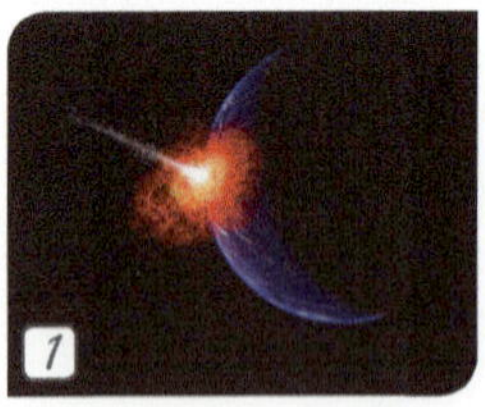
1 An asteroid hit the Earth and made a crater.

☐ The carnivores didn't have food, so they died.

☐ The impact caused tidal waves.

B 8.01 Read the article and check your predictions.

WHAT ON EARTH HAPPENED?

Sixty-six million years ago, during the time of the dinosaurs, something happened that changed our planet forever. A meteorite hit the Earth near the Yucatan Peninsula of Mexico and created a crater that was 185 km wide. The impact caused an explosion equal to about 10 million Hiroshima bombs. This caused a chain of events that resulted in mass extinctions of life on Earth.

Scientists almost all agree that the meteorite was the main cause of these mass extinctions. They now think they understand what happened after the meteorite hit. First, if you had been within 1,000 km. of the impact site, you would have been killed by a massive ball of fire. Almost immediately after the impact, there were earthquakes and 300-meter-high tidal waves all over the planet. About eight minutes after the impact, debris from the explosion would have started to fall out of the sky. A lot of the debris was on fire, and this caused massive forest fires. A few minutes later, there would have been 965-km-per-hour winds caused by the quickly heating air. These winds would have destroyed everything they came into contact with.

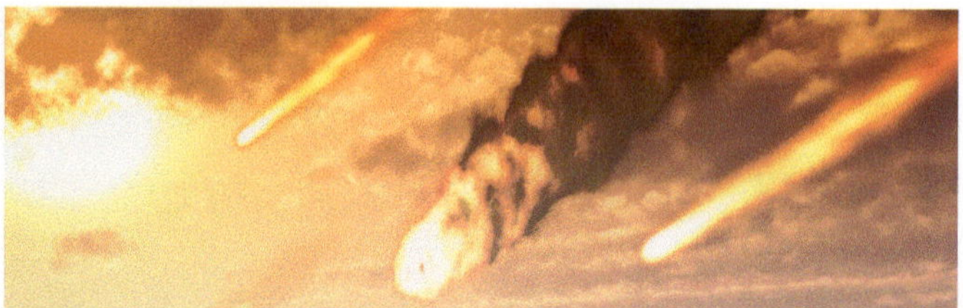

Common theories suggest that if you had been far enough away, you would have survived the explosion. However, in a few days, you would have seen the sky get very dark because of the carbon soot that filled the atmosphere. The soot blocked the sunlight for months and perhaps for years. Without sunlight, plants began to die. When the plants died, there was no food for the herbivores, so they died, too. When the herbivores died, the carnivores didn't have food, so they also died.

It is interesting to try to imagine what would have happened if the meteorite had *not* crashed into Earth. Some scientists think dinosaurs might have survived. They believe they could have adapted to slow changes in climate over many years. Just imagine ...

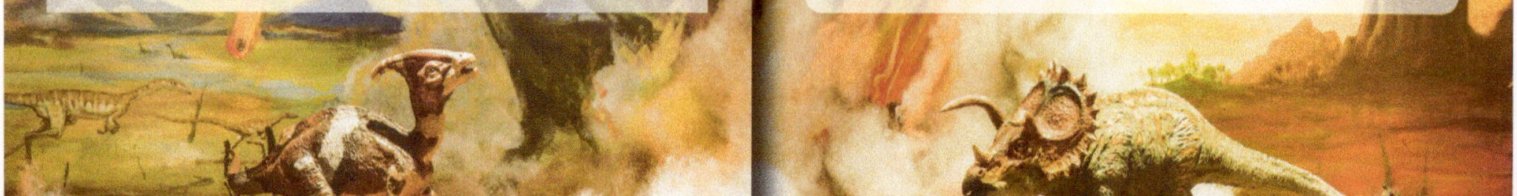

C IN GROUPS THINKING SKILL—Analyze **Infer the answers to these questions. Explain the reasons for your answers.**

1 Did all life on Earth disappear after the asteroid crashed?
2 Do all scientists agree on what caused the dinosaurs to become extinct?

GRAMMAR third conditional

A Choose the sentences with the same meanings. Then choose the correct options in the rule.

1 First, if you had been within 1,000 km of the impact site, …
  a You were not within 1,000 km of the impact site.
  b You were within 1,000 km of the impact site.
2 If you had been far enough away, you would have survived the explosion.
  a Your survival in the past was certain.
  b Your survival in the past was not certain.
3 .... others think dinosaurs might have survived.
  a The dinosaurs' survival in the past was certain.
  b The dinosaurs' survival in the past was not certain.
4 … they could have adapted to slow changes in climate over many years.
  a Their adaptation was certain.
  b Their adaptation was not certain.

To make the third conditional, use *if* + **present** / **past** perfect and *would/might/could have* + **present** / **past** participle.

For more practice, go to page 152.

B Write third conditional sentences for the situations.

1 A meteorite hit the Earth. The dinosaurs didn't survive.
If a meteorite hadn't hit the Earth, the dinosaurs might have survived.
2 There were no humans on the Earth at that time. They didn't die from the meteorite crash.
____
3 The soot in the air blocked the sun. Temperatures became much cooler.
____
4 Dinosaurs didn't have food after the meteorite crashed. They disappeared in a few years.
____

C IN PAIRS **Take turns reading your sentences. Did you have similar ideas?**

SPEAKING

A IN PAIRS **How would history have been different if certain events had or had not happened? Write down three examples in your notebook.**

If the 1969 moon landing hadn't been successful, people might not have gone to the moon again.

B IN GROUPS **Share your ideas. Discuss whether you agree with your classmates' speculations. Use the Confident Communicator box to help you.**

CONFIDENT COMMUNICATOR
KEEP TALKING

To express possibility or probability, use *maybe* or *probably*:
Maybe *humans wouldn't have gone to the moon again if the moon landing hadn't been successful. (possibility)*
Humans ***probably*** *wouldn't have gone to the moon again if the moon landing hadn't been successful. (probability)*

Life in Space

VOCABULARY space

A Complete the sentences with the words from the box.

outer space | International Space Station | space capsule | spacecraft | space shuttle | zero gravity

1 People have been traveling into space on ____________ for over fifty years.
2 The first person who traveled to ____________, the area outside Earth's atmosphere, was Yuri Gagarin, in 1961.
3 In the 1970s, the first ____________ was developed, a vehicle that could go to space and return several times.
4 A ____________ is a compartment or cabin where the astronauts live during a space flight.
5 In the 1990s, the US, Russia, Japan, and Europe built the ____________ (ISS) to discover more about human life in space.
6 One of the effects of living in ____________ is that people get taller!

LISTENING

A IN PAIRS **What do you think the challenges of living in a space capsule would be? Discuss.**

B 8.02 **Listen to an interview about life in space. Were your ideas correct?**

C 8.02 LISTENING SKILL—Listen for specific information **Listen again and complete the notes.**

1. Number of times Karen has flown into space:
2. Number of times she has been to the International Space Station (ISS):
3. How you sit down in space:
4. Why Karen has short hair:
5. Where spacecraft may go in the future:
6. What the Earth looks like from outer space:

D IN GROUPS THINKING SKILL—Question **Decide what the astronaut meant when she made this statement about observing Earth from outer space.**

"You can see the oceans and the continents, but no countries, of course, and that can make you think differently about our world."

MAKE IT REAL

The International Space Station is often referred to as the *ISS*. It is common in English to refer to companies and institutions by their initials. Can you think of any more examples?

PRONUNCIATION consonant clusters with /s/

A 8.03 **Underline the consonant cluster with /s/ in each word. Listen and practice.**

1 host 2 guest 3 space 4 sleep 5 just 6 school 7 student 8 desk

GRAMMAR indirect questions

A Read the examples of direct and indirect questions and complete the rules with the correct options.

Direct questions	Indirect questions
What is life like at zero gravity?	Can you tell us what life is like at zero gravity?
How do you drink water?	Could you explain how you drink water?
Will the US have space shuttles again in the future?	Do you know if/whether the US will have space shuttles again in the future?

1. Direct questions have the verb *be* or the auxiliary (*will*, *did*, etc.) **before** / **after** the subject.
2. Indirect questions have the main verb **before** / **after** the subject.
3. Indirect questions in the simple present or simple past **have** / **don't have** the auxiliary *do/did*.

For more practice, go to page 153.

B Rewrite the direct questions as indirect questions.

1. How big is the International Space Station?
   Could you tell me ______________________________?
2. What do astronauts in the ISS do?
   Can you explain ______________________________?
3. Will the ISS ever return to Earth?
   Do you think ______________________________?

C IN GROUPS Take turns asking and answering the questions from B.

SPEAKING

A IN PAIRS Read the facts and look at your notes from LISTENING C. Use the information in the web page and your own ideas to think of questions to ask an astronaut. Include indirect questions.

ZERO GRAVITY FACTS

- You lose muscle mass, so you have to exercise a lot to build muscles.
- You breathe in things that are floating in the air, so you have to be careful about things like crumbs from food, drops of water, or hair from shaving.
- It's hard to sleep. You have to sleep in a special sleeping bag with arm bags so that your arms don't float.

B IN PAIRS Role-play your interview for another pair. Use the Confident Communicator box to help you.

A: Can you tell me what you like and don't like about life in space?
B: Well, I really like … I don't like … or … very much because … .
A: That's interesting. And do you know if you will go to space again?

CONFIDENT COMMUNICATOR
KEEP TALKING

To make a question sound more polite, especially in a formal situation like an interview, use at least some indirect questions: *Can you tell me why you didn't like the experience?* Instead of *Why didn't you like the experience?*

Do We Need Space Exploration?

LISTENING

A IN GROUPS **Discuss the reasons for space exploration. How many different things do space programs do?**

B 8.04 LISTENING SKILL—Listen for main ideas **Listen to a panel discussion about space exploration. Then answer the questions.**

1 Are the people on the panel in favor of or against space exploration?

____

2 What does Seth, the astronaut, say space exploration is mainly about?

____

3 What does the second guest, Lauren, say that satellites do?

____

4 What does the third speaker, Cristina, focus on in her comments?

____

5 What does the last speaker, Mike, say the space program is like?

____

C 8.04 THINKING SKILL—Recall **Choose the speaker who discussed each point. Compare with a partner. Then listen and check.**

1 The space program encourages young people to study. Seth / Lauren / Cristina / Mike
2 The space program gave us cell phone cameras. Seth / Lauren / Cristina / Mike
3 The space program makes us safer. Seth / Lauren / Cristina / Mike
4 The space program is not only about astronauts. Seth / Lauren / Cristina / Mike

VOCABULARY space program inventions

A **Label the pictures with words from the box.**

cordless vacuum	foil blanket	home insulation
memory foam	water filter	wireless headset

1

____

2
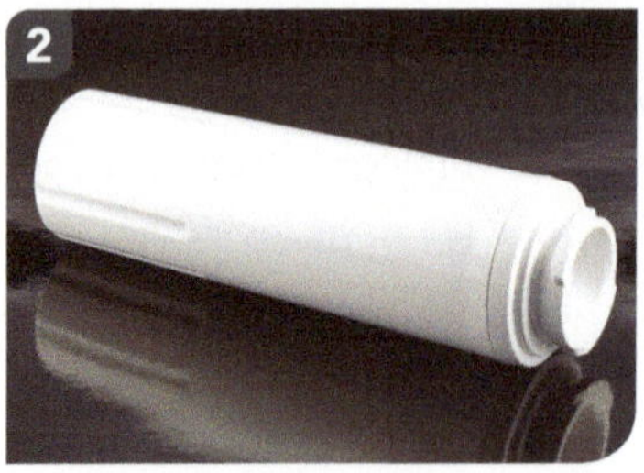
____

3

____

4
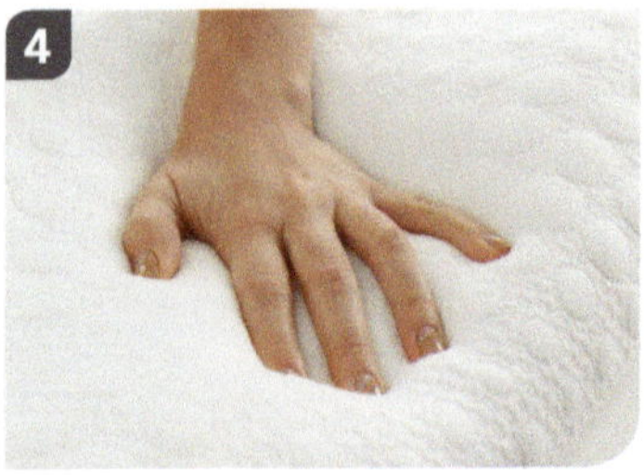
____

5

____

6

____

B IN GROUPS **Discuss which of the contributions from space exploration you have used.**

WRITING

A **Read the opinion posted on a blog site. Then choose the statements that best reflect the writer's opinion.**

Stop Exploring Space!

It's time to stop exploring space. It is true that space exploration has developed technology that is used in many ways on Earth. However, I feel certain that if the technology hadn't been invented for the space program, it would have been invented anyway. The main problem with space exploration is the cost. If we hadn't spent billions of dollars on space exploration, we could have already stopped world hunger. In addition, space travel is dangerous. Astronauts become ill from a number of health problems from being in zero gravity for long periods of time. Furthermore, we don't know what dangerous viruses might be in space—it could be dangerous for Planet Earth. Also, some kinds of rockets use enormous amounts of fossil fuel.

Many people argue that we need to learn about our universe. Nevertheless, I am convinced that we should spend our energy and our money on ways to make our lives better here on Earth.

1 **a** He thinks that we wouldn't have had some technologies if we hadn't had a space program.
b He thinks we would have developed our technologies even without a space program.
2 **a** He thinks we should spend money to stop world hunger instead of on space exploration.
b He thinks we have almost stopped world hunger.
3 **a** He thinks being in space is very dangerous.
b He thinks people will live in space in the near future.
4 **a** He thinks we should look for new sources of fossil fuel on other planets.
b He thinks space exploration uses too much fossil fuel.

B **Look back at the blog. Find words and phrases that connect ideas.**

To add ideas: *and*, __________, __________, __________
To contrast ideas: *but*, __________, __________

C **You are going to respond to the blog with the opposite point of view. Write notes to plan your response.**

Opening statement: __________
Arguments from the blog you disagree with: __________
Other reasons to support space exploration: __________
Closing statement: __________

D **Write your blog post. Use connecting words and phrases from B to structure your response.**

E IN PAIRS **Read each other's blog posts. Did you use similar arguments?**

SPEAKING

A **Decide whether you are for or against space exploration in the future. Make a list of your arguments. Use ideas from this lesson or your own ideas.**

B IN GROUPS **Discuss your opinions from A. Ask questions to clarify your classmates' reasons for their opinions. Use the Confident Communicator box to help you.**

A: I think space exploration is a waste of time.
B: Can you tell me why you think that?

CONFIDENT COMMUNICATOR
KEEP TALKING

To ask someone to clarify the reasons for their opinions, use these phrases:
Can you tell me why you think …?
Why do you think …?
What makes you believe …?

Language and Life

Reason Effectively – Space Team

A IN PAIRS **What challenges/problems/difficulties would people living on Mars face? Discuss.**

B 8.05 **Read the description of what life would be like on Mars. Does it include any of your ideas from A? What other challenges does it include?**

Life on Mars

Artist's rendition of an ecosystem on Mars.

Traveling to Mars is hard. Living on Mars is even harder. First, there are serious environmental issues. One problem is radiation. Astronauts on the International Space Station get 10 times more radiation than on Earth, and the radiation in deep space could be even stronger. One possible solution is ice-covered domes because ice partly blocks radiation. The second problem is the effects of low gravity on the human body. People's bones and muscles become weaker if they are in low gravity for a long time. It is necessary to use weights and do heavy exercise to prevent this. A third problem is that people will have to live in a closed ecosystem. They have to stay inside a dome or a spacesuit at all times. There is no fresh air, so there is a danger of pollution or contamination by bacteria or viruses.

Life on Mars will also have psychological difficulties. First, there will be very few people on Mars, at least at the beginning, so there will not be many choices of friends. There will be no restaurants, cafés, or parks, so there will be few options for social activities, and life could be very boring. Second, the living spaces will be very small. People will be living very close to each other. Life will not be very comfortable. Water will be very limited, so people will have to take 30-second showers and almost never wash their clothes. Plants cannot grow on Mars, so all food will be dried or in cans. Also, most food tastes the same at low gravity. Finally, communication with Earth will be very hard. Cell phones and other voice communications will be impossible, so the only communication will be through email. It will take 20 minutes for an email to reach Earth, and another 20 minutes to get a reply, and most of us are used to very fast communication with our friends and families.

C IN GROUPS **You are going to choose the first three people who will live on Mars for two years. What characteristics and experience are important? Make a list.**

Characteristics	Experience
calm	*background in science*

D IN GROUPS Read the descriptions of the candidates for the Mars mission. Analyze and evaluate each description. Discuss the characteristics and experience you listed in C and relate them to each candidate. Consider the candidates' pros and cons and choose the best candidate.

MARTIN
MALE, 28
USA
COMEDIAN
NOT MARRIED

Competes in sports competitions and marathons. Now doing a TV show where he uses humor to teach people about nutrition. Very friendly, but friends say he talks too much!

Specializes in rare tropical diseases. Has lived in the jungles of northern Colombia and central Africa. Lived by herself for a year on a remote Pacific island. No time to do sports or socialize with people because her work is so important.

SUSANA
FEMALE, 45
COLOMBIA
MEDICAL RESEARCHER
NOT MARRIED

ARI
MALE, 35
RUSSIA
DOCTOR
MARRIED

Works at a family medicine clinic in Moscow. Practices general medicine, but specializes in respiratory diseases in children. Grows vegetables and rides his bicycle in his free time. Work and city living make him feel stressed; he relaxes by walking and bicycling in the countryside on weekends. Wife and two children support his decision to go to Mars for two years.

Designs large urban office buildings and specializes in green buildings with solar energy, rainwater collection systems, and air pollution cleaning systems. Loves decorating; skilled at house repairs. Loves living in Nairobi because it's an exciting city with many things to do. Has many friends and a very active social life. Married for two years; hopes to have children in the future.

ASHA
FEMALE, 32
KENYA
ARCHITECT
MARRIED

CLAUDIA
FEMALE, 50
BRAZIL
PSYCHIATRIST
MARRIED

Specializes in stress disorders. Uses herbs, meditation, and exercise therapy to help her patients. Works well with patients because she has had a lot of stress in the past. Grows her own herbs. Learned about herbal medicine when she lived in a small village in the Amazon where there was no electricity, running water, or communication with the outside world.

E IN GROUPS As a class, discuss which candidates you chose and which factors—experience, skills, other factors—most influenced your group's decision about the candidates.

A: Can you explain why you think Susana is better than Ari?

B: Susana has more experience with unusual diseases. If Ari had done more research on those types of diseases, he would have been a better candidate than Susana, but I think her experience is important.

F Which factors most influenced your group's decision about the candidates—experience or skills? Did any other factors, such as gender, age, or nationality influence your decision? If so, which ones?

G Discuss the questions.

1 What process did your group use to evaluate and select the three candidates? Were you happy with the process?
2 What steps are necessary in order to reason effectively?
3 How do reasoning skills help you at college or at work?

MAKE IT DIGITAL

Do research to find out about someone who went on a space mission. What skills did they have?

VOCABULARY review

SCORE: / 10

A Complete the sentences with words from the box.

asteroid	cordless vacuums	debris	extinction	ISS
outer space	soot	spacecraft	tidal waves	zero gravity

Millions of years ago, a/an **1** ________ hit the Earth and caused the **2** ________ of many species of animals and plants. The impact caused giant **3** ________ from the ocean and fires that filled the air with black, smoky **4** ________.

People started traveling into **5** ________ in the 1960s, and now people from different countries live on the **6** ________ for months at a time. Astronauts travel there in a Russian **7** ________. It is hard to live at **8** ________ because everything floats. If there is any **9** ________ in the air, it can get into the air filters and damage them. Space programs have given us many everyday inventions, like memory foam, home insulation, and **10** ________.

GRAMMAR review

SCORE: / 10

A Write the correct verb forms to make third conditional sentences. More than one answer may be possible.

1 If a meteorite ________ (not hit) Earth, maybe the dinosaurs ________ (live) for longer.
2 If the meteorite ________ (hit) the Earth more recently, people ________ (die).
3 My uncle ________ (be) an astronaut if he ________ (grow up) in the US.
4 If I ________ (know) about last night's TV show on space programs, I ________ (watch) it.

B Rewrite the direct questions as indirect questions in your notebook.

1 Are there any good documentaries about space exploration?
2 How big is the International Space Station?
3 Where did the meteorite hit?
4 Why did mammals survive after the meteorite?
5 Have other meteorites hit the Earth?
6 Will we live on other planets in the future?

16–20 correct: You can talk about events in the past and their impact on today. You can ask questions and discuss space exploration. You can use the third conditional and make indirect questions.
0–15 correct: Look again at the Vocabulary and Grammar sections in the unit.

TOTAL SCORE: / 20

WHAT DO YOU KNOW NOW? Look back at page 77 and add the words you know now to the boxes.

FOLLOW A PRO SPACE

Take the quiz about space. Go to Follow A Pro on page 134 to find the answers.
Then learn about astrobiology.

1 The hottest planet in our solar system is …
a Mercury. **b** Venus. **c** Mars.

2 Scientists think there may be a planet made of …
a diamonds. **b** gold. **c** silver.

3 One day on Venus is longer than one … on Earth.
a week **b** month **c** year

4 A NASA space suit costs about … dollars.
a five hundred thousand **b** one million **c** twelve million

UNIT 9

The World of News

WHAT DO YOU ALREADY KNOW?

1 Think of words you know about media and the news. Write the words.

2 **IN PAIRS** Share and compare your ideas. Add more words to your lists.

Media/News

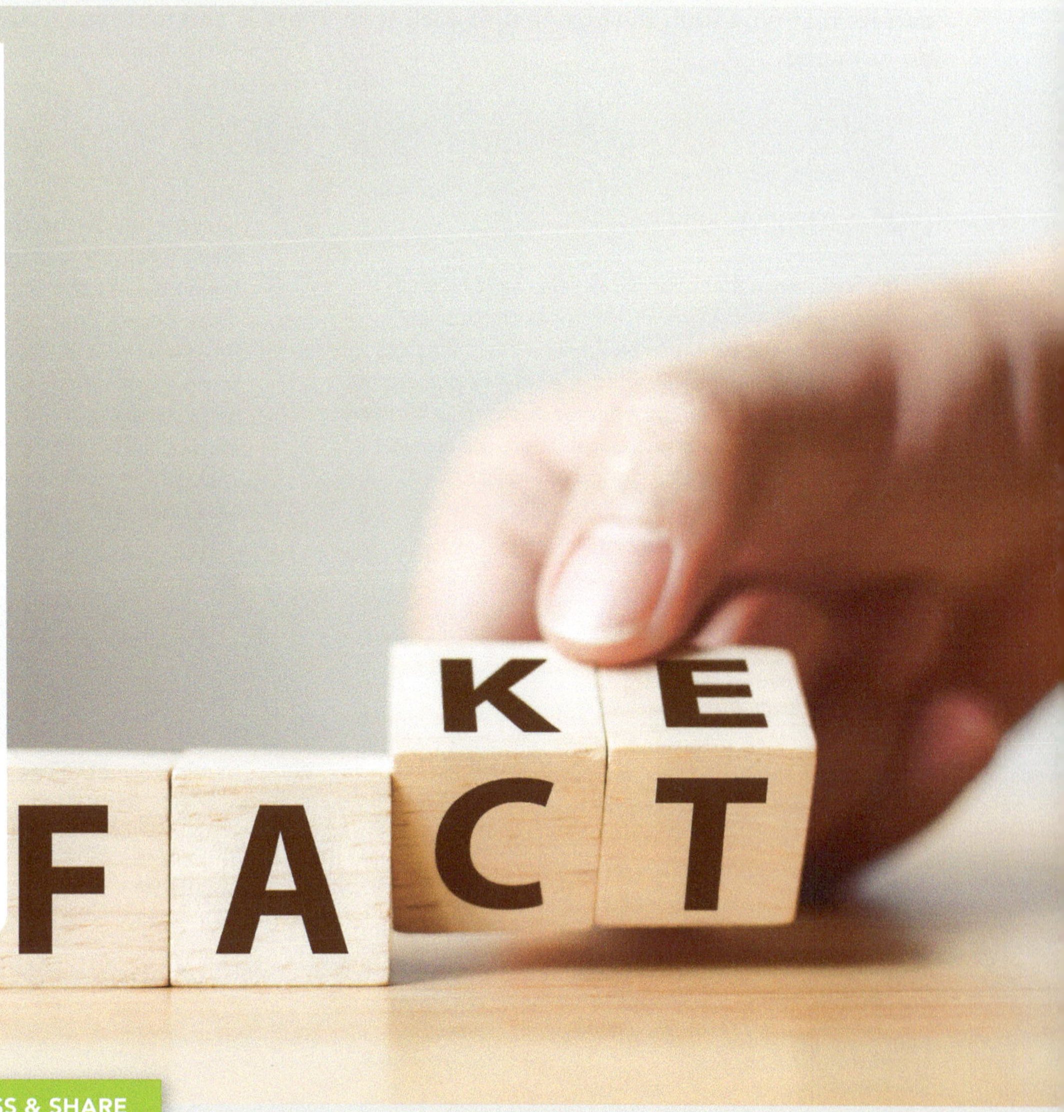

VIDEO

DISCUSS & SHARE

3 **IN GROUPS** Watch the video and answer the question.

SYM The news—how much is too much?

In this unit, you will ...

- give your opinions on fake news, journalists and citizen journalists, compare real and fake news stories, and role-play a job interview for a news career.
- use thinking skills: analyze, apply, and deduce.
- read about developments in news.
- use strategies and language to ask for an opinion, interrupt politely, and introduce new information about your skills and experience.
- use problem-solving skills to discuss the pros and cons of solutions to a problem.
- learn tips to make notes.

LESSON 1 News in the 21st Century

READING

A How interested are you in the news? Share your view with the class.

1 Very interested. I like to know what's happening in the world.
2 Pretty interested. Some things interest me more than others.
3 Not interested at all. Events in the news aren't really part of my life.

B 9.01 READING SKILL—Identify text types Read the texts. Write the correct text type from the box next to each text. There is one text type you do not need.

blog post | email | online article | review | tweet

Changing Times

It's no surprise that newspaper sales have fallen in recent years and TV news audiences are smaller because of the **effect** of 24/7 online news sites. It's too early to say how this will affect the way we present the news, but it's such an important **industry** that it's likely to survive technological change. There will always be journalism and a need for good journalists.

1 ______________________

I never buy newspapers these days. What's the point? News is reported so quickly because it changes all the time. I'm not that interested in current affairs, but I read news stories online, and sometimes I watch the news on TV if something "big" is happening somewhere in the world. I see some news items on social media, but the majority are **human-interest stories**, and that kind of story is not interesting enough for me to repost. I'd like to know if anyone here does repost those stories in their newsfeed.
posted by jamiek 12:23

follow

2 ______________________

Citizen Journalists: The Word on the Street
by Amos Hadfield

A must-read for all journalism students is *Citizen Journalists: The Word on the Street* by Amos Hadfield. Citizen journalism is where ordinary people collect, report, share, and comment on news stories via their social media newsfeeds or tweets. It's an interesting **trend** because it's so hard to control. A positive point is that ordinary people can get involved. However, there are some problems. "It isn't easy to limit the spread of fake news" he writes. "**Governments** want more power, but that is also dangerous."

3 ______________________

Amber Spratt @ The Ark

Breaking news! People are here in the thousands—there's such an amazing atmosphere right now. No word from the president yet, but we expect more information soon. #excitingtimes

4 ______________________

GLOSSARY

journalism (n): the activity of reporting the news
fake (adj): not real or true
current affairs (phrase): events that are happening now and that are discussed in news reports

C Read the texts in B again. Complete the sentences with the correct text types.

1 The writer of the ______________ is not interested in the news.
2 The writer of the ______________ is reporting events as they happen.
3 The writer of the ______________ believes that journalism is an important profession.
4 The writer of the ______________ mentions a new way of reporting news.

D THINKING SKILL—Analyze Read text 3 in B again. Compare the arguments in favor of citizen journalism and the arguments against it.

VOCABULARY

A Match the definitions to a word or phrase in bold in READING B.

1 news reports about a person's life or experiences ____________
2 a change that is the result of another action ____________
3 a specific trade or service ____________
4 the groups of people who control a country ____________
5 something popular at a specific time ____________

MAKE IT YOURS

Go online and look at a website where you can read the news in English. What news sections does the website have? Look up any words for the sections that you don't know.

GRAMMAR *so, such, too, enough*

A Complete the sentences from the texts in READING B. Then match with the correct forms.

1 It's an interesting trend because ____________ to control.
2 …there's ____________ right now.
3 … that kind of story is ____________.
4 It's ____________ how this will affect …

a *such* + adjective + noun ____
b (*not* +) adjective/adverb + *enough* ____
c *so* + adjective/adverb ____
d *too* + adjective/adverb ____

Can you find any more examples in the texts?

B Match the words (1–4) with their meanings (a–d).

1 *such/so* ____
2 *too* ____
3 *enough* ____
4 *not enough* ____

a more than needed
b less than needed
c the right amount
d very

For more practice, go to page 154.

C Rewrite the sentences correctly in your notebook.

1 Some news reports are such shocking I can't watch them.
2 Jake is enough shy to succeed as a journalist.
3 My journalism teacher said I don't have to rewrite my report. It is enough good.
4 I think being a journalist must be so an interesting job.

D IN PAIRS Discuss sentences 1 and 4 in C. Are they true for you?

SPEAKING

A Make notes about how young people see the news in the 21st century. Think about the questions.

- What types of news stories are young people interested in?
- Are there are too many news sources?
- Are journalists professional enough?

B IN PAIRS Write three opinion questions about these topics. Use *too*, *so*, *such*, or *enough* in your questions.

- Fake news
- Journalists
- Citizen journalists

Do you think there is too much fake news?

C Go around the class. Ask different students your questions. Encourage them to give reasons for their opinions. Use the Confident Communicator box to help you.

CONFIDENT COMMUNICATOR
KEEP TALKING

Use these phrases to ask for someone's opinion:
Hi, can/could I ask you some questions about …?
Do you mind if I ask you about …?
Could you answer some questions about …?

News Reporting—Who Do You Trust?

VOCABULARY news stories

A Match the underlined words to the correct definitions (a–f).

1 It can be hard to figure out what is fake news. ____
2 If a news headline makes you laugh, it's probably not true! ____
3 We get news from many different sources – newspapers, TV, news websites and social media, for example. ____
4 To prove that a news story is true, compare it to other reports of the story. ____
5 Fake news is not accurate and can be dangerous. ____
6 You should only trust news websites that have a good record of telling the truth. ____

a show that something is true
b people or places we get information from
c understand; find the answer
d the title of a newspaper story
e believe is honest, fair, and reliable
f true; correct; without mistakes

B Complete the sentences with an underlined word from A.

1 The ____________ is "Dangerous Tigers Escape From Zoo!"
2 Which websites do you ____________ for the world news?
3 Can scientists ____________ that there is life on other planets?
4 We need to include information from three ____________ in our report.
5 How do you know this information about national exam results is ____________?
6 It can be difficult to ____________ how to tell a fake news story from a real one.

LISTENING

A 9.02 Listen to Part 1 of a lecture on fake news. Then answer the question.

Why is fake news a "hot topic"? Give two reasons. ____________________

____

GLOSSARY

rumor (n): information that may or may not be true

B 9.03 LISTENING SKILL—Listen for information order Listen to Part 2 of the lecture. Put the steps in the correct order (1–5).

a Research the person who wrote the story. ____
b Question everything you read online. ____
c Check links to other news stories. ____
d Research where the story comes from. ____
e Check if the story is on other websites. ____

C THINKING SKILL—Apply Think about a news item you saw on social media. Use the information you heard in B to establish if the news was real or fake.

GRAMMAR modals of deduction

A Read the sentences from LISTENING B. Choose the correct option in the rule.

If they haven't written anything else for a source you trust, the article **could** spread fake news.
Think to yourself, "This story **might** be true, but it **may not be** 100% accurate."
Or, "This story **can't be** true because certain details don't seem right."

When talking about deductions in the present, use a modal (+ *not*) + the **base infinitive** / **infinitive with *to*** form of the verb.

B **Complete the sentences with words from the box.**

can't could may might must

You're 99% sure the news is fake.	The news **1** ______________ be fake.
You aren't sure if the news is fake or not.	Do you think that story **2** ______________ / **3** ______________ / **4** ______________ be fake?
You're 95% sure the news is true.	The news **5** ______________ be fake.

For more practice, go to page 154.

C **Complete the sentences with the correct modal of deduction. More than one answer may be possible.**

1 Your friend Lola said she would visit you today. There's a knock at the door.
"That ______________ be Lola."

2 You see someone in a store who looks like your cousin Martha. But Martha works abroad as a journalist.
"That ______________ be Martha."

3 You look out of the window. People are carrying open umbrellas.
"It ______________ be raining."

4 You're sure TV news ends at 11 p.m.
"It's midnight. The news ______________ be on TV."

D IN PAIRS **Look at these pictures. What do you think they show? Use modals of deduction to discuss.**

a

b

c

d

This picture must be a …
This might be a …

MAKE IT REAL

You can use *maybe* and *perhaps* instead of *may be*, *could be*, and *might be*:
Maybe it's a/an … *Perhaps they're …*

SPEAKING

A **Read these two news story summaries. Have you heard about them or seen them in the news?**

Story 1:
Some cities around the world now use "silent fireworks" in displays to make the shows more enjoyable for children and less stressful for pets.

Story 2:
A group of penguins is living on an island of ice and plastic waste in the Pacific Ocean.

B IN PAIRS **Work together to decide which might be fake news and which might be true.**

This one can't be a true news story, because …
That one must be fake news, because …

C IN GROUPS **Talk about how you worked out which news story was fake. Use the Confident Communicator box to help you.**

CONFIDENT COMMUNICATOR
REPAIR IT

To interrupt politely, use the following phrases:
Excuse me, can I just interrupt here and say …
Do you mind if I interrupt?
Sorry, can I just add that …

LESSON 3 A News Career

VOCABULARY news careers

A Look at the pictures. Match the careers from the box with the correct pictures.

foreign correspondent	investigative journalist	news anchor	newspaper editor
photojournalist	reporter	sports journalist	translator

1 
______

2 
______

3 
______

4 
______

5 
______

6 
______

7 
______

8 
______

B IN PAIRS Talk about what skills a person needs to do each of the jobs.

A: I think a news anchor needs to feel confident in front of a camera.

B: True. And an investigative journalist must not be afraid to ask hard questions.

PRONUNCIATION /ə/ versus /r/

A 9.04 There are differences in the pronunciation of certain sounds in British English and American English. Listen and notice the difference between the sounds /ə/ and /r/ at the end of these words.

1 anchor 2 translator 3 editor 4 reporter

B 9.05 Listen and choose the sound you hear.

1 anchor a the /ə/ sound b the /r/ sound
2 translator a the /ə/ sound b the /r/ sound
3 editor a the /ə/ sound b the /r/ sound
4 reporter a the /ə/ sound b the /r/ sound

LISTENING

A What do you think the job of foreign correspondent is like? How about a translator in a different country?

B 9.06 Listen to the interview and choose the correct answers.

1 What is Dana McDonald's job?
a foreign correspondent b translator c professor

2 Where does Dana McDonald live?
a England b the US c India

3 What did Peter Marsden study at college?
a Arabic b English and French c journalism

4 Where is Peter from?
a the US b Algeria c India

C 9.06 **LISTENING SKILL—Listen for opinions** **Listen again and decide who expresses the following opinions. Write *D* for Dana, *P* for Peter, or *B* for both.**

Who …

1. worked in a different career in the beginning? ____
2. finds their job quite hard? ____
3. doesn't really speak the language of the country they live in? ____
4. is away from home for long periods of time? ____
5. works for themselves? ____

D **THINKING SKILL—Deduce** **Decide what you would find challenging about being a foreign correspondent or a translator in a different country.**

MAKE IT REAL

To talk about a job that would/wouldn't suit you, use:
I'd make a good/terrible … because I …
e.g., *I'd make a terrible photojournalist because I can't take good pictures!*

WRITING

A **Read this fact file about a person who works as an undercover investigative journalist. Would you like to do a job like this?**

FACT FILE: Undercover investigative journalist
NAME: Faye Garcia [not her real name]
AGE: 32

I work as an undercover journalist. I hide my real identity as a journalist so that I can find out about things. Right now, I'm investigating people in the Congo who illegally trade wild animals. My job is to collect as much accurate information as I can and give that information to the local police. I love it, but it's a hard job. It's essential that the criminals don't figure out who I am. I find that it's hard because my life might be in danger. I have the feeling that other people would hate this job. As for me, I think it's very exciting. In my opinion, it's the most amazing job in the world.

B **Underline four examples in A where the writer gives her opinion.**

C **Choose another news career from this lesson. Write about 100 words on whether you think you would like the job. Use the phrases from B to give opinions.**

SPEAKING

A **IN PAIRS** **Choose a news career from this lesson. Decide what skills and experience a person needs to do this job. Write five questions that an interviewer would ask someone who was applying for the job.**

B **IN PAIRS** **Role-play an interview for the job. Change roles after two or three minutes. Use the Confident Communicator box to help you.**

A: So, why do you think you would make a good reporter?
B: Well, I'm very interested in current affairs and …

C **IN GROUPS** **Talk about how the interview went and who you think did well in the interview.**

CONFIDENT COMMUNICATOR
KEEP TALKING

To introduce important skills and experience that an interviewer hasn't asked about, use the following phrases:
Did I mention that I have experience in / know how to …?
Although I don't have much experience in …, I'm very good at …
I think my experience in … could help in my role as a/an …

Language and Life

Problem Solving – Local News

A IN PAIRS Discuss the questions.

1 Do you ever read a local newspaper (in print or online)?
2 If not, how do you get information about what's happening in your local area?
3 Do you think local newspapers are important? Why or why not?

B 9.07 Read the article about a new local newspaper. Then answer the questions.

No Story Is Too Small

With the rise of social media and online news sites, local newspapers have had a hard time. However, in a group of small towns in the Midwestern United States, print news is fighting back. Gene Nightingale and Matt Emerson, two journalists who were worried about local journalism, decided to start up their own micro newspaper. The newspaper goes on sale once a month and sells around 4,000 copies.

The newspaper is based on the idea that "no story is too small" because they write about small stories, such as how a farmer's field was flooded with water after a pipe burst, and how a new sandbox has been installed in a children's play area.

But it is these "small stories" that are the building blocks for any community. If people are aware of what is happening in their local area, they feel more connected to their community. This connection helps to create strong relationships between people who live in villages, towns, or cities. Whether it is good news, such as a local student winning a national debating competition, or bad news, such as the closure of the town library, the point is that it is news—it is something to discuss and debate and bring people together. Gene and Matt's newspaper provides that essential link.

Local newspapers are in danger. A recent report by the US Bureau of Labor Statistics found that the number of newspaper jobs fell from 458,000 in 1990 (considered to be the start of the internet age) to about 183,000 in 2016. That's a fall of almost 60%. This has an effect on local newspapers in that local news stories are not investigated in the same way. "People depend on Facebook and social media, so what's going on close to home can be ignored by larger newspapers," says Emerson. Local businesses have been very helpful and paid for the first copy of the newspaper. Nightingale and Emerson hope there might be the chance to start up other "micro newspapers" in other small towns over the next few years.

Read more

Burst pipe floods local field

Jenny McGill's winning argument

Town library in danger of closing

1 How often is the paper published? ______
2 What idea is the newspaper based on? ______
3 How many people were working in newspaper jobs in 2016? ______
4 Who helped to pay for the first copies of the newspaper? ______

C **IN PAIRS** **Imagine that you work for a local daily newspaper that has lost sales. Your boss has some suggestions on how to improve sales. Choose the five best suggestions and write them in note form in the first column of the table.**

My tips for improving business

1 *Include more human-interest stories and more photos.*
2 *Encourage citizen journalism where local people write stories that are important to them.*
3 *Include live-blogging on the website to cover breaking news stories. Readers can add audio and video posts.*
4 *Make online stories more personal. Allow readers to choose the news and the area that they are interested in. They receive notifications when news that's important to them happens.*
5 *Have an online-only news service. Readers join and pay a monthly fee as they would with Spotify or Netflix.*
6 *Offer reader discounts at other local businesses, e.g. a discount on a Valentine's Day meal in a local restaurant if you buy the newspaper every day for a week, for example.*
7 *Go from being a daily newspaper to a weekly newspaper.*
8 *Increase the price of the newspaper.*

	Suggestions	Advantages	Disadvantages
1			
2			
3			
4			
5			

D **IN PAIRS** **Discuss the advantages and disadvantages of each of your choices. Write them in the table.**

A: One advantage of using citizen journalists is that they do it for free. We can save money.
B: Yes, that's true, but they might not be very good at writing news stories.

E **Compare your ideas and agree on the best five. Make some other suggestions for ways to improve sales.**

F **Discuss the questions.**

1 Why is it useful to identify the advantages and disadvantages of a solution?
2 What other approaches to solving problems can you think of?

MAKE IT DIGITAL

Go online and find a local news website. Share some examples of interesting or amusing local news with the class.

VOCABULARY review

SCORE: / 10

A Complete the sentences with the correct words. The first letter is given.

1 Right now, I'm working as a s________________ on the magazine *Soccer Special Weekly*.
2 Your facts must be accurate, or your readers won't t________________ you to tell the truth.
3 Whenever there is b________________ around the world, I get an update on my newsfeed.
4 This is a great picture for our article, but will people be able to f________________ what it is?
5 I read the news online, but I'm not interested in h________________ stories about people I don't know.
6 In some countries, the g________________ controls the media, especially television and newspapers.
7 One of the e________________ of online news is that newspaper sales have fallen.
8 Do you speak Spanish, or would you like a t________________ to help you?
9 As an investigative journalist, my job is to try to p________________ that the story I'm investigating is true.
10 Have you seen today's h____________? They've found water on Mars!

GRAMMAR review

SCORE: / 10

A Choose the correct words.

My hero is Nellie Bly. She was **1** so / such an amazing woman. She became one of the world's first investigative journalists, writing articles about female factory workers. Male readers were **2** enough / so shocked to learn that the writer was a woman that Nellie was moved to the women's section of the paper. Nellie thought that writing about fashion and gardening wasn't **3** interesting enough / enough interesting for her. In 1888, her editor suggested she travel around the world in 80 days—something that people thought was **4** such / too dangerous for a woman to attempt. It is **5** so / such amazing that she returned in just 72 days!

B Complete the sentences with the correct modals of deduction.

1 I can't open my email. There ____________ be a problem with my wi-fi.
2 The news report says it's cold, but it ____________ be snowing. It almost never snows in Los Angeles!
3 My phone shows I have one missed call. ____________ it be about the reporter's job I applied for?
4 That newspaper ____________ be mine. My copy is in my briefcase.
5 I'm sure I know that woman. I think she ____________ be the news anchor on our local news channel.

16–20 correct: You can talk about news stories and news careers. You can use *so*, *such*, *too*, and *enough* and modals of deduction.
0–15 correct: Look again at the Vocabulary and Grammar sections in the unit.

TOTAL SCORE: / 20

WHAT DO YOU KNOW NOW? Look back at page 87 and add the words you know now to the box.

STUDY SKILLS MAKING NOTES

Take the quiz about making notes. Go to **Study Skills** on page 135 to find the answers. Then learn more about making notes.

1 When taking notes from a book, it's a good idea to write down every word you read without changing anything.
a True **b** False

2 What is plagiarism?
a writing so fast that you can't read what your notes say
b including someone else's ideas in your essay without mentioning the source

3 You can use your own symbols and abbreviations in both your notes and assignments.
a True **b** False

4 How many sets of notes should you aim to have?
a one **b** two **c** three

UNIT 10

Got It?

WHAT DO YOU ALREADY KNOW?

1 Think about the things you are good at in different areas of your life. Write the things.

2 IN PAIRS Share and compare your ideas. Add more words to your lists.

At home

At school or work

Sports and art

VIDEO

DISCUSS & SHARE

3 IN GROUPS Watch the video and answer the question.

SYM Would you use your talent to express your creativity or make money?

In this unit, you will ...

- talk about your talents and abilities, ask and answer questions for a talent show audition, and share advice on how to succeed in the music industry.
- use thinking skills: question, analyze, and evaluate.
- read about what causes talent.
- use strategies and language to talk about your achievements politely, control your nerves when speaking to a group, and use idioms in informal contexts.
- use communication skills to make judgments and choose winners of a talent contest.
- follow a talent scout to learn about this job and the skills needed to be in this industry.

LESSON 1 Born with Talent?

READING

A **Think about different kinds of great artists. What talents do they have?**

B **10.01 Read the text. Then choose what type of writing you think it is.**

a a blog entry **b** a newspaper article **c** a popular science magazine article

Ask an Expert

Petra Waterhouse from Berlin asks: Are great artists born or made? In other words, is **talent** genetic or is it learned?

Professor Anna Felix answers: 1 I think the short answer is both. Musical ability is a good example here because some people are born with greater **potential** than others, but without hard work and practice, they don't achieve it. **2** A study of 1,211 sets of **identical twins** born between 1959 and 1985 found that even when one twin practiced music regularly and one didn't, it made no difference. In one case, one man practiced for over 20,000 hours more than his twin, but their musical ability was about the same. This goes some way to showing us that at least some talents are genetic. **3** I believe they are part of our DNA and we probably inherit them from our parents. So, thank you, Mom and Dad!

4 A different study by Professor Zach Hambrick investigated 14 studies of top chess players and musicians: could their level of ability be explained by their hours of practice? The answer was "no." **5** Practice only made about a 30% difference to how good these people were. In previous research, Hambrick argues that what is important is the ability to remember things. Having an excellent **memory** can mean the difference between just being smart and being a genius.

6 One **theory** is that it takes 10,000 hours of practice to become an expert at something. There is possibly a degree of truth in this (although this will probably depend on what you are practicing). But if your DNA gives you a love of chess, languages, music, or soccer, I'd **assume** that would make you more likely to be prepared to put in those long hours of practice anyway.

GLOSSARY

genetic (adj): related to chemicals in a cell that are passed from one generation to another
inherit (v): get something (e.g., a talent, a medical condition) from one's parents
genius (n): a very intelligent person

C **READING SKILL—Recognize fact and opinion** **Read the text in READING B again. Are the underlined sentences (1–6) facts or opinions? Write *F* (fact) or *O* (opinion).**

1 ____ 2 ____ 3 ____ 4 ____ 5 ____ 6 ____

D **THINKING SKILL—Question** **Do you think great artists are born or made? What has helped the artists you know become famous?**

VOCABULARY

A **Match the words with their definitions.**

1 assume (v): ____
2 potential (n): ____
3 memory (n): ____
4 talent (n): ____
5 identical twins (n): ____
6 theory (n): ____

a brothers or sisters born at the same time that look exactly the same
b an idea that explains how something happens
c the ability to remember things
d a natural ability for something
e an ability that may be developed in the future
f believe that something is true without proof

MAKE IT DIGITAL

Go online to find profiles of talented people. Make a note of the adjectives that are used to describe them.

GRAMMAR reported speech: statements

A We use reported speech to report something a person has said or written. Read the example from READING B. How does the tense change between direct speech and reported speech?

"I think the short answer is both." (direct speech)
She **said** she thought the short answer was both. (reported speech)

1 ____________________

B Complete the table.

Tense	Tense Change	Direct Speech	Reported Speech (note reporting verb)
simple present	simple past	"Jack is very talented."	She **said** (that) Jack was very talented.
present progressive	**1** ____________	"I'm learning the saxophone."	She **told me** (that) she was learning the saxophone.
present perfect	past perfect	"I have never seen *The X Factor*."	She **admitted** (that) she **2** ____________ *The X Factor*.
simple past	past perfect	**3** "My dad ____________ good at singing."	She **explained** (that) her dad had been good at singing.
future with *will*	*will* becomes **4** ____________	"Macy will be a genius one day."	She **mentioned** (that) Macy would be a genius one day.

C Choose the correct options for the rules.

1 Use quotation marks for **direct speech** / **reported speech**.
2 In reported speech, the verb tense in the noun clause changes to the **past** / **future** form.

For more practice, go to page 155.

D Rewrite the statements in your notebooks using reported speech.

1 "Lyndon is a very talented soccer player." (the coach, say)
2 "I don't really like abstract art." (Alessandro, admit)
3 "We will practice the dance routine this weekend." (the class, promise)
4 "I learned how to draw by watching video clips online." (Alicia, tell me)

SPEAKING

A Think about something that you have learned to do well. Make notes.

- what you learned
- how you learned it
- how you felt about it

B IN PAIRS Take turns talking about the thing you learned in A. Ask and answer questions to find out more. Use the Confident Communicator box to help you.

C IN PAIRS Now work in a different pair. Report what your first partner told you.

Nina said she had learned to windsurf when she was 15 ...

CONFIDENT COMMUNICATOR
KEEP TALKING

To talk about your own achievements without sounding overconfident, use the following phrases:
It took a lot of hard work, but I managed to learn ...
I was really lucky, because I found it easy to ...
I had a really good teacher/tutor/friend who helped me to ...

TV Talent Shows

LISTENING

A **Which TV talent shows are popular in your country? Do you like watching them? Why or why not?**

B **10.02 Listen to short excerpts from a TV talent show. Match the speakers (1–3) with their acts (a–d). There's one act you don't need.**

1 Noel _____
2 Caitlyn _____
3 Bobby _____

a a ventriloquist
b a magician
c a comedian
d a singer

GLOSSARY

audition (n): a short performance so someone can decide if you are good enough to perform at an event

C **10.03 LISTENING SKILL—Identify attitude Listen to the same speakers talking about their experience after the TV talent show auditions. Choose how they think they did.**

1 Noel
a very well b OK c badly
2 Caitlyn
a very well b OK c badly
3 Bobby
a very well b OK c badly

MAKE IT REAL

If you don't do something you were planning to do because you're too nervous or scared, you can use the phrasal verb *chicken out.*
*I was supposed to go to an audition for The Big Break, but I **chickened out** at the last minute.*

D **THINKING SKILL—Analyze Discuss this statement: "Only a small number of people who appear on TV talent shows are really talented." Do you agree or not?**

VOCABULARY phrasal verbs

A **Match the phrasal verbs in bold (1–5) with the definitions (a–e).**

1 Bridget's dance classes are not easy, but she plans to **keep on** going. _____
2 The director **turned down** a lot of people who auditioned for the play. _____
3 When will you **come back** from the audition? _____
4 Please **fill out** this form with your name and contact information. _____
5 Over 100 people **showed up** at the movie studio for the audition. _____

a to arrive at a place
b to return to a place
c to complete a form
d to say no to an offer or request
e to continue doing something

PRONUNCIATION stress in phrasal verbs

A **10.04 Listen to the sentences. Underline the stressed word in each one. Can you notice the difference?**

1 a He filled out the form. b He filled it out.
2 a She turned down the job. b She turned it down.
3 a I gave up dance classes. b I gave them up.

GRAMMAR reported speech: questions

A Read the direct questions and reported questions from LISTENING B. Notice how the tense changes are the same as in reported statements.

1 He asked, "Do you need some water?" → He asked whether I needed some water.
2 He asked, "Are you feeling confident?" → He asked if I was feeling confident.
3 He asked, "How long have you been doing your act?" → He asked how long I'd been doing my act.
4 He asked, "Who are you?" → He asked who I was.

B Choose the correct options to complete the grammar rules.

1 Use *if* or *whether* in reported *yes/no* questions / reported information questions.
2 Use a question word in reported *yes/no* questions / reported information questions.
3 Use / Don't use auxiliary verbs in reported questions.
4 The word order in reported questions is the same as / different from word order in affirmative sentences.
5 Use / Don't use a question mark at the end of reported questions.

For more practice, go to page 156.

C Rewrite the direct questions as reported questions.

1 She asked, "Do you ever watch TV talent shows?" → She asked ______.
2 She asked, "What are you wearing to the audition?" → She asked ______.
3 She asked, "How long have you been waiting?" → She asked ______.
4 She asked, "Who is the best candidate?" → She asked ______.

D IN PAIRS Think about the last time you spoke to a close friend. What did he or she ask you about? Report it to your partner.

Last night, I spoke to my friend Estefan. He asked me if I had done anything interesting …

SPEAKING

A Imagine you are going to an audition for a TV talent show.

Would you …

- sing a song?
- dance?
- do something else?
- tell jokes?
- do a magic trick?

B Write questions that an interviewer might ask you at the audition.

C IN PAIRS Ask and answer the questions from B.

A: Have you been in any other talent shows?
B: No, this is the first time I've auditioned.
A: And how long have you been doing magic?
B: I've been doing magic since I was six.

D IN GROUPS Report what your partner told you using reported speech. Use the Confident Communicator box to help you.

CONFIDENT COMMUNICATOR
KEEP TALKING

You might feel nervous talking to a large group of people or the whole class. To help in these situations, you can try the following things:

- Control your breathing; breathe in and out slowly before you begin.
- Focus on what you are saying and not on your audience.
- Speak slowly.

Making It!

VOCABULARY idioms and sayings connected to success

A Match the idioms (1–6) with the meanings (a–f). Use a dictionary or look online if you need help.

1 be in the right place at the right time _____
2 it isn't what you know; it's who you know _____
3 set your sights on something _____
4 have your heart set on something _____
5 dream big _____
6 be hungry for success _____

a focus on something as your goal
b want something very much
c be lucky because of where you are and when
d make progress in life because of personal connections
e have goals or hopes that are difficult to achieve
f want to do very well

B IN PAIRS Do you know any other idioms about success in English or another language? What are they?

LISTENING

A What special talents or abilities do you think you need to succeed in the music industry?

B 10.05 Listen to this radio call-in show. What does Elsa Hardman do?

a She runs a music website.
b She manages a music store.
c She owns a record company.

C 10.05 LISTENING SKILL—Listen to take notes Listen again and complete the notes. Remember that you don't need to write every word you hear.

Tips to Make It in the Music Industry!

Starting a Record Company:
- *Dream big!*
- *Go out and* **1** _______________
- *Ask people with more experience for* **2** _______________

Finding Work as a Singer:
- *Keep goals* **3** _______________
- *Sing at a local show*
- *Think of yourself as a* **4** _______________
- *Be* **5** _______________

D THINKING SKILL—Evaluate How do people measure success in your country? Discuss the top three things that you think make a person successful.

A: I think the three things that make someone successful are hard work, talent and the people you know.
B: What about luck? You need to be lucky too!
A: But is luck more important than hard work?

WRITING

A Read the informal email. Match the items (a–e) with the underlined parts of the email (1–5).

a informal greeting ____
b informal closing ____
c contraction ____
d informal punctuation ____
e signature ____

New Message

From: Delia Roberts Cc Bcc

To: Henri Martinez

[1] Hi Henri,

I hope [2] you're well. I'm writing to ask a favor. A friend has her heart set on working in the music industry. She's a fantastic singer, but she isn't very confident. I thought since you're a music producer you'd have some advice I can give her before she gives up. Any information welcome [3]!

[4] Thanks for your help!

[5] Delia

Send

B Now read Henri's reply. How is the style of Henri's email different from the email in A?

New Message

From: Henri Martinez Cc Bcc

To: Delia Roberts

Dear Delia,

Thank you for your email. I am pleased to hear that you are well. I have some advice for your friend. She will need to make a recording of her voice and send it to as many producers as possible. We are always looking for new talent, so send it to me, too. We will be able to decide if she has real musical talent.

Yours sincerely,

Henri Martinez

Send

C Rewrite Henri's email giving advice to Delia, but in a more informal style. Use the points in A.

SPEAKING

A IN PAIRS Read the emails you rewrote. Whose email sounded more informal?

B IN GROUPS Report the advice from your partner's email for making it in the music industry. Ask the group: whose advice is the most useful?

A: Jose said that she should use social media to advertise her talents.
B: And Francesca said she should practice at home to improve her confidence.

C IN GROUPS Discuss the statement. Use the Confident Communicator box to help you.

It isn't what you know, but who you know that matters in the music industry.

CONFIDENT COMMUNICATOR
KEEP TALKING

Use only a few, well-known idioms in your informal speaking and writing.
Make sure that you know the meaning of an idiom before you use it.

Language and Life

Communication – Talent Contest

A **Have you or anyone you know ever taken part in a talent contest? What was the experience like?**

B 10.06 **Read the article about the beginnings of TV talent shows. Then answer the questions.**

Talent Contests

A TV talent show audition

The TV talent show *Got Talent*, started by Simon Cowell in 2004, has become a global success story. Viewers watch the shows in 58 countries. In 2014, *Guinness World Records* named it the most successful reality TV show ever. A number of other audition-based shows, such as *The Voice* and *The X Factor*, are also popular with audiences across the planet. And the reason? People love watching as the contestants go from nothing to huge success over a few weeks and months. But how did it all start?

Back in 1934, a radio show called *Original Amateur Hour* began in the US. After some success, it moved to TV in 1948. That show was similar to talent shows today. TV professionals traveled the country looking for entertainers who then went to New York for the auditions. The entertainers would audition for the judges on TV, and if chosen, they would come back and audition again. The audience would vote for their favorite act by phone or by mail. The final competition was at Madison Square Garden and the winners received a trophy and $1,500.

Original Amateur Hour helped to create a number of stars. Frank Sinatra performed on the radio show. Surprisingly, Elvis Presley wasn't successful when he auditioned for the show in Tupelo, Mississippi.

Another talent competition was *Star Search*. *Star Search* was different because entertainers competed in different categories, such as best male singer and best female singer. The prize money was $100,000 for each category. Many well-known pop stars and singing groups auditioned when they were younger, including Justin Timberlake, Destiny's Child, Christina Aguilera, Britney Spears, and Usher.

American Idol started on TV in 2002. Many more TV talent shows followed: *So You Think You Can Dance*, *The X Factor*, *Rockstar INXS*, *The Sing-Off*, *Dancing With the Stars*, and most recently, *The Voice*. Past winners of *Got Talent* include a performing police dog team, acrobats, ventriloquists, wheelchair dancers, and even Rubik's cube puzzle solvers.

1 What did the winners of *Original Amateur Hour* win? ______
2 Who auditioned, but did not get a place, on *Original Amateur Hour*? ______
3 What was different about the format of *Star Search*? ______
4 When did *American Idol* first appear on TV? ______
5 What talents do the past winners of *Got Talent* have? ______
6 Why might these talents be interesting to watch on TV? ______

C IN PAIRS **Talk to your partner and discuss what talents you have.**

A: I have a cool talent. I can play music using glasses of water!

B: Really? That's amazing. I can play guitar.

A: Maybe we could perform together!

D Your class is going to hold a talent contest. Choose three classmates to perform. Decide if you want to be a contestant or a judge and follow the instructions.

Contestants: Get into groups. Explain what you want to do. Choose from one of the following:

- singing
- dancing
- playing an instrument
- reading a poem out loud
- acting out a scene from a movie or theater show
- another talent

Think about the questions you may be asked in the audition and work together to prepare clear and precise answers.

Possible Questions	Possible Answers
I think they might ask me how long I have been playing piano.	*I've been playing piano for five years.*

Judges: Get into groups. Discuss and agree how you are going to give scores for each contestant. Are you going to judge them on:

- talent?
- effort?
- appearance?
- a combination of these things?

Think about what you want to ask in the audition and work together to prepare clear questions.

Possible Questions
I'd like to ask why they want to be in the talent contest.

E IN PAIRS Find a partner from the opposite group (contestants or judges). Report the questions that your group prepared and make sure they are the same.

A: Our group thought you would ask us how long we had been playing an instrument

B: Our group had that question. We also decided to ask you why you wanted to be in the talent contest.

F Return to your groups. Record your questions then hold the talent contest.

Contestants: Perform in front of the judges. Answer any questions as clearly as possible.
Judges: Ask questions that you made a note of.

G Decide on the winner(s) as a class. Explain what you liked about each performance and why.

H Discuss the questions.

1. Were you happy with your questions and answers? Did they help you to communicate clearly?
2. In what other situations might you have to plan questions to ask someone or plan answers to give to someone?
3. What other factors contribute to effective communication?

MAKE IT DIGITAL

Record the talent contest. Decide whose performance was the best. Who definitely has talent?

VOCABULARY review

SCORE: / 10

A Complete the sentences with the idioms from the box.

dream big | hungry for success | in the right place | set his heart on | set his sights on

1 Eliza works hard because she is ________________.
2 Be sure to ________________! Then you will have a goal to work toward.
3 Nat has ________________ a singing career. He even has a manager!
4 I was ________________ at the right time, and I got a record deal while I was at music school.
5 Sam has ________________ being a rock star when he leaves school!

B Complete the sentences with a phrasal verb from the box that means the same as the verb in parentheses.

come back | fill out | keep on going | make up | show up

1 If you forget the dance steps in the show, ____________ (invent) your own steps.
2 The theater doors don't open until 8 p.m., so you should ____________ (return) then.
3 To enter the talent show, you need to ____________ (complete) an application form.
4 If you've failed your music exam five times, ____________ (continue) until you pass!
5 Auditions for the talent show start at 10 a.m., so please ____________ (arrive) just before then.

GRAMMAR review

SCORE: / 10

A Rewrite the numbered sentences in your notebook as reported speech. Use the verbs in parentheses.

Kyle: **1** I'm doing a project about unusual talents (tell). **2** Do you know anyone who has one? (ask)
Dan: **3** My cousin Elena has a cool talent. (say)
Kyle: **4** What can she do? (want to know)
Dan: **5** She can juggle. (explain)
Kyle: **6** Where did she learn to do that? (ask)
Dan: **7** She took a circus class. (say) **8** Have you ever taken a circus class? (ask)
Kyle: **9** I'm not good at that kind of thing! (admit)
Dan: **10** Most people aren't. (say)

16–20 correct: You can talk about your talents and abilities and use phrasal verbs and idioms connected to success. You can use reported statements and questions.
0–15 correct: Look again at the Vocabulary and Grammar sections in the unit.

TOTAL SCORE: / 20

WHAT DO YOU KNOW NOW? Look back at page 97 and add the words you know now to the boxes.

FOLLOW A PRO ENTERTAINMENT

Take the quiz about entertainment. Go to Follow A Pro on page 136 to find the answers. Then read about the entertainment industry.

1 Which country has the most televisions, with approximately 400 million?
a Russia **b** China **c** the US

2 In what year was the first in-flight movie shown?
a 1925 **b** 1945 **c** 1965

3 Which Hollywood actor was first spotted by a talent scout having an argument in a bank?
a Jennifer Lawrence **b** Natalie Portman **c** Charlize Theron

4 How many boys auditioned for the leading role in the first Harry Potter movie?
a 160 **b** 1,600 **c** 16,000

UNIT 11

Money in the Bank

WHAT DO YOU ALREADY KNOW?

1 Think about words you know related to money and finances. Write the words.

2 IN PAIRS Share and compare your ideas. Add more words to your lists.

Money/Finances

VIDEO

DISCUSS & SHARE

3 IN GROUPS Watch the video and answer the question.

SYM Is it better to save for the future or enjoy your money now?

In this unit, you will ...

- discuss who you would employ if you were a millionaire, share ideas about what to do with a fortune, and compare your budget with that of a partner.
- use thinking skills: question, apply, and recall.
- read about the gig economy.
- use strategies and language to talk about imagined future situations, collaborate on creative ideas, and politely refuse to answer a question.
- use collaboration skills to manage a budget.
- learn tips for personal development.

LESSON 1 The Gig Economy

READING

A Do you know what the "gig economy" is? Can you figure out what it is from the pictures?

B 11.01 READING SKILL—Read for the main idea Read the job ad, article, and business profile. Match a title with each one.

a Every Day is Different! b Calling All Computer Game Fans … c Changes to Our Working and Home Lives

1 ______ We're **hiring** in your area! Would you like to earn some extra cash? Are you happy to do freelance work from home?

If the answer is "yes," then give Reviews4U a call at 800-555-3210. We're a software company that needs gamers to test our new range of exciting PC games. We'll pay $40 for each gaming review you send to us. No **contract**, no stress, and hours that work for you.

2 ______ Today's workers no longer expect to have the same job for life. The gig economy means that more and more people are working for themselves, offering their services and time **in exchange for** cash, but with no contract, no **pension**, and no vacation or sick pay. The way we take care of chores has changed at home, too. We have people take care of our gardens and yards, we make someone else walk our dogs because we're too busy to do it ourselves, and we get people to decorate our apartments. We have our groceries delivered and we get our houses cleaned. Interestingly, there are things that we used to get *others* to do in the past that we now do *ourselves* because of changes in technology. Now, we book our own flights online instead of getting a travel agent to do it for us. We also manage our own money online without the help of a bank clerk.

GigGetters

3 ______ CeeCee Rogers, a tech worker in New York City, was **laid off** in 2018. She knew it might take a long time to find another job in her field.

"I wasn't sure what to do," explains CeeCee. "When I lost my job, it was a big shock. Luckily, I found out about GigGetters and I signed up with them. They have me do various gigs so I can make money while I'm looking for a more **permanent** job. I enjoy it. No day is the same!"

C Read the texts again. Write *True* or *False*.

1 The job at Reviews4U pays the same amount of money every month. ______
2 Working for Reviews4U would mean working in an office. ______
3 Text 2 includes information about disadvantages for workers in a gig economy. ______
4 CeeCee wants to work for GigGetters for as long as possible. ______

GLOSSARY

freelance (adj): not employed by a particular company, but working for them on a temporary basis

D THINKING SKILL—Question What are the advantages of gig work? What are the disadvantages?

VOCABULARY

A Complete the sentences with a word or phrase in bold in READING B.

1 My friend gave me a skirt that didn't fit her ____________ a brown jacket that I never wear.
2 I was ____________ a month ago, so I'm looking for another job.
3 When people retire from work, they usually get a regular amount of money called a ____________ from the company or government.
4 Did you sign a ____________ with your company when you started?
5 Dave has a temporary job, but he's looking for something ____________.
6 This restaurant is ____________ chefs and servers.

MAKE IT YOURS

Go online or use a dictionary to find job advertisements in English for your chosen career. Are most companies hiring permanent workers, temporary workers, or gig workers?

GRAMMAR causatives with *have, get,* and *make*

A Underline examples in Text 2 in READING B of things we pay people to do for us and things we do ourselves.

B Complete the grammar rules with forms from the box.

base form of verb (x 2) infinitive past participle

1 Use *have* or *get* to talk about paying or asking someone to do something for you.
subject + *have/get* + object + ____________ → I have/get my house cleaned.
2 Use *make* when you force or persuade someone to do something.
subject + *make* + object + ____________ → I made my brother clean his room.
3 Use *have someone do something* to talk about someone who does a job for you.
subject + *have* + person + ____________ → We had a mechanic fix the car.
4 Use *get someone to do something* when you ask, persuade, or pay someone to do something for you.
subject + *get* + person + ____________ → They got a vet to check their dog's health.

For more practice, go to page 156.

C Complete the sentences with the correct forms of the words in parentheses.

If you think being one of the world's wealthiest people sounds like fun, think about all the staff you'd need to hire just to keep your life in order! You'd need **1** ____________ (get / housekeeper / clean) the house. You'd have to **2** ____________ (have / nanny / take care of) your children and a private tutor **3** ____________ (make / them / do) their homework. But think of the advantages! When you came home at the end of a long day, you could **4** ____________ (have / your meal / cook) by your personal chef and **5** ____________ (make / butler / bring) your slippers for you before you put your feet up in front of the TV!

D IN PAIRS Talk about things you have, get, or make other people do for you.

SPEAKING

A You have an unlimited amount of money. Make notes about what you would get these people to do for you.

- a hairdresser
- a mechanic
- a chef
- a dog walker

B IN PAIRS Talk about your ideas. Use the Confident Communicator box to help you.

C IN GROUPS What jobs would you like to have people do for you and what jobs you would prefer to do yourself?

CONFIDENT COMMUNICATOR
START TALKING

To start a conversation about things you dream of for the future, use:
You know what I'd do if I were …?
You know what I'd do if I had enough money? I'd have a chef cook all my meals.

Giving Away Money

VOCABULARY money verbs and nouns

A Read the definitions. Write the related nouns. Use a dictionary if needed.

Verb	Noun (thing)	Noun (person)
donate: to give something such as money to a charity	**1** ____________: an amount of something such as money given to a charity	**2** ____________: a person who donates something
contribute: to give something such as money to help achieve something	**3** ____________: a gift or payment you make to help achieve something	**4** ____________: a person who contributes something

B IN GROUPS Do you know individuals who have donated large sums of money to a particular cause in your country or abroad? Discuss.

Examples: George Soros Bill and Melinda Gates Oprah Winfrey Alcario and Carmen Castellano

LISTENING

A IN PAIRS Do you ever donate money to charity? What kind of charities do you support?

1

animal charities

2
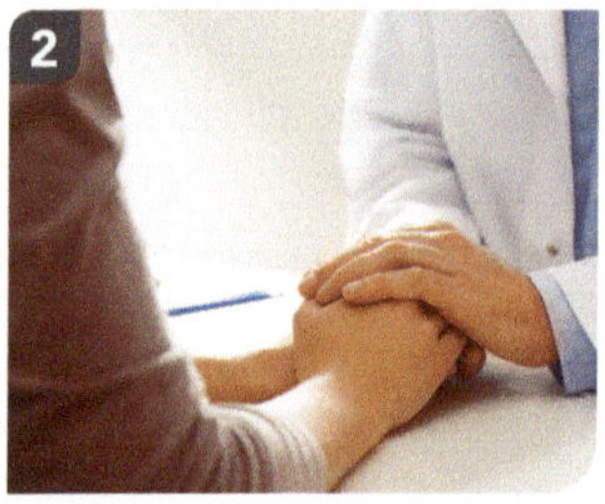
charities that help people with health problems

3

educational charities

4

environmental charities

5

charities that provide food, water, or housing

B 11.02 LISTENING SKILL—Listen for specific information Listen to an interview. Then complete the sentences.

1 The interviewer says that George Soros has donated over ____________ billion dollars to charity.
2 The charity called *Rainbows* helps ____________.
3 Pat says that people can offer to work in the charity's thrift ____________.
4 Danny says you can do online ____________ to help charities.
5 Danny says an organization called ____________ helps people who need food.
6 Pat's charity has received ____________ thousand dollars in foreign currency collected on planes.

GLOSSARY

campaign manager (n): a person who organizes ways to make money for a charity, organization, or political party
volunteer (n): a person who is not paid for the work they do
foreign currency (n phr): money from another country

C 11.02 IN PAIRS Compare your answers. Then listen again and check.

D THINKING SKILL—Apply Is it better to donate time or money to a charity? Give reasons.

GRAMMAR verbs with gerund, infinitive, or both

A Read the examples from LISTENING B. Notice how some verbs are followed by the infinitive (*to* + base form of verb), the gerund (verb + *–ing*), or both.

Many people decide **to give** cash …
Some people prefer **doing** these events
Have you considered **playing** games online?

B Complete the rules with one of the verbs underlined in the examples from A. Then complete the example sentences.

1 Some verbs (such as ____________ *agree*, *want*, *offer*, etc.) are followed by infinitives.
EXAMPLE: Last year, my cousin did a 10k fun run and now, I really ____________ **to do** one too.

2 Some verbs (such as ____________ *suggest*, *deny*, *keep*, etc.) are followed by gerunds.
EXAMPLE: For a charity event, my friend ____________ **raising** money by playing games online.

3 Verbs that describe feelings (such as ____________ *dislike*, *like*, *love*, *hate*, etc.) can be followed by both gerunds and infinitives.
EXAMPLE: I could never run a marathon! I absolutely ____________ **running**.

For more practice, go to page 157.

C Complete the text with the infinitive or gerund form of the verb in parentheses. If both forms are possible, write both.

Inheriting money can be hard, especially when the person who dies leaves instructions about what the person must (or mustn't) agree **1** ____________________ (do) to get the money. Leona Helmsley, a hotel owner, left $12 million to her dog when she died. However, she gave instructions that two of her grandchildren would only inherit money if they promised **2** ____________________ (visit) their father's grave regularly. Henry Budd of London, who died in 1862, hated **3** ____________________ (see) men with mustaches so much that he refused **4** ____________________ (leave) money to his two sons unless they avoided **5** ____________________ (grow) facial hair. It seems some people just like **6** ____________________ (give) instructions even in death!

D IN PAIRS Complete the sentences with information that is true for you. Discuss with your partner.

1 I dislike ____________________
2 I sometimes help ____________________
3 I avoid ____________________
4 I really love ____________________
5 I always refuse ____________________

SPEAKING

A Imagine that you have inherited $1 million. Would you spend it, save it, or give it to charity? Make notes.

B IN GROUPS Share your ideas. Give specific information about what you would do with the money. Use the Confident Communicator box to help you.

CONFIDENT COMMUNICATOR
START TALKING

When you collaborate on creative ideas, it's good to start by going around the group, giving everyone the chance to talk about their ideas without interruptions. That way, everyone in the group can express their ideas with the full attention of everyone else.

LESSON 3 Spending Money

VOCABULARY paying for things

A Label the pictures (1–6) with phrases from the box.

ATM / cash machine | cash | change | contactless payment | credit card | debit card

1 

2 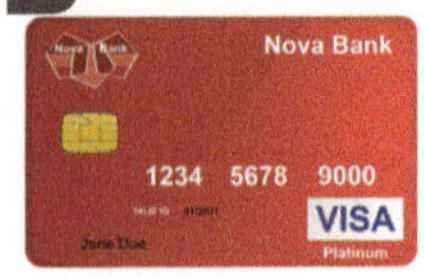

3 

4 

5 

6 

B IN PAIRS Talk about what you use to pay for different things.

A: I usually use cash to pay for lunch.

B: I sometimes use a debit card when I buy clothes.

PRONUNCIATION /tʃ/ versus /ʃ/

A 11.03 Listen to how these words are pronounced. Notice the difference between the /tʃ/ and /ʃ/ sounds.

change   cash machine

B 11.04 Practice saying these sentences. Then listen and check.

1 Do you have any change?
2 I'm going to use the cash machine.

LISTENING

A What do you spend money on? How do you manage your money?

B 11.05 LISTENING SKILL—Listen for the main idea Listen to a radio show. People are talking about the ways they manage their money. Match the speakers (1–4) with the ways to manage money (a–d).

1 Speaker 1 ____
2 Speaker 2 ____
3 Speaker 3 ____
4 Speaker 4 ____

a pays someone else to manage their money for them.
b says that they mostly use debit cards when they shop.
c uses traditional ways of managing their money.
d uses an app to help them manage their money.

C 11.05 Listen again and choose the correct speakers.

Which speaker …

1	isn't very good at managing money?	1	2	3	4
2	rarely uses a credit card?	1	2	3	4
3	would rather earn money than manage it?	1	2	3	4
4	likes to keep a physical record of her/his spending?	1	2	3	4
5	uses computer programs to manage her/his money?	1	2	3	4
6	uses their smartphone to manage her/his money?	1	2	3	4

MAKE IT REAL

To *splurge* means to spend a lot of money. *Maria used her birthday money to splurge on expensive new shoes.*

D IN PAIRS THINKING SKILL—Recall Try to remember how much money you spent yesterday. What did you spend it on? How did you pay?

A: I really don't remember. I know I bought a soda and a sandwich.

B: Is that it? I'm sure you bought more than that.

WRITING

A **A friend is visiting you from abroad. Read her email. What does she need advice about?**

1 restaurants   2 sightseeing   3 money

New Message

How are you doing? I'm really excited about seeing you in a few weeks. Can you give me some advice?

- Should I bring cash with me? If so, how much do you think I'll need per day for food, shopping, sightseeing?
- Should I change my dollars into the local currency here or wait until I'm there?
- Can I use my debit card or credit card at the ATMs?
- Please let me know what you think is best. A list of do's and don'ts would be great.

See you soon!
Amelia

Send

B **Think about Amelia's questions. Add advice to the table.**

Do's	Don'ts
change some money before you arrive	bring too much cash

C **Write an email to Amelia. Include the information from your table in B.**

D **IN PAIRS Share your emails. Did your partner answer all of Amelia's questions?**

SPEAKING

A **Find out what the average income is for people in your country per month. Write it in the table. Then fill in the amounts of money you think you would need to spend per month on these things.**

Item	Amount	Item	Amount	Item	Amount
rent/mortgage	1	food	2	clothes	3
entertainment/going out	4	travel/transportation	5	phone	6
household bills (water, gas, electricity, etc.)	7	other	8		

1 Total monthly income: ______________   2 Total monthly spending: ______________

B **IN PAIRS Compare the amount of money you imagine you would spend on each thing.**

A: I think I would spend about $100 a month on food.

B: Really? I think I'd need to spend more than that. I wrote $150.

C **IN GROUPS Report to the group what you have learned about your partner's budget. What advice would you give to people who have spent too much? Use the Confident Communicator box to help you.**

Rico enjoys eating out. He thinks he'd spend between $60 and $100 a month. Maybe he should eat out less.

CONFIDENT COMMUNICATOR

KEEP TALKING

Money can be a hard topic to talk about. There are phrases you can use to refuse, politely, to answer questions you aren't comfortable with:

I'd rather not answer that question, if you don't mind.
That's a personal question. I'd rather not say.
I'm sorry, but that isn't information I want to share.

Language and Life

Collaborate – A Budget

A **Are there any businesses near you that were set up by local people? What kinds of things do they sell? Are they popular?**

B 11.06 **Read the newspaper article about two friends who set up a business. Answer the questions.**

Business Profile: KylieBelle's Bakery

Meet Annabelle Eggers and Kylie Howell, a pair of high school friends who recently set up KylieBelle's Bakery, a bakery and coffee shop on the North Shore. The pair both left successful careers in law to start their own business. But things didn't get off to a good start.

"It hasn't been easy," Kylie explains, when we meet up at the bakery on a Sunday morning. "I don't think we realized how much hard work it would be. We thought we'd be doing the jobs we love all day, which for us is making cakes and serving customers. But actually, there's a lot more involved, like accounting. Also, we had an awful first day." The pair had to close the bakery after a serious fire in their kitchen on the day they opened. "It was terrible," admits Annabelle. "We thought we might not be able to afford to open again after the accident. We were both in tears."

Luckily, a local resident, Marlene Parks, offered to help by investing over $10,000 in the business. "I was looking for a small business to invest some money in," says Marlene. "And who doesn't love a nice bakery in their local area? I hope the business does really well and I wish Annabelle and Kylie lots of luck." The women used the money to get builders to repair the kitchen, and the bakery reopened two weeks later.

"Thanks to Marlene, we were able to get the business open again. We need to pay her back, obviously, but it meant we could start making money. The business is doing really well. We're going to have a new seating area built outside so we can serve more of our cakes. People love our white chocolate cheesecake!"

1 What profession did Annabelle and Kylie use to work in? ____________________

2 What happened on the first day the bakery opened? ____________________

3 How did the women get money for builders to repair the kitchen? ____________________

4 What are they planning to build outside and why? ____________________

C **IN PAIRS** **Imagine you want to open a small business in your city or town with your partner. You have a budget of $10,000 to get the business started. Together, discuss the questions and reach an agreement for each point.**

1 What kind of small business will you open?
2 Where will it be located?
3 What is the rent?
4 What will you call it?
5 What product or service will you sell?
6 How much will the product or service cost?
7 What kinds of payment will you accept (cash, credit cards, debit cards)?
8 What kinds of problems do you think the business might have?
9 What can you do about these problems?

D **IN PAIRS** **Before you open the business, you need to decide which jobs you can do yourself and which you are going to get someone else to do for you. Decide together and write the jobs and the costs in the correct column.**

Jobs we can do ourselves	Jobs we need to get someone else to do	Expected costs for jobs other people will do
delivering leaflets	*installing new kitchen equipment*	

E **Underline the jobs in D that will cost a lot to have someone else do. Could you do any of them yourself? Negotiate with each other to decide who could do which job.**

F **IN GROUPS** **Share your ideas. Find out which businesses are within the $10,000 budget.**

G **Discuss the questions.**

1 Did you and your partner work well together? How did you overcome any disagreements?
2 In what other situations might you have to collaborate and agree on a solution?

MAKE IT DIGITAL

Find and read an online article about starting a new business. What other things should you consider that were not discussed in this lesson?

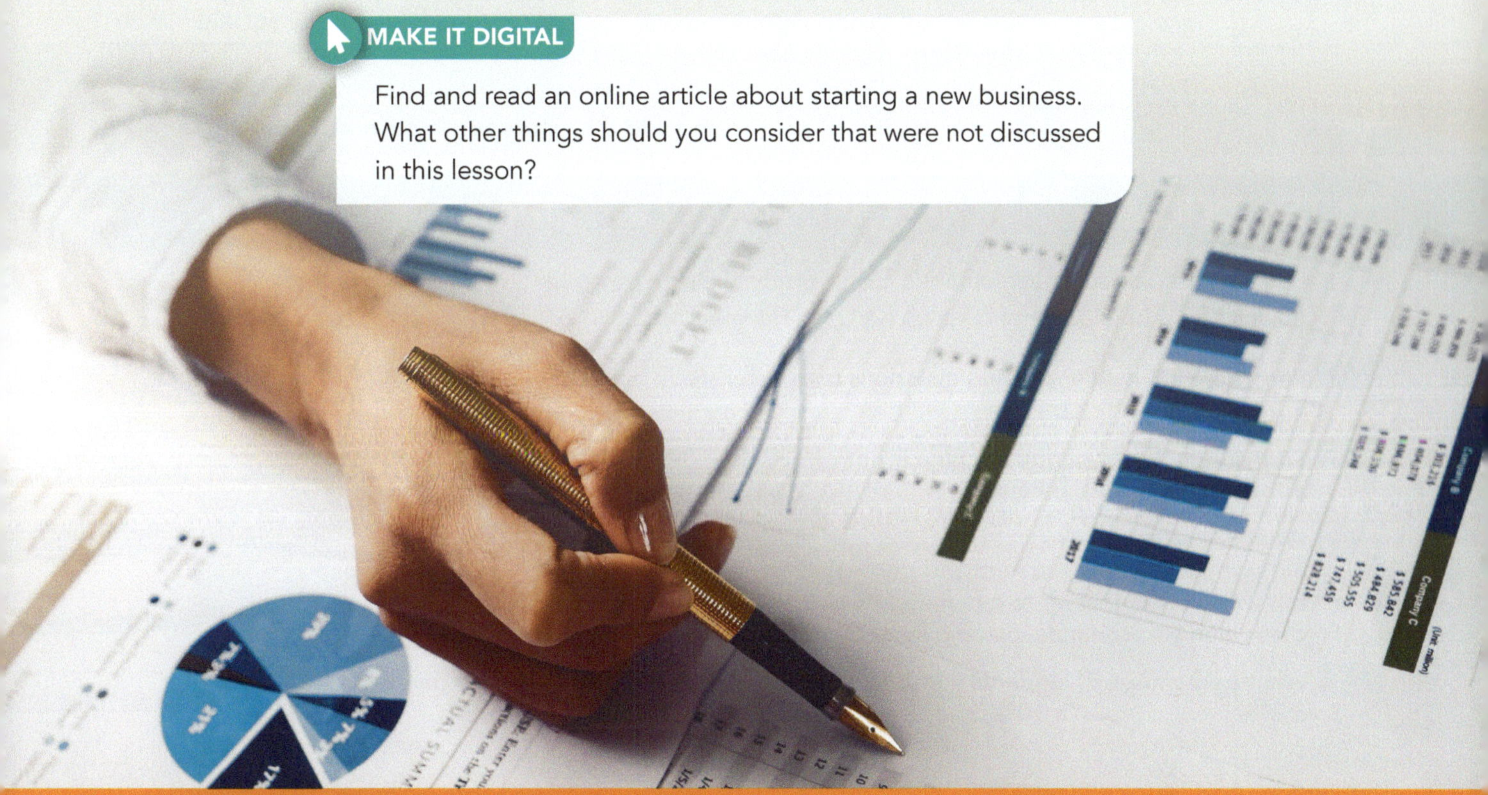

VOCABULARY review

SCORE: / 10

A Complete the sentences with words from the box.

contract contribution donor pension permanent

1 In some countries, you can receive a ________________ from the government at the age of 60.
2 Did you sign a ________________ when you started your new job?
3 This is a ________________ job, so you'll have a fixed schedule.
4 A generous celebrity ________________ has given $1 million to this charity.
5 Did you make a ________________ to any charities last year?

B Choose the five correct answers to complete the sentences.

1 I don't like borrowing money, so I don't have any **credit** / **debit** cards.
2 Do you have any **ATMs** / **cash**? This machine doesn't accept **change** / **contactless** payments.
3 The **credit card** / **ATM** isn't working so I haven't got any **cash** / **cash machines** at all.

GRAMMAR review

SCORE: / 10

A Choose the correct words.

1 She is **having** / **making** her hair cut at the hairdresser at the moment.
2 Did you **have** / **get** a mechanic fix your car?
3 They are **getting** / **making** a painter to decorate their new bathroom.
4 Mom **made** / **got** the kids mow the lawn before they had lunch.
5 Will he **get** / **have** a taxi to take him to the airport at 3 a.m.?

B Complete the sentences with the correct forms of the verbs in parentheses. Write both forms where possible.

1 My manager has agreed ________________ (give) me time off when I move.
2 I've decided ________________ (save) some money every month for a vacation.
3 Marcus promised ________________ (not/spend) a lot of money on his fiancée's Christmas gifts.
4 I prefer ________________ (pay) for things with my debit card rather than with a credit card.
5 I avoid ________________ (waste) money buying things I don't need.

16–20 correct: You can talk about money and paying for things. You can use *have*, *make* and *get* and verbs with the gerund, infinitive, or both.
0–15 correct: Look again at the Vocabulary and Grammar sections in the unit.

TOTAL SCORE: / 20

WHAT DO YOU KNOW NOW? Look back at page 107 and add the words you know now to the box.

STUDY SKILLS PERSONAL DEVELOPMENT

Take the quiz about personal development. Go to **Study Skills** on page 137 to find the answers. Then learn more about personal development.

1 Recording yourself answering questions is a useful study technique.
a True **b** False

2 Studying for short periods of time is not effective.
a True **b** False

3 What is overlearning?
a It's when you work too hard and get very tired.
b It's when you go over to a friend's house to study.
c It's when you continue learning something even when you think you've already learned it.

4 What percentage of students admit to studying for exams at the very last minute?
a 99% **b** 90% **c** 65% **d** 51%

UNIT 12

Inside Advertising

WHAT DO YOU ALREADY KNOW?

1 Think about ads you like. Write words to describe them.

2 IN PAIRS Share and compare your ideas. Add more words to your lists.

Ads:

DISCUSS & SHARE

VIDEO

3 IN GROUPS Watch the video and answer the question.

SYM Does advertising work?

In this unit, you will ...

- discuss the advertising of energy drinks, talk about ads that you like and dislike, and debate the effects of advertising.
- use thinking skills: evaluate, symbolize, and induce.
- read about advertising controls around the world.
- use strategies and language to make sure everyone has a turn in a discussion, get a discussion back on track, and paraphrase to clarify what someone has said.
- use media-literacy skills to make a TV ad.
- follow a digital copywriter to learn about this job and the skills needed to be in this industry.

Advertising Regulations

READING

A Are there any ads that you dislike? Why don't you like them?

B 12.01 Read the article. Then answer the questions.

Advertising Around the World: Who Controls What?

As you might expect in the modern world, more and more advertising is being controlled by strict rules. In the US, the Federal Trade Commission (FTC) makes sure that all ads are accurate. In the UK, this is done by the Advertising Standards Agency (ASA), which in 2017 received about 30,000 **complaints** about ads. The job of these agencies is to decide if certain rules are broken by advertisers. **1** ______ The FTC and the ASA decide if the ad can be shown or if it has to be **removed**.

Ads that you might think aren't very offensive can cause lots of complaints. **2** ______ People felt that this ad might encourage bad habits in children. In 2017, another TV ad for fried chicken that showed chickens dancing to rap music was **criticized** for being offensive to vegetarians and vegans. The request was turned down by the ASA.

Each country has different rules about what they allow. A famous series of billboard ads made by a fashionable Italian clothing company caused problems in countries where they appeared. One ad, showing a very young baby, shocked a lot of people. In Sicily, the company was ordered by the town officials to remove the ad. **3** ______ It was given a prize by the Swiss General Poster Association, and a hospital in Bologna asked **permission** to display the ad on its walls.

Some ads have been **banned**, not for showing offensive images, but for the way they market the product. A well-known soft drink ad campaign, which had been seen by millions, was removed for showing a famous celebrity sharing her drink with a police officer at a protest event. **4** ______

GLOSSARY

offensive (adj): causing people to feel upset or embarrassed
billboard (n): a large board for ads in an outside public space

1. What is the name of the organization that controls ads in the US? ______
2. What did viewers not like about the fried chicken ad? ______
3. What type of company produced an ad showing a newborn baby? ______

C READING SKILL—Identify missing sentences Match the sentences (a–d) to lines 1–4 in the article.

a It is interesting that what shocks some people is loved by other people.
b The message is just as important as the image.
c These might include making false promises about the product or using offensive images.
d A TV ad showing people talking with their mouths full of food received the most complaints in the ASA's history.

D THINKING SKILL—Evaluate Consider this statement: "Advertising doesn't really have an effect on the things I choose to buy." Is this statement true for you?

VOCABULARY

A Match the words in bold in READING B with the definitions.

1. ______ (v): officially stated that people must not do or say something
2. ______ (n plural): written or spoken statements in which someone says they are not happy with something
3. ______ (v): said what you thought was bad or wrong about something
4. ______ (n): the right to do something that someone with power gives you
5. ______ (v): taken away from a place

MAKE IT DIGITAL

Research online for examples of ads that have been banned. Do you think that they should have been banned?

GRAMMAR passive voice: other tenses

A Read the examples of the passive voice from READING B. Find five other examples of passive sentences in the article.

... more and more advertising is being controlled by strict rules. (present progressive passive)
The job of these agencies is to decide if certain rules are broken by advertisers. (simple present passive)
... was criticized for being offensive. (simple past passive)
Some ads have been banned ... (present perfect passive)
... which had been seen by millions ... (past perfect passive)

B Choose the correct options.

1 Use the passive voice to show that the action is **more** / **less** important than the person doing the action.
2 Use the passive voice when you **know** / **don't know** who did the action.
3 Only use the passive voice with **transitive** / **intransitive** verbs.

For more practice, go to page 158.

C Complete the text with the correct passive forms of the verbs in parentheses. More than one form may be possible.

An ad for an electronic device **1** ________________ (change) recently following a complaint. Alexa, as she **2** ________________ (know) around the world, tried to order cat food when she heard her name on a cat food ad. The ad, which shows the device **3** ________________ (use) in different situations by different people, confused Alexa into making the order. A complaint **4** ________________ (receive) by an advertising complaints organization. Amazon agreed that Alexa did place an order for the cat food, but the order **5** ________________ (cancel) by the customer. Customers now have to confirm their orders. The orders **6** ________________ (remove) immediately from their shopping carts if customers do not confirm them.

D IN PAIRS Think about a recent ad campaign that you like. Describe it to your partner. Can he or she guess the ad? Who is it made by? Where is it advertised? How long has it been advertised?

This ad is made by a fast food company. It's been shown on TV for about six months, but the actors have been changed recently.

SPEAKING

A IN PAIRS Should energy drinks be advertised on TV and in magazines? Complete the table and give reasons.

For	Against

B IN GROUPS Decide whether you are for or against advertising energy drinks on TV or in magazines. Take turns presenting your opinion and giving reasons. Use the Confident Communicator box to help you.

CONFIDENT COMMUNICATOR
KEEP TALKING

To make sure everyone in a group has a turn in a discussion, use phrases like this:
Can we hear someone else's opinion?
What do you think, [name]?

LESSON 2 How Does Advertising Work?

VOCABULARY advertising campaigns

A Match the job responsibilities (1–6) with the meanings (a–f). Use a dictionary if needed.

1 come up with a slogan ____
2 promote a product ____
3 design the logo ____
4 launch the product ____
5 identify the target market ____
6 manage the budget ____

a think of words or phrases to sell a product
b figure out which groups of people will buy a product
c attract people's attention to a product
d start selling a new product
e control the money spent on a project
f create a memorable image connected to a product

LISTENING

A IN PAIRS Look at the magazine ads. What are they trying to tell you about the product? Who is the target market?

B 12.02 Listen to an excerpt from an interview with a marketing executive. What does he consider in ad campaigns? Choose the correct answers.

The man says that …
1 they identify their target market using **five** / **six** / **seven** different categories.
2 in ads for younger people, the music is **slower** / **faster** / **calmer** than in ads for older people.
3 ads for people over the age of **40** / **50** / **60** often have calmer music.
4 the more you write slogans, **the harder** / **the faster** / **the easier** it gets.

C 12.03 LISTENING SKILL—Listen for inference Listen to the ad. Then answer the questions.

1 What is the ad for? ____
2 Who is the target market? ____
3 Why is the ad appropriate for this market? ____

D THINKING SKILL—Symbolize Sketch as many logos as you can in two minutes. Why do you think these logos stick in your mind?

GRAMMAR comparative and superlative adverbs

A Look at the phrases in bold in the sentences from LISTENING B. Which adverbs are comparative? Which are superlative? Write C or S.

1 … one of the first things we have to do **the most carefully** is identify our target market. ____
2 And in TV or radio ads directed at older people, the actors usually **speak more seriously** and less quickly. ____
3 "These running shoes will help you **run faster**!" ____

B Choose the correct options to complete the grammar rules.

1 Most comparative adverbs are formed with … + adverb.
  a *more* b *the most*
2 Most superlative adverbs are formed with … + adverb.
  a *more* b *the most*
3 Most short adverbs, such as *fast* and *hard*, end in *–er* in the comparative and *–est* in the …
  a superlative. b infinitive.
4 The verb usually goes … the adverb.
  a before b after

For more practice, go to page 159.

C Complete the sentences with the correct forms of the words in parentheses.

1 In commercials for younger people, the actors talk _______________ (quick) than in commercials for older people.
2 Ad campaigns work the _______________ (successful) when they have a clear target market.
3 They're working _______________ (careful) on this ad campaign than the last one.
4 Our products are selling more _______________ (slow) than we'd like them to.
5 The people in that ad sing _______________ (badly) than I thought possible!

MAKE IT REAL

There are different ways of talking about TV *ads*. You can talk about *ads* or *commercials* (all informal) or about *advertisements* (more formal).

D IN PAIRS Talk about ads.

Which ones …
1 do you see most often?
2 work the most successfully?
3 make the product look better than it actually is?

SPEAKING

A Think about an ad you like and an ad you dislike. Complete the table with notes about them.

	Ad I Like	Ad I Dislike
Product		
Logo		
Slogan		
Target market		
Kind of ad (print, TV, billboard)		
People, activity, or music in ad		

B IN GROUPS Talk about ads you like and dislike. Suggest improvements for the ad you dislike. Use the Confident Communicator box to help you.

A: Why don't you like this commercial?
B: I think the people in the ad speak too quickly. I think they could speak more slowly.

CONFIDENT COMMUNICATOR
REPAIR IT

If a discussion goes "off topic," you can use the phrases to get the discussion back on topic:
Going back to what I was saying earlier about *advertising.*
Let's get back to talking about *how to improve this ad campaign.*
You were saying that *you didn't like this ad.*

LESSON 3 The "Unreal" World of Advertising

VOCABULARY discourse markers

A Write the discourse markers from the box next to the correct functions.

although	as well as	for instance	such as
as a result	due to	in addition	whereas

Function	Examples
Adding information	also, too, and, furthermore, **1** __________, **2** __________
Giving examples	for example, **3** __________, **4** __________
Giving reasons	because, so, therefore, **5** __________, **6** __________
Contrasting different ideas	but, however, on the one hand, on the other hand, **7** __________, **8** __________

B Choose the correct options.

1 A: Do you always change channels when the commercials come on?
B: Not always, **because** / **although** I actually like watching some of them.

2 A: Did you know that this ad was banned in many countries?
B: I know. But **in addition** / **as a result**, the fast food chain became even more popular!

3 A: Ads for products **such as** / **due to** soft drinks shouldn't be shown during kids' movies.
B: I completely agree.

4 A: **As well as** / **Whereas** all the pop-up ads on Facebook, I get a lot of spam email, too.
B: Yeah, me too. It's really annoying.

LISTENING

A IN PAIRS **Compare the pictures. Which one has been photoshopped (changed to look different)? How do you know?**

B 12.04 LISTENING SKILL—Recognize discourse markers **Listen to four people giving their opinions about advertising. Then match each speaker with the discourse marker that he or she uses (a–d).**

1 Speaker 1: _____ a due to
2 Speaker 2: _____ b such as
3 Speaker 3: _____ c as a result
4 Speaker 4: _____ d although

GLOSSARY
edit (v): to make changes to a photo to make it look better

C 12.04 **Listen again and decide which speaker (1–4) has a positive opinion of advertising and which speaker has a negative opinion.**

(+) opinion ____________________

(–) opinion ____________________

D THINKING SKILL—Induce **Decide if people generally believe what companies say about their products.**

PRONUNCIATION filler sounds and words

A 12.05 **Listen to the sentences from LISTENING B. Underline the filler sounds and words that the speakers use. Why do you think they use them?**

1. Situations that people can, um, understand and connect with.
2. I felt quite angry, hmm …
3. You might think ad companies would, you know, check the images carefully …
4. It's like, when I'm shopping, what makes me pick up certain things and buy them?

B **Think about your language. What filler sounds and words do you use?**

WRITING

A **Read the essay prompt and one student's answer to it. Has the student answered the question? Why or why not?**

PROMPT: "Photoshopped images should be banned in ads." Discuss the arguments for and against this statement.

In recent years, some advertising companies have been criticized for using photoshopped images in their advertising campaigns. For example, it's common for the pictures in ads for some products—beauty products, for instance—to be edited to make the people in the ads appear perfect. The ad companies use computer technology to change the shape of people's bodies. Due to this trend, young people can have health problems because they try to look like the people in the ads. As a result, photoshopping ads has already been banned in some countries. In France, for example, photoshopped images are not shown in magazines or on billboards. I agree that it should now be banned in the rest of the world, too.

B IN PAIRS **Can you think of any arguments in favor of photoshopping images in ads? Make notes.**

C **Write a for-and-against paragraph about photoshopping. Use ideas from A and the notes you made in B. Try to include some discourse markers from VOCABULARY A.**

SPEAKING

A **What is your opinion on the following question: "Do the images used in advertising have a positive or negative effect on people?" Make notes.**

B IN GROUPS **Discuss your ideas, giving examples and reasons. Use discourse markers to connect your ideas. Use the Confident Communicator box to help you.**

CONFIDENT COMMUNICATOR

KEEP TALKING

Use the following phrases to paraphrase and clarify what someone else has said in a debate or discussion:

So, what you're saying is that these ads make people feel uncomfortable?

Am I right in thinking that you think ads do have a negative effect on people?

If I understand correctly, you're saying that ads don't have any negative effects?

Language and Life

Media Literacy – A TV ad

A 12.06 **When a company has an idea for a TV ad, they make a storyboard. Read the article and then choose the correct options.**

STORYBOARDS:
WHAT YOU NEED TO KNOW

A Simple Guide

Have you ever come up with the most fantastic idea for an ad—or perhaps a home-made video—but had a problem getting your ideas down on paper? Then you need a storyboard!

WHAT IS A STORYBOARD?

A storyboard is a series of sketches, drawn in the style of a comic. It shows every scene of the ad. It shows what characters are in the scene, what they are doing, and what they are saying. A good storyboard will help you imagine the ad. It shows the production team what to photograph and in what order. It communicates ideas without long, wordy descriptions. As more people become involved in making the ad and give their opinions, the storyboard may develop and change.

HOW TO MAKE A STORYBOARD

A storyboard doesn't have to be complicated. Here's how to make one:

STEP 1: MAKE A TEMPLATE
Draw a series of **squares** or **rectangles** on a plain piece of paper, one for each scene. Leave room underneath the squares or rectangles for notes. You can also find free storyboards online.

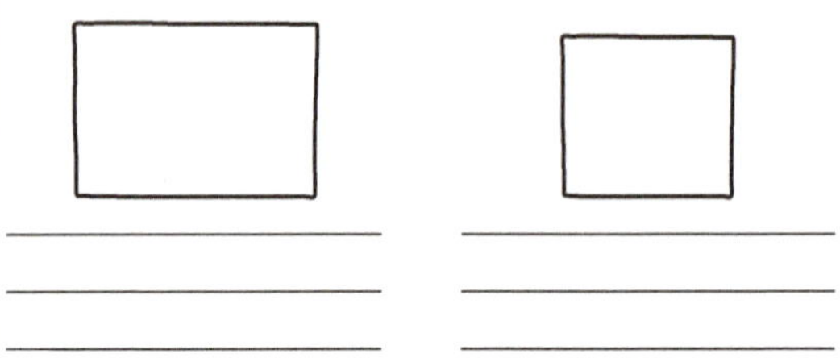

STEP 2: DRAW THE STORY
Don't worry if you aren't very good at drawing. You can use **simple stick figures** in the boxes. Show any movement with an **arrow** or **short parallel lines**.

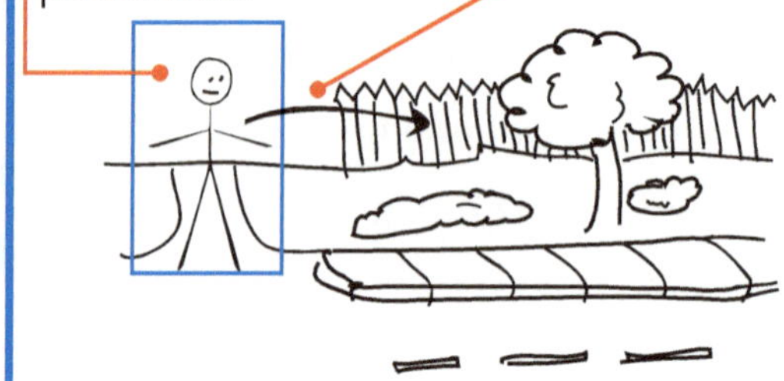

"Hey! Wait for me!"
Camera: Pans to the right from this angle as person walks. *Background music: Should have an upbeat tempo.*

STEP 3: ADD THE DIALOGUE
Write any dialogue underneath the pictures. You can also make a silent video where no dialogue is necessary.

STEP 4: ADD NOTES
These might include instructions for camera angles, descriptions of the actions in the scene, or ideas for music.

Good luck!

1 You make a storyboard at the start / end of an ad campaign.
2 A storyboard contains long / short written descriptions.
3 You need / don't need to be a good artist to draw a storyboard.
4 Storyboards have to / don't have to include dialogue.

B **IN PAIRS** **Look at the storyboard for an ad. Take turns describing what you think is happening in each of the scenes.**

C **IN PAIRS** **Discuss the following questions.**

1 What product do you think the ad is trying to sell?
2 Who is the biggest market?
3 What message is the ad trying to communicate?
4 Do you think the ad works? Why or why not?

D **IN GROUPS** **Make a storyboard for a TV ad.**

1 Choose a product. It can be real or imaginary.
2 Identify the target market.
3 Discuss your ideas and message for a TV ad.
4 Make a storyboard for a TV ad.

MAKE IT DIGITAL

Turn your storyboard idea into an ad. Decide which parts you are playing, practice any dialogue, and record your ad!

E **Present your storyboards as a class.**

F **Discuss the questions.**

1 Whose ad do you think would be the most successful. Why?
2 What are the key factors of a successful ad?

VOCABULARY review

SCORE: / 10

A Complete the text with words or phrases from the box.

although | as a result | budget | comes up with | identify | in addition | launch | logo | such as | whereas

My job is to manage ad campaigns for a large grocery store. We need to develop an ad campaign for party food **1** ________________ snacks and drinks. **2** ________________ in the past, ads for food were designed to appeal mostly to women, nowadays we have to **3** ________________ our target market more carefully. **4** ________________, we spend a lot more time researching who buys our products. The creative team **5** ________________ a slogan for the new ad and the design team makes the **6** ________________ that goes on our party food packaging. **7** ________________, I have to manage the **8** ________________ to make sure we don't spend too much money. Today, we will have a meeting to discuss how we are going to **9** ________________ a new product in the market. **10** ________________ the different teams sometimes disagree about the best way to advertise a product, we usually produce a great ad!

GRAMMAR review

SCORE: / 10

A Rewrite the sentences using the passive voice in your notebook.

1 They showed this ad for the first time this year.
2 An artist designed that logo.
3 Some governments have banned that ad.
4 We are launching the product in the early fall.
5 The creative team had developed the storyboard.

B Choose the correct options.

1 Ed is **the harder / the hardest** worker on the design team.
2 The man in the soap ad sings **more beautifully / the beautifullest** than the woman.
3 Aiden draws **more slow / more slowly** than Mark.
4 Melanie presented her ideas **more confidently / most confidently** than Juan.
5 The ad campaign for cookies worked **most / more** successfully than that for brownies.

16–20 correct: You can talk about advertising and advertising campaigns. You can use the passive voice and comparative and superlative adverbs.
0–15 correct: Look again at the Vocabulary and Grammar sections in the unit.

TOTAL SCORE: / 20

WHAT DO YOU KNOW NOW? Look back at page 117 and add the words you know now to the box.

FOLLOW A PRO ADVERTISING

Take the quiz about advertising. Go to Follow A Pro on page 134 to find the answers. Then learn about advertising.

1 What did the first ad shown on British TV advertise?
a dog food **b** toothpaste **c** hamburgers

2 Pepsi's TV ad campaign in 2002 was the most expensive ever. How much did it cost?
a \$8.1 million **b** \$81 million **c** \$108 million

3 What event did the first billboard ad in New York advertise?
a a circus **b** a baseball game **c** a music performance

4 In most wristwatch ads, what time is shown on the watch?
a 8:40 **b** 10:10 **c** 12:00

UNIT 1

STUDY SKILLS

A Read what students have to say about time management challenges. Which of the challenges do you face most often?

EFFECTIVE TIME MANAGEMENT

1 _____ Radu I guess social media is my biggest obstacle to getting things done. It's just too easy to take time out and see what my buddies are doing. Before I know where I am, I've gotten myself involved in some kind of debate, or—and this happens more often—find myself scrolling through the vacation pictures of someone I barely know.

2 _____ Deepali I find that I lose concentration too easily. I start off well, but after an hour I don't feel like I'm taking anything in anymore. How can I stay focused?

3 _____ Katia Time just disappears. It's always the same—I start off feeling like I have all the time in the world. Then it gets to deadline time and I have no idea where the days and hours have gone! I wind up doing everything too fast and my grades aren't great as a result.

4 _____ Roberto I feel like I spend a lot of time reading online. The internet's a huge place and it's easy to get lost. The problem is that I'm never sure if the stuff I'm reading is actually any good.

5 _____ Simone I can focus on my studies if there are no distractions. The problem is that I get so many messages from friends, and they might think it's rude if I don't reply right away. Well, it is a bit rude, isn't it?

B Match the problems in A (1–5) to the pieces of advice (a–e).

a Turn your phone off when you are studying, or keep it on silent.
b Reward yourself with social media time at the end of a study session, but go offline when you are trying to complete a task.
c Before you start reading an article online, make sure that it comes from a source that you can trust.
d Be systematic in planning your schedule. Decide what needs to be done urgently and what is not so important. Be realistic about how long it takes you to complete tasks, and leave yourself enough time.
e Study in short periods (45 minutes is realistic), and reward yourself with 5 to 10 minutes of relaxation between study periods.

C Complete the tips with words from the box. Can you think of two more strategies for managing your time effectively? Write them below.

deadlines realistic schedule

Make a list of all your **1** _____________. Write them on a calendar or in a planner so you can see how much time you have.
Be **2** _____________ about how long it takes you to do things. It's better to overestimate than underestimate.
Reward yourself for hard work by setting aside time for relaxation in your **3** _____________.
4 ____
5 ____

MAKE IT HAPPEN

Make a study plan for the coming month with your assignment deadlines and the exam dates. Write down the days and times you will be in class and decide how much time you need for independent study. Include time for hobbies, relaxation, and sleep in your schedule. Compare your schedule with that of your partner and give your partner feedback.

D IN PAIRS Talk about what you can do to become better at managing your time. Mention any specific challenges you face. Listen to your partner and offer advice based on what you have learned in this lesson.

E THINKING SKILL—Apply Explain why time management skills are so important in study, work, and life in general. Why does the "good time management skills" requirement appear so often in job advertisements?

Answers to the quiz on page 16
1 b and c 2 b 3 c 4 b

UNIT 2

FOLLOW A PRO

A Read about a wildlife photographer's job. Answer the questions below in your notebook.

A WILDLIFE PHOTOGRAPHER

Jeff Richards works as a freelance wildlife photographer.

"These days, everyone has a camera on their phone, and there are images all around us. If you're going to make a living as a wildlife photographer, you need to be able to take pictures that are different and that really stand out. And that means getting into an animal's habitat to get close to it. A wildlife photographer needs to be an expert at using photographic equipment, but you also need to understand animal behavior. When you understand an animal, you can look ahead, know where it's going to be and how it's going to act, and be ready to take your shot. Physical fitness is very important, too, since you may need to put yourself in an unusual position to get the shot that is going to sell.

When I'm not on a shoot, the rest of my time is spent editing images, contacting clients, and planning future trips. It takes a long time to build up a career in this very competitive area, so you need to understand how to run a business as well as having a good eye for a picture. You need to be patient when you're trying to get the right shot of an animal, and you need to apply the same patience to your career. It's not necessarily the right career for someone who wants instant success."

1 Why do your pictures need to stand out and be different?
2 What does a wildlife photographer need to be able to predict?
3 Why does it help to be physically fit?
4 Apart from photographic skills and knowledge of animals, what other area does a wildlife photographer need to understand?
5 Why might this not be a good career for someone who wants instant success?

B Discuss the questions as a class.

1 What do you imagine is the hardest thing about being a wildlife photographer?
2 Do you think you have the right skills to be a wildlife photographer? What could you do or not do?

VIDEO

WATCH THE VIDEO AND FOLLOW A MARINE BIOLOGIST.

C IN GROUPS Answer the questions.

1 What does the person do? ____________________
2 Where does the person work? ____________________
3 What skills does the person need for the job? ____________________
4 What is the focus of the person's research? ____________________
5 On how many projects is the person currently working? ____________________
6 What is the most exciting part of the person's job? ____________________

D IN GROUPS Check your answers to the quiz on page 26 and discuss the questions.

1 Do you know anyone who works with animals? Explain what you think his or her job is like.
2 What other jobs working with animals do you know about?
3 What do you think are the most enjoyable things about working with animals? What are the least enjoyable?
4 What skills does a veterinarian need? Is it a career you would consider?
5 Are there any opportunities to work with animals where you live? If so, what are they?

Answers to the quiz on page 26
1 b 2 c 3 c 4 a

STUDY SKILLS

A Read the conversation between Soren and Tania.

MAKING A PRESENTATION OR GIVING A TALK

Soren: How's your talk going, Tania? Are you nearly ready?

Tania: It's going well, I think! I'm doing mine on the advantages and disadvantages of artificial intelligence.

Soren: Wow. That's really interesting. So, are there more advantages or disadvantages?

Tania: Whoa, hold on! I haven't gotten to that part yet. Right now, I'm just writing the history.

Soren: That's just the history? That's over 30 pages! How will you remember all that?

Tania: Ha, ha! I won't! I'll just type the information on my presentation and read it to the audience. It's much easier than remembering it all.

Soren: I see. But didn't Mr. Elmwood say the talk should be 10 minutes maximum?

Tania: Yeah, I know! Don't worry, though, I talk really fast when I get excited about something!

Soren: Well, be careful you don't write too much, or you won't have time to say it all. I mean, look—you've written 30 pages and you haven't even started writing about the advantages and disadvantages yet.

Tania: That won't take long. I mean, everyone knows that there are only advantages to artificial intelligence, right? No one thinks there are disadvantages.

Soren: Well, you certainly seem confident.

Tania: I don't really get nervous about talks, especially when I'm talking about my favorite subject. It'll be great!

B Select four pieces of advice that you think would be most useful for Tania.

1 If possible, speak from notes written on note cards or from memory.
2 Choose a subject that you are interested in or feel strongly about.
3 Make sure your research and preparation are balanced.
4 Don't speak too fast. Pause and take a breath after each point you make.
5 Be aware and respectful of the fact that some audience members may not share your point of view.

C Match the tips about oral presentations in B (1–5) to the explanations (a–e).

a This means that your talk will flow better and that you will be able to make eye contact with your audience. _____
b Audience members are likely to stop listening if they feel their point of view is not being respected. _____
c This will make you seem calmer and more professional. Your voice will sound stronger, too. _____
d This will show that you are well prepared and not biased. _____
e This means that your enthusiasm will be noticeable and that people will enjoy listening to you. _____

D IN PAIRS Discuss your experiences giving talks. Talk about your strengths and weaknesses and decide what further tips you would add to the list in B. Think about the following points.

- Developing your main argument
- Providing a clear structure
- Opening and summing up
- Including effective visual aids
- Answering questions
- Engaging with the audience

E THINKING SKILLS—Apply Think about a memorable talk you have listened to. Why was it memorable? What techniques did the speaker use to engage with the audience?

MAKE IT HAPPEN

Prepare an oral presentation on something you are interested in. Use the tips from this lesson to help you plan, structure, and deliver your talk.

Answers to the quiz on page 36
1 c 2 b 3 a 4 a

UNIT 4

FOLLOW A PRO

A Read about a PR professional's job. Answer the questions below in your notebook.

A PR PROFESSIONAL

Companies have messages about their brands that they want to communicate to members of the public. They use advertising for some of those messages. They also employ or hire PR (public relations) professionals. PR professionals work with journalists and other people in the media. They are responsible for communicating positive stories about a company and its products.

PR professionals need to be good at networking. They need contacts in many areas of the media. They need to know who they can persuade to run a story in a way that makes their business look good. This is particularly important when something negative happens to the company, such as people losing their jobs. The PR professional is the person who tries to explain the reason behind what is happening in a positive way.

Successful PR professionals have to express themselves clearly and have very good writing skills. They spend a lot of time producing press releases, fact sheets, and other documents that give journalists the starting point for their reports and articles. They can make a big difference to the stories that appear in the media. PR professionals also tell the stories behind their companies and brands through events such as press conferences or open houses. The PR professional is an important connection between a business and the public.

1 What is the main role of a PR professional?
2 Why does a PR professional need to be good at networking?
3 When is a PR professional's job particularly important?
4 What communication skills does a PR professional need to have?
5 How do PR professionals help journalists?

B Discuss the questions as a class.

1 What do you think PR professionals enjoy most about their job?
2 Would you be a good PR professional? Why or why not?

VIDEO

WATCH THE VIDEO AND FOLLOW A TRANSLATOR/INTERPRETER.

C IN GROUPS Answer the questions.

1 What is the person's job? ______
2 What skills does the person need for the job? ______
3 Where has the person worked as a translator? ______
4 How many languages does the person speak? ______
5 What is the person's first language? ______
6 Why does the person prefer doing interpretation instead of translation? ______

D IN GROUPS Check your answers to the quiz on page 46 and discuss the questions.

1 What careers in communication do you know about?
2 Would you be interested in any of those careers? If so, which ones?
3 Do you know anyone who works in communication? If so, what do you think his or her job is like?
4 What personal qualities do you need to work in PR?
5 What qualifications do you need to work in PR?

Answers to the quiz on page 46
1 c 2 b 3 a 4 a

UNIT 5

STUDY SKILLS

A Time yourself as you read this text as quickly as you can. What environmental problem is described in the text? What possible solutions are given?

IMPROVING READING SPEED

Let's imagine a typical morning. You leave your home for college or work. On the way, you stop and buy yourself a bottle of water. Perhaps you'll be given a plastic straw to drink it with. At lunch, you choose a nice healthy salad in a plastic box—or a sandwich wrapped in plastic. Maybe you'll eat the salad with plastic cutlery. On the way home, you'll stop off at the store for some groceries, probably also wrapped in plastic. All this plastic is used just once before you throw it away and forget all about it.

Here's the problem: plastic never fully biodegrades. It simply breaks down into smaller particles, which can be absorbed by our bodies. This has serious effects on our health; scientific research has linked plastic to cancer, birth defects, infertility, and a weakened immune system. Plastic is also a huge problem for marine animals, who can get tangled up in plastic rope or choke on pieces of plastic packaging. One million sea birds and 100,000 marine mammals are killed every year by plastic in our oceans.

In fact, 50% of plastic is used just once and then thrown away. Single-use plastic is probably one of the easiest things we could cut out of our lives to make a really big difference. Carry your own thermal flask for your coffee or hot drink, and carry your own water bottle. When shopping, try to choose as many items as you can that are not wrapped in plastic. There are lots of online challenges you can take part in to help you get motivated—or why not try a "no single-use plastic" challenge with a friend? You could also ask your college campus and local businesses to become "no single-use plastic" zones.

If each one of us committed to cutting out single-use plastic, we could fix one of the most serious environmental problems of our time.

B Match the sentence halves to make tips about improving reading speed.

1 Reading improves with practice, so you should _____
2 If you move your finger down the page while you read, _____
3 Active reading strategies such as predicting will _____
4 Putting a colored filter over the page can _____
5 Reading larger chunks of text at one time _____
6 If a nonfiction text looks hard, you should _____

a you will train your eyes to move more quickly down the text.
b start with something easier on the same subject.
c make the words easier to read.
d help you find the information you are looking for more quickly.
e is less tiring for your eyes and will help you to read for longer periods.
f look for subjects that interest you and read more for pleasure.

C Read the text in A again. This time, try to use as many of the tips from B as you can.

D IN PAIRS Which of the tips do you find most useful? Discuss your ideas with a partner.

Malin: I followed the tip about moving my finger down the page as I read. That definitely helped.
Theo: I tried reading larger chunks of text at one time, but I don't think it made a difference. I forgot what I had read!
Malin: I'm going to try that idea next time!

E THINKING SKILLS—Apply What makes a person a good reader? Apart from reading speed, what other ways can we use to measure our skills in this area?

MAKE IT HAPPEN

Work with a partner. Look online and choose a text at an appropriate level that you think your partner would find interesting. Ask your partner to read the text using some of the tips outlined in these lessons. Share your findings in a group.

Answers to the quiz on page 56
1 b 2 b 3 b and d 4 a

UNIT 6

FOLLOW A PRO

A **Read about an archeologist. Answer the questions below in your notebook.**

AN ARCHEOLOGIST

Many people think archeologists work outside, discovering the secrets of ancient civilizations in the mountains of Peru or the deserts of Egypt. Well, that's true, but is archeology really just about that? Archeology is a part of the larger field of anthropology, which is the study of human culture. Archeologists study structures and objects from ancient civilizations to try to understand what the ancient cultures were like and how ancient people lived. To be an archeologist, you will need a master's degree or a PhD. Your studies will include a large amount of research and probably some fieldwork. The chance of making a great discovery is what most archeologists dream of. However, even when it happens, archeologists have to carefully analyze their findings, to prove their importance. If you want to find out more about archeology before you spend a lot of time and money getting advanced degrees, research what an archeologist does online. You need to understand that archeologists do not all work in exciting places. Most of us work at places like historic sites, national parks, museums, or universities. We also often do not have regular working hours. We might work seven days a week for several weeks if there is an important project. We also have to work in all kinds of weather at all times of day. Archeology is an interesting job, and sometimes it's exciting, but you have to study a lot to become an archeologist, and you have to work very hard when you get a job!

1. What field is archeology a part of?
2. What do archeologists study? Why?
3. What do archeologists most want to achieve?
4. What is a good way to find out more about archeology before you decide to study it?
5. Where do archeologists work?

B **Discuss the questions as a class.**

1. In what ways is archeology a hard job?
2. Is archeology an important field in your country?

VIDEO

WATCH THE VIDEO AND FOLLOW A MECHANICAL ENGINEER.

C **IN GROUPS Answer the questions.**

1. What does the person do? ____________
2. What skills does the person need for the job? ____________
3. Where does the person often work? ____________
4. What kind of special equipment does the person use? ____________
5. Does the person work alone or in a team? ____________
6. Is the person happy with the job? Why? ____________

D **IN GROUPS Check your answers to the quiz on page 66 and discuss the questions.**

1. What old or ancient civilizations were in your country? Have you ever visited any of their sites? If so, which ones?
2. What other archeological or historical sites in the world would you like to visit?

Answers to the quiz on page 66
1 a 2 c 3 b 4 a

UNIT 7 STUDY SKILLS

A Read the essay. Which of the questions is the writer trying to answer? What is your answer to that question?

STRUCTURING YOUR WRITING

a Describe a time you made a serious mistake. What did you learn from it?
b If you don't make mistakes, you'll never learn. In your opinion, is this true?

Consider the achievements of the last hundred years. People have gone to space, invented the internet, and made incredible breakthroughs in medicine. Is it possible that in each of these attempts, the first try was successful? Of course not. We know that these achievements were only possible through trial and error—in other words, through making countless mistakes.

It's important to remember this in our own lives. Often, we believe that we need to do everything right the first time. This belief is generated by the images of perfection in magazines, on TV, and on social media.

However, this desire to get everything right the first time is dangerous. Take a man who has just started to play the violin, for example. How many wrong notes will he have to play before he plays something that is enjoyable to listen to? Or a woman who is learning to juggle? How many balls will she drop before she keeps them all in the air?

People who aspire to live a life free from mistakes will never take risks, never challenge themselves, and never learn anything new. They will turn down opportunities to avoid looking a fool. This will result in a safe life free from embarrassment and risk, but it will also result in regret at wasted opportunities.

Mistakes are seen as a form of failure but they can be really positive. Mistakes help us learn, and it is for this reason that I believe that they are not just important but desirable.

B Read the essay again. Check (✓) the correct sentences.

1 ☐ The essay is organized into paragraphs.
2 ☐ Each paragraph contains several different ideas.
3 ☐ The writer develops a clear argument, moving logically from point to point.
4 ☐ The writer doesn't provide any evidence to support her ideas.
5 ☐ The writer begins with an introduction and ends with a conclusion.

C Match the headings (1–4) to the tips for structuring essays (a–d). Then write your own tips under each heading in your notebook.

1 Divide your main idea into topics ____
2 Rearrange your notes ____
3 Write an outline plan ____
4 Organize the information into paragraphs ____

a Use separate sheets of paper for each topic.
b Plan your introduction, conclusion, and the main body of your essay.
c Each paragraph should have one main idea with supporting details or evidence.
d Spread your notes out on the table so that you can easily see them.

D IN PAIRS Think about the last essay you wrote. Tell your partner about the process you went through to structure your essay. What would you do differently next time?

E THINKING SKILLS—Apply What do you find most challenging about structuring an essay? How can you develop this skill for future assignments?

✓ MAKE IT HAPPEN

Choose one of the essay questions in **A** and write a short essay (500 words maximum) with your main idea divided into topics, each in their own paragraph.

Answers to the quiz on page 76
1 b 2 3, 4, 1, 5, 2 3 a, b, c

UNIT 8 FOLLOW A PRO

A Read about an astrobiologist. Then choose *True* or *False*.

AN ASTROBIOLOGIST

I'm an astrobiologist, which might sound like a job in a science-fiction movie! Actually, it's not science fiction. Astrobiologists study if life exists in other places in the universe besides Earth. We study how life originated, and how life could exist in extreme environments. There is an enormous variety in the jobs astrobiologists do. Some develop computer models to predict what life would be like on other planets. Others study life in extreme climates like the freezing Arctic, the Atacama Desert, or the deepest oceans. Some astrobiologists use high-tech radio telescopes to listen for signals from aliens. To be honest, I think that would be boring because so far, all the communication from outer space has come from our own satellites. Most astrobiologists work in an office or a lab and do research on elements like carbon, nitrogen, phosphorus, and iron. The results of the research help create the computer models that predict whether a specific planet or solar system could have life.

To work in astrobiology, you need a degree in a related field such as biology, chemistry, physics, astronomy, geology, mathematics, or information technology. You might think that all astrobiologists work at NASA in the US, but in fact, there are astrobiology jobs in many other parts of the world, including Europe, Australia, Mexico, and South America. There are jobs with NASA projects, at universities, or at private foundations. If you are interested in the origin of life, and the possibility of life on other planets, astrobiology might be the career for you.

1	Astrobiologists mostly work in science-fiction movies.	True / False
2	Astrobiologists study the history of life.	True / False
3	There are many different types of jobs in astrobiology.	True / False
4	The writer thinks listening for alien communications is an exciting job.	True / False
5	You have to live in the US to work in astrobiology.	True / False

B Discuss the questions as a class.

1 Why do you think the writer says that astrobiology sounds like a job in a science-fiction movie?
2 Would any of the astrobiology jobs mentioned in the article interest you? If so, which ones?

VIDEO WATCH THE VIDEO AND FOLLOW AN ASTRONOMER.

C IN GROUPS Answer the questions.

1 What is the person's job? ______
2 Where does the person work? ______
3 What skills does the person need for the job? ______
4 What specific subjects does the person study for the job? ______
5 Why does the person use special equipment in the job? ______
6 What does the person say is the best part of the job? ______

D IN GROUPS Check your answers to the quiz on page 86 and discuss the questions.

1 If you had a lot of money, would you want to be a "space tourist"? Why or why not?
2 What do you think the most important reasons for space exploration are?

Answers to the quiz on page 86
1 b 2 a 3 c 4 c

STUDY SKILLS

A **Esme and Marley are taking a course on the history of popular music. Read their notes about Motown music. Whose notes are more likely to be an effective study aid?**

MAKING NOTES

1 Esme

Motown is often described as "the sound that changed America." It was founded by an American songwriter called Berry Gordy (?) who got a loan of $800 (?) from his family to set the company up with. He wanted to set the record company up in recognition of the warm, soulful, and talented people he grew up with. Motown success stories included Smokey Robinson & The Miracles, Michael Jackson and the Jackson 5, Marvin Gaye, Diana Ross & The Supremes (?), and many more.

Motown was the first African American record label to achieve widespread recognition and acclaim.

2 Marley

From Billy Robson's "Sound of America," pps 35–37

Motown founded by Am. songwriter Berry Gordy from Detroit—1st Af/Am label to achieve widespread acclaim

Detroit called Motor City=name Motown

Acts: Smokey Robinson & Miracles, Michael Jackson & Jkson 5, Diana Ross & Supremes, etc.

B **Write *E* (Esme) or *M* (Marley).**

1. The writer has noted down the sources. _____
2. The writer has tried to copy down every word. _____
3. The writer has highlighted the most important information. _____
4. The writer is not totally sure how correct the notes are. _____

C **Match the sentence halves to make tips about taking notes.**

1. Before you start making notes, _____
2. Make a list of questions you want to find answers to _____
3. It's a good idea to label and number pages _____
4. Use sticky notes so that you can _____
5. Use abbreviations because this will _____

a draw up a mind map so you can see what you already know about the subject.
b write down ideas as you think of them or add ideas to charts or posters.
c save you a lot of time.
d as this will make it easier to cross-reference your notes.
e as this will make your notes more focused.

D IN PAIRS **Think about notes you have taken from lectures or books. How could you improve your note-taking technique?**

E THINKING SKILLS—Apply **What do you find hardest about taking notes? How can you ensure that your notes are as effective as possible?**

MAKE IT HAPPEN

Go online and find a podcast on a subject that interests you. Take notes using the tips from **C**. When the podcast has finished, look at your notes. How can you make them clearer? How can you make the key information stand out?

Answers to the quiz on page 96
1 b 2 b 3 b; Use symbols and abbreviations in notes, but not in assignments. 4 a; Visual familiarity will help you to remember the content of your notes.

UNIT 10

FOLLOW A PRO

A Read about a talent scout's job. Answer the questions below.

A TALENT SCOUT

Meet Jeni Mills, a talent scout from Chicago.
Jeni says: "I started out working in theater production for musical shows on Broadway, which was a fantastic job to go to after college, where I majored in music and dance. But then I decided I wanted a change. I saw an ad for an international cruise ship company that was looking for a talent scout to find the best acts for their cruise ship shows. These shows are really popular, and the audience expects to see something special. While I know a lot of people in the entertainment industry from my work on Broadway, I want to find acts that are a little different, but still amazing. So, a few times a week I go to small gigs—shows at small theaters and local comedy and music clubs—and try to find the most talented people. I organize auditions and get the best acts to come back and try to impress a live theater audience before we offer them work on the ship. I've found wonderful magicians and amazing dancers, singers, and comedians. I've been doing the job for five years now and I love it. The only negative is that the hours are long, but I'm meeting interesting people all the time."

1 What job did Jeni do before she became a talent scout? ____________________
2 What did Jeni study in college? ____________________
3 Where does Jeni find the acts for her shows? ____________________
4 How long has Jeni been working as a talent scout? ____________________
5 What does Jeni not like about her job? ____________________

B Discuss the questions as a class.

1 Would you like to be a talent scout? Why or why not?
2 What do you think it would be like to work on a cruise ship?

VIDEO

WATCH THE VIDEO AND FOLLOW A MUSICIAN.

C IN GROUPS Answer the questions.

1 What does the person do? ____________________
2 What skills does the person need for the job? ____________________
3 What is the person's schedule? ____________________
4 How many instruments does the person play? ____________________
5 What is the person's favorite music style? ____________________
6 What is the most exciting part of the person's job? ____________________

D IN GROUPS Check your answers to the quiz on page 106 and discuss the questions.

1 Do you know anybody who works in the entertainment industry? If so, what do they do?
2 What kinds of live entertainment are popular in your country?
3 What skills do you think a talent scout needs?
4 What type of acts (e.g., music, dance, comedy, magic) do you think require the most talent? Why?
5 Can you think of any professions other than the entertainment industry where talent scouts work? If so, what are they?

Answers to the quiz on page 106
1 b 2 a 3 c 4 c

UNIT 11

STUDY SKILLS

A Read the conversation. Is this study session productive? What challenges are the friends facing?

PERSONAL DEVELOPMENT

Marco: Ah, I love study nights! It's so much more fun than reviewing my notes on my own. More pizza, anyone?
Jill: Yeah, it is good fun, Marco, but we need to focus now.
Liz: Sure, Jill. We can't let this delicious pizza get cold, though, can we?
Jill: I guess not … It's just that the exam is in only two weeks.
Marco: We're probably going to fail it, Jill. No one does well in Mr. Leaper's class.
Liz: Yeah. He's right. I guess we can try again next year, though, right?
Jill: Don't say that! I've been trying to study all month. This is my first night out of the house in weeks!
Liz: Hmm. You are looking really pale, Jill. Are you eating well?
Jill: I don't have time to eat! And I'm not hungry, to be honest. I'm way too stressed out.
Marco: Well, I studied all day yesterday. I sat at my desk for six hours. I'm not sure if I learned much, though. The view from my window is pretty cool …
Liz: Lucky you, having the time to look out the window! I'm just so busy … Getting the bus to work, working, looking after my brother. He's been sick this week, so I've been taking care of him …
Marco: Yeah, if only we had more time! Speaking of time, that new series everyone is talking about starts in 10 minutes. I know we haven't finished but we've done a lot, right?

B Which student would benefit from each piece of advice? Write *M* (Marco), *J* (Jill), or *L* (Liz).

1 Add your favorite TV shows to your timetable. Use TV shows as a reward for finishing a study session. _____
2 Surround yourself with people who are positive and will encourage you. _____
3 Seek help from a professional counselor at college if you feel you can't deal with things. _____
4 Always carry your notes with you and study on the bus or while you wait. _____
5 Study with friends if you struggle to study alone, but make sure you use the time constructively. For example, explain something to your friend and see how well your friend understands your explanation. _____
6 Keep an exam question in your head and write points down as they occur to you. _____

C Match each piece of advice (1–4) to a way to follow it (a–d).

1 Get organized and focused. _____
2 Manage your time carefully. _____
3 Stay healthy. _____
4 Use exam papers from past years. _____

a Brainstorm answers to past questions.
b Create a realistic schedule.
c Include regular exercise in your schedule.
d Make flashcards with key information.

D IN PAIRS Role-play the study session in A. Make it more positive and productive.

Lucille: Why don't we take a break and have some ice cream?
Rob: Why don't we wait until we've finished this chapter? Hey, can I try explaining what I've just read to see if I've understood it?
Lucille: Sure!

E THINKING SKILLS—Apply What do you find hardest about studying for tests? What are your challenges, and how can you improve your study habits?

✓ MAKE IT HAPPEN

Talk about your study habits with your partner. Share what you think you are doing well and talk about the areas you need to improve.

Answers to the quiz on page 116
1 a 2 b; It can be very effective. 3 c 4 a

UNIT 12 FOLLOW A PRO

A Read about a digital copywriter's job. Answer the questions below in your notebook.

A DIGITAL COPYWRITER

There are many different jobs in advertising. Bruno Torres is a digital copywriter. He tells us more about his career.

Bruno says: "People are always asking me what a digital copywriter's job is. I think it's because it's one of those "behind the scenes" jobs. It's a very important job—especially for the advertising industry. My team develops advertising campaigns. My main job is to check all of the online materials—the headlines, slogans, emails, and social media ads. I check spelling and grammar, obviously, but I also make sure that the advertising material is easy to understand and that it sells the product! I usually work on at least two or three projects for different campaigns at the same time, so I need to be focused and organized. It's also very important that I meet my deadlines and finish the work by a certain date. Advertising is about creating trends so I have to make sure I know what is important to young people—style, fashion, how things look—that's a major part of it. People don't just buy a product—they buy into a lifestyle. People also ask how I got started in my career. Well, I majored in media studies and worked as a journalist for three years. Then I changed to this career because it seems more interesting. I hope to become a creative director one day and be in charge of the whole advertising campaign from start to finish."

1 Why do people often ask Bruno what a digital copywriter's job is?
2 What is the main part of Bruno's job?
3 How many projects does Bruno usually work on?
4 What job did Bruno do before he became a digital copywriter?
5 What does Bruno want to do in the future?

B Discuss the questions as a class.

1 Would you like to work in advertising? Why or why not?
2 What would you like about being a digital copywriter? What would you dislike? Explain.

VIDEO

WATCH THE VIDEO AND FOLLOW A VIDEO EDITOR.

C IN GROUPS Answer the questions.

1 What is the person's job? ______
2 Where does the person work? ______
3 What skills does the person need for the job? ______
4 What are the person's main responsibilities? ______
5 Has the person worked with someone famous? If yes, who? ______
6 What does the person say is the best part of the job? ______

D IN GROUPS Check your answers to the quiz on page 126 and discuss the questions.

1 How important do you think good language skills are to a digital copywriter's job?
2 What other skills do you think a digital copywriter needs?
3 Would you be good at a job with deadlines? Why or why not?
4 What advertising campaigns have succeeded in your country? Why?
5 What is the most effective medium for advertising: TV, magazines, the internet, billboards, or something else?

Answers to the quiz on page 126
1 b 2 a 3 a 4 b

Irregular Verbs

Infinitive	Simple past	Past participle
be	was/were	been
become	became	become
begin	began	begun
break	broke	broken
bring	brought	brought
build	built	built
buy	bought	bought
catch	caught	caught
choose	chose	chosen
come	came	come
cost	cost	cost
cut	cut	cut
do	did	done
draw	drew	drawn
drink	drank	drunk
drive	drove	driven
eat	ate	eaten
fall	fell	fallen
feed	fed	fed
feel	felt	felt
find	found	found
fly	flew	flown
get	got	gotten
give	gave	given
go	went	gone
grow	grew	grown
hang	hung	hung
have	had	had
hear	heard	heard
hit	hit	hit
hold	held	held
hurt	hurt	hurt
keep	kept	kept
know	knew	known
leave	left	left
let	let	let
lose	lost	lost
make	made	made
meet	met	met
pay	paid	paid
put	put	put
read	read	read
ride	rode	ridden
ring	rang	rung
rise	rose	risen
run	ran	run
say	said	said
see	saw	seen
sell	sold	sold
send	sent	sent
set	set	set
sing	sang	sung
sit	sat	sat
speak	spoke	spoken
stand	stood	stood
stick	stuck	stuck
take	took	taken
teach	taught	taught
tell	told	told
think	thought	thought
throw	threw	thrown
understand	understood	understood
wake	woke	woken
wear	wore	worn
win	won	won
write	wrote	written

Pronunciation Symbols

Vowels

ɪ	did
ɛ	bed
æ	bad
ʌ	cup
ʊ	book
ə	banana
i	feed
ɑ	father, box
ɔ	tall
u	student, food
ɝ	shirt, birthday
eɪ	date, table
aɪ	cry, eye
ɔɪ	boy
oʊ	comb, post
aʊ	about, how

Consonants

p	park, happy
b	back, hobby
t	tea
d	die
k	came, kitchen, quarter
g	game, go
f	face, photographer
v	vegetable
θ	thing, math
ð	then, that
s	city, summer
z	please, goes
ʃ	she, shop
ʒ	leisure
h	hot, who
tʃ	chicken, watch
dʒ	jacket, orange
m	men
n	sun, know
ŋ	sung, singer
w	week, white
r	rain, writer
l	light, long
j	yes, use, music

Grammar Review

A Complete the news report with the simple past or the past progressive form of the verbs in parentheses.

There was a fire last night at 10:20 p.m. on East Coast Road. While Jon and Lisa Hawes **1** ______________ (watch) TV in their living room, their five-year-old son **2** ______________ (play) with matches in his bedroom. He **3** ______________ (light) a small fire and then, afraid, **4** ______________ (run) into the bathroom. While his parents **5** ______________ (come) to check on him, they **6** ______________ (smell) smoke. They **7** ______________ (try) to put the fire out, but it was already too big. They found their son, **8** ______________ (call) the fire department, and got out of the house safely.

B Choose the correct options.

Tyler: I really like your apartment. It gets **1 any / a lot of** light.

Miguel: Yeah, but there isn't **2 enough / too many** space for all my stuff. And I'd like to move **3 somebody / somewhere** closer to school.

Tyler: But this is a great neighborhood. There are **4 some / any** great restaurants and cafés here.

Miguel: I know, but there's **5 too many / too much** noise around here on the weekends. It feels like **6 anybody / everyone** is out on the street at night.

Tyler: You live alone, right? Have you ever thought about getting a roommate?

Miguel: I've considered it **7 a few / a little** times, but I really like living by **8 myself / ourselves**.

C Complete the sentences with the correct superlative form of the adjective in parentheses.

1 My cat is the ______________ (lazy) animal I've ever seen.
2 That was the ______________ (risk) thing I've ever done.
3 Rush hour is the ______________ (bad) time to get a seat on the bus.
4 Craig is the ______________ (creative) person in class.
5 Maria is the ______________ (kind) of my three sisters.
6 Ines is the ______________ (good) person to have as a study partner.

D Rewrite the sentences to include the verb in parentheses.

1 You are not allowed to come in. (can't)

____

2 Do you want to go with me? (would)

____

3 I'll possibly be late to the ceremony. (may)

____

4 Will you book a hotel room for me? (could)

____

5 I don't think I'll be able to come. (might)

____

6 Our flight lands in 30 minutes. (will)

____

E Complete the sentences with the simple past or the present perfect form of the verb in parentheses.

Although he is just a teenager, Brandon Iverson **1** ____________ (be) a businessman for much of his life. At age 10, he and a friend **2** ____________ (sell) old toys and games online. When he was 13, they **3** ____________ (establish) their own financial education company. A year later, they **4** ____________ (publish) a book on how to succeed as a young entrepreneur. They **5** ____________ (make) a lot of money since then. A few years ago, Brandon **6** ____________ (start) another online company selling T-shirts, jogging pants, and hoodies. The company **7** ____________ (do) well since its launch. Recently, he **8** ____________ (become) a popular speaker at schools around the country, and he is enjoying this new venture.

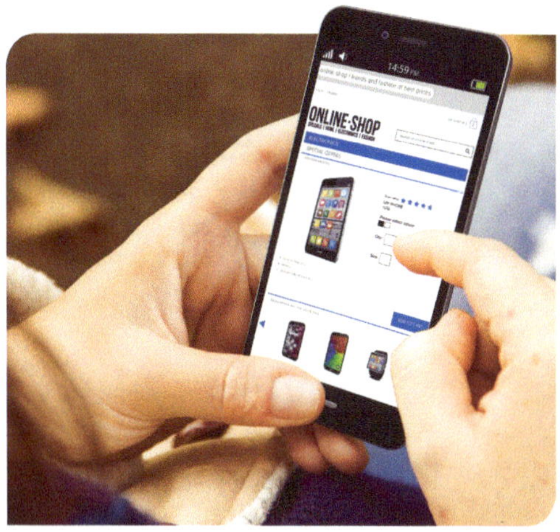

F Unscramble and write the sentences.

1 Jesse / degree / gotten / yet / hasn't / his / .

____

2 ever / Lila / promotion / a / gotten / has / ?

____

3 here / since / worked / 2017 / has / Peter / .

____

4 applied / Erica / for / already / job / has / the / .

____

5 our / read / I / just / benefits / about / have / .

____

6 been / Tina / has / month / team / a / leader / for / .

____

G Choose the correct option.

1 Many people are interested in **cooking** / **to cook** these days.
2 Why doesn't Claire want **flying** / **to fly** a kite with her friends?
3 Henri enjoys **making** / **to make** things with wood.
4 David really dislikes **cleaning** / **to clean** his apartment.
5 We really hope **seeing** / **to see** you at the park this weekend.
6 **Having** / **To have** a potluck meal sounds like a great idea!
7 Where did you and Ethan decide **going** / **to go** last night?
8 Would you like **coming** / **to come** over for a barbecue tonight?

H Complete the sentences with the correct form of the verb in parentheses.

1 Fur coats ____________ (not wear) much nowadays.
2 Children may develop health problems if they ____________ (eat) too much food.
3 These days, most hotel reservations ____________ (make) online.
4 If we ____________ (not be) friends, I would be angry with you.
5 When my parents were young, milk ____________ (sell) in bottles.
6 If the weather doesn't improve, we ____________ (not have) a picnic.
7 Cotton ____________ (use) in clothing such as blue jeans and T-shirts.
8 I ____________ (meet) my cousin at the airport tomorrow.

Grammar Reference

UNIT 1 — stative and dynamic verbs

Function

We use stative verbs such as *seem*, *know*, and *understand* to describe states. They are not usually used in progressive tenses. We use dynamic (action) verbs like *walk*, *run*, and *play* to describe actions. Some stative verbs, like *be*, *think*, and *have*, and verbs of the senses, like *see*, *smell*, *taste*, and *hear*, can also be used as dynamic verbs, though the meaning of the verb changes.

Form

Stative verbs	Dynamic verbs	Stative or dynamic
Juan **likes** climbing. I **don't understand**. She **wants** to leave now. I **don't know** how to play this.	He **runs** every day. **Don't laugh** at me. **We're playing** a video game. They **are using** new technology.	I **think** she's amazing. She**'s thinking** about her work. This pasta **tastes** delicious. She**'s tasting** the soup.

A Write *S* (stative) or *D* (dynamic) for each verb.

1 eat ______
2 climb ______
3 know ______
4 seem ______
5 drink ______
6 want ______
7 sleep ______
8 hate ______
9 use ______
10 believe ______
11 laugh ______
12 understand ______

B Complete the sentences with the simple present or the present progressive form of the verb in parentheses.

1 I ______________ (know) how to use this software.
2 ______________ you ______________ (like) to climb mountains?
3 My sister Sara ______________ (have) a disability.
4 Our teacher ______________ (think) we should use phones in class.
5 She ______________ (not understand) what I'm saying.
6 What ______________ you ______________ (think) about?
7 ______________ you ______________ (read) anything interesting right now?
8 They ______________ (not have) a very good day today.

UNIT 1 — expressing ability

Function

We can express general ability in the present with *can* or *am/is/are able to*. We can express general ability in the past with *could* or *was/were able to*. To express a particular ability, we can use phrases such as *manage* (+ infinitive) and *succeed in* (+ gerund).

Form

Present ability	Past ability
I can speak two languages. I can't speak three languages.	He could play the violin at the age of five. He couldn't play the violin at the age of three.
I'm able to remember people's faces easily. I'm not able to learn people's names easily.	He was able to play the French horn 10 years ago. He was not able to compose music 10 years ago.

A Choose the correct option.

1 People who **can** / **able to** speak two languages are often valued by employers.
2 When I was young, I **am** / **was** able to develop an ear for music.
3 They have succeeded **in learning** / **to learn** Portuguese.
4 She managed **in learning** / **to learn** the guitar without a teacher.

5 Can you **play** / **to play** the piano without looking at the piano keys?
6 He **has succeeded** / **was able to** learn the Korean alphabet in only two hours.
7 Benjamin is able **hear** / **to hear** a song once and remember all the words.
8 Not many people **succeed in** / **manage to** become professional musicians.

B Rewrite the sentences in a different way.

1 I couldn't swim until I was a teenager. *I wasn't able to swim until I was a teenager.*
2 He can name a hundred different kinds of fish. ____________________
3 Are you able to sing as well as your mother? ____________________
4 We weren't able to take private music lessons. ____________________
5 I can't explain the difference between a viola and a violin. ____________________
6 Could you speak English when you were young? ____________________

UNIT 2 — tag questions

Function

We use tag questions for two main purposes: to invite someone to agree with our opinion and to confirm information that we think is correct.

Form

Sentences with *be* form tags with *be*. Sentences with modals form tags with the modal. Sentences with other verbs form tags with forms of *do* or *have*. When the verb in the main part of the sentence is positive, the verb in the tag is negative. When the verb in the main part of the sentence is negative, the verb in the tag is positive.

Affirmative verbs	Negative verbs
Horses **are** intelligent, **aren't they**?	That dog **isn't** very smart, **is it**?
He **is feeding** the elephant, **isn't he**?	That horse **isn't** tame, **is it**?
You **love** animals, **don't you**?	Pigeons **don't use** tools, **do they**?
She **swam** with dolphins, **didn't she**?	The cat **didn't pass** the mirror test, **did it**?
They**'ve been** to a zoo before, **haven't they**?	He **hasn't ever** had a pet, **has he**?
Parrots **can** talk, **can't they**?	We **shouldn't do** tests on animals, **should we**?

A Match the sentence beginnings (1–8) to the sentence ends (a–h).

1 You don't like to visit zoos, ____
2 Dogs are very smart, ____
3 You can't train a cat to do tricks easily, ____
4 She volunteered at a dog rescue center, ____
5 You didn't have a pet as a child, ____
6 Chimpanzees can learn sign language, ____
7 He doesn't want to see the dolphin show, ____
8 Monkeys don't make good pets, ____

a did you?
b can you?
c does he?
d can't they?
e do you?
f didn't she?
g do they?
h aren't they?

B Complete the sentences with a tag question.

1 Dogs are more intelligent than cats, ____________________?
2 You don't need to feed snakes every day, ____________________?
3 A fish doesn't require as much care as a bird, ____________________?
4 Cats should not eat chocolate, ____________________?
5 You've worked with animals before, ____________________?
6 You care about animals as much as I do, ____________________?
7 It's not a good idea to feed fish more than once a day, ____________________?
8 We need to teach children not to harm animals, ____________________?

Grammar Reference

UNIT 2 — articles

Function

We use indefinite articles (*a*, *an*) before nouns to indicate the nouns are general. We use the definite article (*the*) before nouns to indicate they are specific. Sometimes we do not use any article at all.

Form

Use	Example
Use *a/an* with a singular countable noun when being general.	A veterinarian takes care of animals.
Use *a/an* when mentioning a singular countable noun for the first time. You can add an adjective between the article and the noun.	I heard there is a new veterinarian in town.
Use *the* with a singular countable noun when being specific.	The school counselor talked to us about careers.
Use *the* with a singular countable noun when referring to all members of a group in a general way.	The elephant is known for its intelligence, loyalty, and strength.
Use *the* with plural countable nouns when being specific.	The jobs that involved working with animals sound interesting.
Use *the* when there is only one of something.	Wolves sometimes seem to howl at the moon.
Use no article with plural countable nouns when talking generally.	Dolphins and whales are very intelligent.
Use no article with singular uncountable nouns when talking generally.	Stress can be an issue when working with animals.

A Choose the correct article. If no article is needed, choose X.

Have you ever thought about getting **1 a / the** job at **2 an / the** animal rescue shelter? **3 X / The** work can sometimes be hard, but it is **4 a / the** rewarding experience for **5 X / the** right person. Shelter managers often need to spend time raising funds in **6 X / the** community, so they depend on **7 X / the** volunteers to help out with animal care. The job pays as much in satisfaction as in **8 X / the** money.

B Complete the sentences with *a*, *an*, *the*, or *X* (no article).

1 We're thinking of getting ____________ pet, but we're not sure what kind.
2 My sister studies whales that migrate from ____________ Arctic Ocean.
3 I know several people who work as ____________ dog walkers.
4 Did anyone ever find ____________ dog that went missing in the neighborhood?
5 I don't think working as ____________ animal trainer is the right job for me.
6 Where can I get ____________ information on veterinary schools?

UNIT 3 — future time clauses (*after, as soon as, before, until, when*)

Function

We can use a time clause to talk about a possible future event. The time clause is introduced with a subordinating conjunction such as *after*, *as soon as*, *before*, *until*, or *when*. The time clause in the simple present tense can come before or after the main clause in the simple future tense. When the time clause comes first, add a comma after it.

Form

Main clause	Time clause
I will tell you my opinion I won't believe that story	after you tell me yours. until I check its source.

Time clause	Main clause
After you tell me your opinion, Until I check its source,	I will tell you mine. I won't believe that story.

A Complete the sentences with the simple present or simple future form of the verb in parentheses.

1 When I call you tomorrow, I ________________ (have) some good news.
2 The class will be quiet as soon as the teacher ________________ (come) in.
3 I ________________ (not be) able to finish this report until I get home.
4 After the students ________________ (finish) class, they will go out for a snack.
5 Don't worry. Sarah ________________ (finish) the presentation before she leaves the office.
6 The company ________________ (not hire) any new employees before the New Year.

B Combine the two sentences into one using the subordinating conjunction in parentheses. Be sure to use correct verb tenses in the clauses.

1 I (get) to work today. I (talk) to my boss about a raise. (after)
____

2 She (finish) this report. She (be) a lot happier! (when)
____

3 He (not provide) feedback on my paper. He (see) the final version. (until)
____

4 I (help) my colleague with her project. I (leave) the office today. (before)
____

5 I (purchase) a new computer. I (save) enough money. (as soon as)
____

6 You (need) help with your essay. I (be) happy to help you. (if)
____

UNIT 3 — present perfect progressive

Function

In some cases, we can use either the present perfect simple or the present perfect progressive tense with no change in meaning. In other cases, there is a difference in meaning or emphasis. We use the present perfect simple primarily to express that an action is completed or to emphasize its result. We use the present perfect progressive to emphasize the duration or continuous nature of an action. Stative verbs (*know*, *believe*, *understand*, etc.) are generally not used in the present perfect progressive.

Form

Present perfect simple (emphasizes completion or result of action)	**Present perfect progressive** (emphasizes duration or continuous nature of action)
I've worked here since 2017.	I've been working here since 2017.
Voice recognition software has improved.	Voice recognition software has been improving.
Humans have used machines for many years.	Humans have been using machines for many years.

Use	Example
Use the present perfect progressive for an action that began in the past and continues into the present.	Brian has been working on artificial intelligence for over 10 years.
Use the present perfect progressive to focus on an action that may or may not be completed.	Bethany and I have been working on our presentation.
Use the present perfect progressive to talk about an action that is temporary.	They have been working a lot of hours at the lab recently.

A Complete the sentences with the present perfect progressive form of the verb in parentheses.

1 I ______________________ (try) to understand this new software.
2 Lisa ______________________ (not come) to our science study group lately.
3 Scientists ______________________ (work) on AI technologies for many years.
4 Our math class ______________________ (get) harder and harder.
5 Gina ______________________ (study) really hard for the past month.
6 We ______________________ (not go) to the gym much lately.

B Unscramble and write questions using the present perfect progressive.

1 been / have / what / lately / you / doing
____

2 video games / been / have / they / playing
____

3 coming / recently / has / been / Aaron / to class
____

4 learning / have / been / why / they / how to / code
____

5 been / money / you / have / saving / for college
____

UNIT 4 — infinitives with *to*

Form and Function

Some words are followed by a *to* infinitive (*to* + verb).

Form and Use	Example
Use an infinitive to express a purpose to mean *in order to*.	I went to the bookstore (in order) to look for a book on public speaking.
Use an infinitive after some verbs (*agree*, *like*, *prefer*, *need*, *want*, etc.).	I don't really like to speak in a group that I don't know well.
Use an infinitive after some adjectives (*easy*, *happy*, *hard*, *good*, *ready*, etc.).	It's not easy to find good research material for some presentations.
Use an infinitive after some verbs (*warn*, *advise*, *persuade*, *tell*, etc.) and an object.	He persuaded me to use visual aids in my presentation.

A Choose the correct option.

1 Our teacher **agreed** / **told** us to watch the Steve Jobs documentary.
2 I didn't **agree** / **warn** to participate in the conference call today.
3 She would **prefer** / **say** to work alone on this week's project.
4 My roommate **persuaded** / **liked** me to go to the lecture.
5 Jason **went** / **ready** to check out a book from the library.
6 I would be **easy** / **happy** to help you with your presentation.

B Complete the sentences with the infinitive form of the verbs in the box.

apply be communicate copy find improve listen see

What separates a good leader from a great one? Look to history **1** ____________ the answer—Martin Luther King Jr., Mahatma Gandhi, Oprah Winfrey, Steve Jobs. It is easy **2** ____________ that communication was central to their success. They all used their own communication style **3** ____________ ideas. They used their gifts to persuade others **4** ____________. People who want **5** ____________ great communicators can do so. It's a skill anyone can learn **6** ____________ in various aspects of their lives. So if feel you are ready **7** ____________ your communication skills, be true to yourself. People who try **8** ____________ the successes of others are never successful.

UNIT 4 — separable and non-separable phrasal verbs

Function

A phrasal verb is a combination of a verb plus a particle (a small word like a preposition) that means something different from the verb and the particle. Phrasal verbs that take an object can be separable or inseparable. For separable phrasal verbs, if the object is a noun, it can go between the verb and the particle or after the particle. If the object is a pronoun, it can only go between the verb and the particle, but not after the particle. For non-separable phrasal verbs, a noun or pronoun can only go after the particle. Three-word phrasal verbs are non-separable.

Form

Separable phrasal verbs	Non-separable phrasal verbs
I need to clean up the house. I need to clean the house up. I need to clean it up. ~~I need to clean up it.~~	I ran into Jeff at the mall. I ran into him at the mall. ~~I ran Jeff into at the mall.~~ ~~I ran him into at the mall.~~
Other examples: *fill out, throw away, pick up, turn off, put off, try on, turn down, ask out, call off, get across, make up*	**Other examples:** *take care of, call off, come across, count on, stick to, get rid of, keep up with, run out of, cut back on*

A Choose the correct sentence.

1 a You need to stick to your original plan. **b** You need to stick your original plan to.
2 a I really should cut down on sugar. **b** I really should cut down sugar on.
3 a Let me know if you come my notes across. **b** Let me know if you come across my notes.
4 a Can you help me clean this up? **b** Can you help me clean up this?
5 a If you like the jacket, try on it. **b** If you like the jacket, try it on.
6 a Let's put off this for another day. **b** Let's put this off for another day.
7 a I forgot to call back her again. **b** I forgot to call her back again.
8 a You know you can always count me on. **b** You know you can always count on me.

B Rewrite the sentences. Change the underlined noun to the pronoun in parentheses.

1 You can always count on <u>Maggie</u>. (her) ________________________
2 I need you to fill in <u>this form</u> now. (it) ________________________
3 Who takes care of <u>your children</u>? (them) ________________________
4 Try to get across <u>your key points</u>. (them) ________________________
5 Can you please turn down <u>the radio</u>? (it) ________________________
6 It's hard to keep up with <u>Estefan</u>. (him) ________________________
7 It's not too late to call off <u>the meeting</u>. (it) ________________________
8 It's time to get rid of <u>your bad habits</u>. (them) ________________________

UNIT 5 — review of conditionals

Function

Conditional sentences express the idea that an action in the main clause can only take place if a condition in the *if* clause is fulfilled. The word *unless* is also used in conditional clauses to express a negative condition.

- The zero conditional is used for situations that are real, and it is often used for general truths about the present. Both clauses are in the simple present tense.
- The first conditional is used for situations that are possible or likely in the future. The main clause is in the future tense, and the *if* clause is in the simple present tense.
- The second conditional is for unreal, hypothetical situations, or situations that are not true. The main clause is in the past tense, and the *if* clause uses *would* + *(not)* + the base form of the verb. If the verb is *be* in the main clause, *were* is used for both singular and plural objects.

Form

Zero conditional	First conditional	Second conditional
If water reaches 100 degrees, it boils. When it rains a lot in a short time, you get a flash flood. Plants die unless they get enough water.	A lot of crops will die if we don't get rain. If sea levels rise, a lot of people will need to move. If we don't do something, climate change will get worse.	If it weren't so rainy, I would go for a walk. Our oceans would be less polluted if we used less unrecyclable plastic. If we used greener energy, the world would be a better place.

A Choose *GT* (general truth), *PS* (possible situation), or *HS* (hypothetical situation) for each sentence.

1 If I had more time, I would volunteer at the aquarium. GT PS HS
2 When the sun goes down, it gets dark. GT PS HS
3 Unless it rains, we'll go to the beach tomorrow. GT PS HS
4 You waste heat if you leave your windows open. GT PS HS
5 We will have 10 members if you join our group. GT PS HS
6 People would use less fuel if they traveled less. GT PS HS

B Choose the correct form of the verb in parentheses.

1 If you ______________ (push) that button, it lights up.
2 If the winds get stronger, we ______________ (have) a hurricane.
3 What would you do if you ______________ (see) a tornado?
4 There ______________ (not be) any class tomorrow unless it stops snowing.
5 Ice melts when it ______________ (reach) a certain temperature.
6 The world ______________ (be) a better place if people cared more for each other.
7 The forest fire will be out of control unless the firefighters ______________ (get) there soon.
8 If it ______________ (snow) again this spring, I would be really surprised.

UNIT 5 — present and future hopes and wishes

Function

We can use the verbs *hope* and *wish* to talk about present and future hopes and wishes.

Form

Form and Use	Example
Use *hope* (+ subject) + simple present, present progressive, or *can* to express something that you want and expect to be true in the present.	I hope a lot of people are attending the march to save the environment today.
Use *hope* (+ subject) + simple present, *will*, or *can* to express something that you want and expect to happen in the future.	I hope our government can find a way to reduce the cost of a university education.
Use *wish* (+ subject) + *would* or *could* to express something that you would like to happen in the future, but that probably won't.	I wish more people would get involved in trying to solve our country's problems.
Use *wish* (+ subject) + simple past to express something that you would like to be true in the present, but that isn't now.	I wish people spent less money on unnecessary electronics.

A Unscramble and write the sentences.

1 I / like / you / environmental poster / my / hope ________________
2 fossil fuels / used / they / she / wishes / fewer ________________
3 stop / will / he / hopes / global warming ________________
4 help / we / our campaign / wish / you / could / with ________________
5 money / some / can / you / I / donate / hope ________________
6 our ideas / wish / reject / I / you / wouldn't ________________

B Choose the correct option.

1 I hope I **get** / **would get** a job with a green company.
2 I wish people **will care** / **would care** more about our environment.
3 Do ever wish you **can change** / **could change** just one law?
4 I hope businesses **are listening** / **would listen** to the eco-needs of their customers.
5 I wish I **major** / **had majored** in environmental science.
6 She hopes other students **can help** / **could help** in her letter-writing campaign.
7 He wishes more people **appreciate** / **would appreciate** the dangers facing our environment.
8 Our teacher hopes her students **will participate** / **would participate** in the Earth Day celebrations.

UNIT 6 — past perfect

Function

We use the past perfect to show that one past action happened before another action in the past. The past perfect is formed with *had* + past participle.

Form

Affirmative statements	Negative statements
I had read all my email by the time I ate breakfast. All of Marta's friends had gotten cell phones before she did. They knew the city well, as they had visited it several times previously.	I failed the history exam because I hadn't studied very hard. Before Ian went to Tokyo, he had never seen so many people. They didn't get into the theater because they hadn't booked a ticket in advance.

A Choose the action (a or b) that happened first.

1 **a** Karl had owned his baseball card collection for 30 years, **b** so he felt bad about selling it.
2 **a** People had had cell phones for years by the time **b** the iPhone hit the market.
3 **a** Steve didn't understand the talk because **b** he hadn't read the speaker's book.
4 **a** When I got to the train station this morning, **b** the train had already left.
5 **a** Many people had attempted to fly before **b** the Wright Brothers made their first successful flight.

B Complete the sentences with the correct form of the verb in parentheses. Use one simple past verb and one past perfect verb in each sentence.

1 I ______________ (know) how to use the new software because I ______________(try) it before.
2 Luckily, I ______________ (save) my document before my computer ______________ (crash).
3 We ______________ (not be) to Los Angeles before, so we ______________ (get) lost right away.
4 The plane ______________ (leave) by the time I ______________ (get) to the airport.
5 Cars ______________ (be) expensive before the assembly line ______________ (make) them affordable.

UNIT 6 — defining relative clauses

Function

A defining relative clause usually comes immediately after the noun or noun phrase it describes. It gives information that defines or identifies the person, thing, time, or place.

Form

Use	Example
Use *that* to refer to a thing.	A car that drives itself sounds like an amazing idea.
Use *who* to refer to a person.	The employee who designs new software is over there.
Use *where* to refer to a place.	I live in a large city where there is a lot of innovation.
Use *when* to refer to a time.	That was a time when things were much simpler.

A Complete the sentences with *that, who, where,* or *when.*

1 This camera ______________ is on my smartphone is better than some expensive cameras.
2 Can you think back to a time ______________ you weren't connected 24/7?
3 That arcade is the place ______________ I first learned how to play video games.
4 Please give me the name of the person ______________ sold you this 3-D printer.
5 The late 20th century was a time ______________ there were great innovations in communications.
6 Do you know the name of the person ______________ first climbed Mount Everest?
7 I want a cell phone ______________ fits neatly into my front shirt pocket.
8 The usual place ______________ my friend and I hang out is the mall.

B Find and correct one error in each sentence.

1 This is the place when everyone gets their SIM cards. ______________
2 This is the card where will get you a 30% discount. ______________
3 I know a guy builds websites for free. ______________
4 Think of an everyday product who you can't live without. ______________
5 She lived at a time who people made their own clothes. ______________
6 Do you know the woman standing by the door is? ______________

UNIT 7 — *should/shouldn't have*

Function

We use *should* + (*not*) + *have* + past participle to talk about past regrets. We often use it to give advice or a recommendation about something that did or did not happen in the past.

Form

Form and Use	Example
Use *should have* + past participle when something didn't happen in the past, but it was a good idea.	He should have listened carefully. (= He didn't listen carefully.) They should have apologized. (= They didn't apologize.)
Use *shouldn't have* + past participle when something happened in the past, but it was a bad idea.	She shouldn't have told a lie. (= She told a lie.) They shouldn't have said those things. (= They said those things.)

A Match the statements (1–6) to the responses (a–f).

1 She spilled coffee on her computer. _____
2 They told me about my surprise party. _____
3 She bought a leather jacket for $600. _____
4 They were very late for the meeting. _____
5 She kept her library books too long. _____
6 They bought 30 lottery tickets. _____

a They should have been there on time.
b She should have been more careful.
c She should have returned them sooner.
d She shouldn't have spent so much.
e They shouldn't have wasted their money.
f They shouldn't have let me know.

B Complete the sentences with *should have* or *shouldn't have* and the past participle of the verb in parentheses.

In 1997, a Canadian beverage company introduced a soda called Orbitz. The product's appearance looked attractive, but the taste wasn't very popular. It was removed from sale a year later.

1 The company ______________________ (make) it taste better.
2 The company ______________________ (spend) so much money on the product's appearance.
3 The company ______________________ (try) to promote it in different ways.

In 2000, Netflix suggested that they manage Blockbuster's online component, while Blockbuster continued to sell videos in its stores. Blockbuster said no and went bankrupt, while Netflix continues to thrive.

4 Blockbuster ______________________ (take) Netflix's offer more seriously.
5 Blockbuster ______________________ (refuse) Netflix's offer.
6 Blockbuster ______________________ (accept) Netflix's offer.

KFC's advertising slogan in the US has been "Finger Lickin' Good" since the 1950s. When it was translated into Putonghua for the Chinese market, it was translated as "Eat Your Fingers Off."

7 KFC ______________________ (get) a better translator.
8 KFC ______________________ (use) a different slogan for the Chinese market.
9 KFC ______________________ (test) the translation on a few people in the Chinese market.

UNIT 7 — past perfect for wishes about the past

Function

We use *wish* + past perfect to talk about wishes or regrets about the past. We use this when we want to be able to change a situation in the past, but cannot do so.

Form

Affirmative	Negative
I wish I had saved more money for college. He wishes he had gotten better grades in school. They wish they had bought a better car.	I wish I hadn't said that. Juan wishes he hadn't eaten so much. They wish their neighbors hadn't gotten a dog.

A Complete the sentences with *had* or *hadn't* and the past participle form of the verb in parentheses.

1 Susan's hair is too short. She wishes she ______________ (cut) it.
2 My cousins pay too much in rent. They wish they ______________ (move) somewhere cheaper.
3 Bob's gym membership is expensive. He wishes he ______________ (get) his own gym equipment to use at home.
4 I don't like my meal. I wish I ______________ (order) something else.
5 My sister returned my skirt with holes in it. I wish I ______________ (lend) it to her.
6 Ellen's not comfortable at the party. She wishes she ______________ (come).
7 The Smiths bought their son a desktop computer. He wishes they ______________ (buy) a laptop.
8 This sweater is really hot. I wish I ______________ (wear) a T-shirt.

B Find and correct one error in each sentence.

1 I wish I had live off campus in college. ______________
2 He wish he hadn't gotten married so late. ______________
3 She wishes her parents had allow her to go to the party. ______________
4 They wish they gotten to know their old neighbors better. ______________
5 I wish I hadn't sit at the back of the class. ______________

UNIT 8 — third conditional

Function

We use the third conditional to talk about events that did not happen in the past. They are hypothetical, so we imagine the effects of past conditions that did not happen. The verb in the *if* clause is in the past perfect, and the verb in the main clause is *would/could/might have* + past participle.

Form

Form	Example
If + (subject) + *had* + past participle, (subject) + *would/ could/might* + *have* + past participle.	If he had gone to the space station, it would have been a dream come true.
If + (subject) + *had* + past participle, (subject) + *would/ could/might* + *not have* + past participle.	If Anna had realized there were so few jobs in astrophysics, she wouldn't have chosen that career.
If + (subject) + *hadn't* + past participle, (subject) + *would/ could/might* + *have* + past participle.	If he hadn't been bad at science, he could have become an astronaut.
If + (subject) + *hadn't* + past participle, (subject) + *would/ could/might* + *not have* + past participle.	If she hadn't passed the fitness test, she wouldn't have gone into space.

A Choose the correct option.

1 We **won't** / **wouldn't** have learned as much about dinosaurs if we hadn't found so many fossils.
2 If our course had made learning about dinosaurs fun, I would **learn** / **have learned** more.
3 If they **would have** / **had** located the dinosaur skull, it would have been on the news.
4 They might **find** / **have found** more fossils if they had stayed on-site longer.
5 If the dinosaur **had** / **might have** been any bigger, it wouldn't have fit in the museum.
6 The movie might not have been so popular if they **didn't use** / **hadn't used** so many special effects.

B Complete the third conditional sentences with the correct form of the verb in parentheses. Use *would* in the main clause.

1 The space station ________________ (not be) a success if we ________________ (not work) together.
2 If they ________________ (not abandon) the rocket launch, it ________________ (be) a disaster.
3 The dinosaurs ________________ (not die out) if a meteorite ________________ (not hit) the Earth.
4 He ________________ (not make) that mistake if he ________________ (follow) the instructions.
5 If NASA ________________ (not invest) in the space program, astronauts ________________ (not go) to the moon.
6 If the Mars rovers ________________ (crash), we ________________ (not get) such amazing pictures.

UNIT 8 — indirect questions

Function

Direct questions usually begin with an auxiliary verb (*does, is*), a modal verb (*can, should*), or a *wh-* word (*what, where*). Indirect questions are more formal and polite. We use them when we speak to someone we don't know well, or in more formal or professional settings. They begin with phrases that help "soften" the question.

Form

Use	Direct question	Indirect question
In an indirect *wh-* question with *be*, *be* goes after the subject.	How old is the space station?	Do you know how old the space station is?
In other indirect *wh-* questions, there are no auxiliary verbs (e.g., *do, does, did*).	Where does an astronaut sleep?	Can you tell me where an astronaut sleeps?
In indirect *yes/no* questions, *if* or *whether* is added.	Does it get hot in space?	Do you know whether it gets hot in space?
In indirect *yes/no* questions with a modal, *if* or *whether* is added.	Can people live on Mars?	Could you explain if people can live on Mars?

A Use direct questions to complete the indirect questions about travel to Mars.

1 Who will go from Earth to Mars? Do you know ________________?
2 Is it a one-way trip? Can you tell us ________________?
3 How long does it take to get to Mars? Do you have any idea ________________?
4 Can people on Mars grow their own food? Do you know ________________?
5 How did you become interested in Mars? Can you tell us ________________?
6 Have you ever seen a spacecraft? Could you please tell us ________________?

UNIT 9 — *so, such, too, enough*

Function

Words like *so*, *such*, *too*, and *enough* are used to add emphasis and to indicate degree.

Form

Form and Use	Example
Use *so* + adjective/adverb to mean "very."	It was so kind of you to publish my story.
Use *such* + (article) + adjective + noun to mean "very."	That is such great work! That was such an interesting story.
Use *too* + adjective/adverb to say there is more than is needed.	The print in this newspaper is too small.
Use adjective/adverb + *enough* to say there is the right amount.	The vocabulary in this news article is easy enough.
Use *not* + adjective/adverb + *enough* to say there is less than is needed.	Those sources are not reliable enough.

A Choose the correct option.

It may be **1 too / enough** early to say that traditional news is dead, but things are changing **2 so / such** fast. Journalism is **3 so / such** an amazing field to work in, and I am **4 so / too** proud to work in print media. But our paper is not big **5 such / enough** to survive the competition from citizen journalists. It's becoming **6 too / enough** hard. We traditional journalists simply cannot get our stories out fast **7 too / enough**. I hope most of us will survive **8 such / enough** hard times.

B Complete the sentences with words from the box.

enough so such too

1 Fake news is ______________ a big problem these days.
2 Sometimes it is ______________ hard to tell real news from fake news.
3 Many people believe what they read much ______________ easily.
4 Some people are not critical ______________ of what they read or hear.

UNIT 9 — modals of deduction

Function

Making a deduction means using the information available to guess or draw a conclusion about something. Modals of deduction include *must*, *could*, *might*, *may*, and *can't*. We use these modals to express how sure we are about something in the present.

Form

Form and Use	Example
Use *must* + verb when you are very sure that something is true because there is strong evidence for it.	That story must be true. The author is well known and always trustworthy.
Use *may* / *might* / *could* + verb when you think something is possibly true, but there is not enough evidence to be certain.	That story may/might/could be fake. There isn't a source and the writing seems very biased.
Use *can't* + verb when you are very sure that something is not true because there is strong evidence against it.	That story can't be true. Every story on this website has already been proven to be fake.

A Match the sentence halves to make deductions.

1 Pedro slept only an hour last night. He ______
2 Diana owns six cars. She ______
3 Bianca got 100% on her exam. She ______
4 Bryan isn't at his desk. He ______
5 Caroline is wiping her eyes. She ______
6 Kendra is out of the country now. That ______
7 Eric just ate a big lunch. He ______
8 Victor just moved to this city. He ______

a can't be hungry again.
b might be at home.
c could be upset about something.
d can't know many people yet.
e must have a lot of money.
f must be tired.
g can't be her.
h must be happy.

B Choose the correct option.

1 Tim is a professional soccer player. He **must** / **may** be in great shape.
2 There's something bright in the sky. It **must** / **could** be a spaceship.
3 My phone battery **must** / **can't** be dead. I just charged it 10 minutes ago.
4 You **must** / **can't** know David. You were in the same class together.
5 My car won't start. It **must** / **may** not have enough gas.
6 I can't find Eduardo anywhere. He **might** / **can't** be at home.

UNIT 10 — reported speech: statements

Function

When we report what someone says using a verb in the past, the tense of the reported sentence often shifts to one of the past tenses.

Form

Tense shift in reported statements	Direct statement	Reported statement
simple present ➔ simple past	Josh has a lot of talent.	She said (that) Josh had a lot of talent.
present progressive ➔ past progressive	Allie is playing the drums.	He told me (that) Allie was playing the drums.
simple past ➔ past perfect	Mark auditioned for the part.	They stated (that) Mark had auditioned for the part.
present perfect ➔ past perfect	Cecile has not been on TV before.	She admitted (that) Cecile had not been on TV before.
future with *will* ➔ *would*	Ina will win the competition.	They predicted (that) Ina would win the competition.

A Read the situation and complete the sentences using reported speech.

You missed the planning meeting for the school talent show. Your friend Sheila attended and told you what people said.

1 Tina is thinking about doing a comedy routine. Sheila said that ______________________
2 Les and Dina are very nervous. She explained that ______________________.
3 Maya has performed in Europe. She mentioned that ______________________.
4 Greg has been practicing his routine nonstop. She stated that ______________________.
5 Sebastian performed a modern dance. She told me that ______________________.
6 Ken and Suzie will compete as a couple. She mentioned that ______________________.
7 Antonia wants to make her parents proud. She said that ______________________.
8 Greg and Maya will tie for the win. She predicted that ______________________.

UNIT 10 — reported speech: questions

Function

As in reporting sentences, when reporting questions the tense in the reported question often shifts to the past. For reported questions, include the *wh-* question word for information questions and add *if* or *whether* for *yes/no* questions. The information after the *wh-* word or *if/whether* follows the word order of a statement, not a question. Note that the pronouns often need to change in reported questions.

Form

Direct information questions	Reported questions
She asked me, "When did you graduate?"	She asked me when I had graduated.
He asked her, "What have you recorded?"	He asked her what she had recorded.
Direct *yes/no* questions	**Reported questions**
He asked me, "Do you have any advice?"	He asked me if/whether I had any advice.
She asked us, "Will you ever retire?"	She asked us if/whether we would ever retire.

A Rewrite the direct questions as reported questions. Be sure to change the pronouns if needed.

1. Sarah asked him, "What did you enjoy most?"
   Sarah asked him ________________.
2. Kevin asked Wendy, "Did you watch the competition?"
   Kevin asked her ________________.
3. Jesse asked Mia, "Have you ever sung live before?"
   Jesse asked her ________________.
4. Anita asked Antonio, "How long have you had a band?"
   Anita asked him ________________.
5. We asked Lila, "Will you do magic tricks?"
   We asked her ________________.
6. Sam asked me, "Do you have much experience?"
   Sam asked me ________________.
7. I asked Jeff, "How many instruments do you play?"
   I asked him ________________.
8. Pete asked Nina, "Who is your greatest inspiration?"
   Peter asked her ________________.

UNIT 11 — causatives with *have, get,* and *make*

Function

We use causative verbs such as *have*, *get*, and *make* to talk about things that someone else does for us or for another person. This includes paying, asking, or persuading the person to do it.

Form

Form and Use	Example
Use *have/get* + (object) + past participle to talk about paying or asking someone to do something for you.	I often have/get my house cleaned when I'm at work.
Use *make* + (person) + base form of the verb when you force or persuade someone to do something.	She makes her children do chores around the house.
Use *have* + (person) + base form of the verb to talk about someone who does a job for you.	We have a mechanic check our car once a month.
Use *get* + (person) + infinitive when you ask, persuade, or pay someone to do something for you.	He usually gets his mother to cut his hair for him.

A Read Kyle's to-do list for the week. Choose the correct option.

1 Get my sister **to drive** / **drove** me to the post office.
2 Have Abigail **look** / **looked** over my English essay.
3 Get someone **to give** / **gave** me feedback on my website.
4 Have my computer **to check** / **checked** for viruses.
5 Get my old watch **fix** / **fixed** at the mall.
6 Have Ben **take** / **took** a new passport picture for me.
7 Make my roommate **clean** / **to clean** his room.
8 Have new software **install** / **installed** on my computer.

B Complete the sentences with the correct form of the words in parentheses.

1 I want to ____________________. (have / my hair / cut) at a beauty salon.
2 Do you know where I can ____________________ (get / my jacket / clean)?
3 Is it expensive to ____________________ (have / someone / shop) for you?
4 My older sister sometimes ____________________ (make / me / do) the housework for her.
5 Mr. Chan usually ____________________ (make / his son / shop) for groceries.
6 It's a good idea to ____________________ (get / your teeth / check) every six months.
7 I like to ____________________ (have / my friends / tell) me if my clothes don't look good on me.
8 You shouldn't ____________________ (get / your little brother / do) your chores.

UNIT 11 — verbs with gerund, infinitive, or both

Function

Some verbs are followed by an infinitive (*to* + base form of verb). Some verbs are followed by a gerund (verb *–ing*). Some verbs are followed by either form.

Form

Use	Examples
Some verbs are followed by infinitives.	She offered to help out at the rescue center. Other verbs: *agree, decide, manage, plan, promise, refuse, volunteer, want*
Some verbs are followed by gerunds.	She enjoys teaching life skills to new immigrants. Other verbs: *avoid, dislike, consider, delay, finish, miss, practice, recommend*
Verbs that describe feelings can be followed by both gerunds and infinitives.	They would love to work on a cruise ship. They would love working on a cruise ship. Other verbs: *dislike, hate, like, prefer*

A Write if the verb is followed by an infinitive (*I*), a gerund (*G*), or both (*B*).

1 consider ______
2 want ______
3 like ______
4 continue ______
5 promise ______
6 recommend ______
7 finish ______
8 agree ______
9 manage ______
10 hate ______
11 prefer ______
12 miss ______

B Complete the sentences with the infinitive or gerund form of the verb in parentheses. If both forms are possible, write both.

1 This website recommends ______________________ (give) donations through charities.
2 I would really like ______________________ (volunteer) with an animal shelter.
3 Have you ever considered ______________________ (donate) money to a zoo?
4 My parents promised ______________________ (take) me out for a celebration dinner after I graduate.
5 His mother avoids ______________________ (use) her credit card for small purchases.
6 Why did you decide ______________________ (become) a financial planner?
7 Maeve continued ______________________ (work) until she was 75 years old.
8 How do you manage ______________________ (save) money on such a small salary?

UNIT 12 — passive voice: other tenses

Function

The passive voice is used to focus on who or what receives an action rather than the agent of the action. It makes writing more impersonal and formal.

Form

Form	Active statements	Passive statements
Simple present passive: subject + *is/are* + past participle	Companies spend billions of dollars on advertising every year.	Billions of dollars are spent on advertising every year.
Present progressive passive: subject + *is/are being* + past participle	Companies are advertising more products through pop-up computer ads.	More products are being advertised through pop-up computer ads.
Simple past passive: subject + *was/were* + past participle	The company developed a new ad.	A new ad was developed by the company.
Present perfect passive: subject + *has/have been* + past participle	People have criticized the ad because of its negative images.	The ad has been criticized because of its negative images.
Past perfect passive: subject + *had been* + past participle	Governments had banned the commercial in over 60 countries.	The commercial had been banned in over 60 countries.

A Choose the correct option.

Got Milk? was a famous US ad campaign. The first Got Milk? ad **1 is** / **was** shown in 1993. In 2002, that ad **2 was** / **has been** named one of the best commercials of all time. Since then, it **3 has** / **had** been featured in books on advertising and case studies. It **4 is** / **was** being studied by students of marketing to this day. Over the years, many famous celebrities **5 was** / **were** featured in the campaign. By the time the campaign **6 was** / **has been** discontinued, it **7 was being** / **had been** seen by hundreds of millions of people. The campaign **8 has** / **have** been credited with greatly increasing milk sales.

B Rewrite the active sentences in the passive voice. Do not include the person or thing that performs the action in your sentence.

1 People criticized the company's ads. ______________________
2 They have called the ads offensive. ______________________
3 The company has now discontinued the ads. ______________________
4 The company lost a lot of money. ______________________
5 The company is using different ads now. ______________________

UNIT 12 — comparative and superlative adverbs

Function

We can use comparative and superlative adverbs to describe changes or make comparisons between things.

Form

Form	Adverb	Comparative	Superlative
Adverbs ending in *–ly*	quickly	more quickly (than)	the most quickly
Adverbs with the same form as the adjective	hard	harder (than)	the hardest
	late	later (than)	the latest
	fast	faster (than)	the fastest
Irregular adverb forms	often	more often (than)	the most often
	well	better (than)	the best
	badly	worse (than)	the worst

A Complete the sentences with the comparative form of the adverb in parentheses.

1 I think viewers will remember the new slogan ________________ (easily).
2 Focused online ads appear ________________ (often) than they used to.
3 The magazine ad did ________________ (badly) than the TV ad.
4 The people at our ad company are working ________________ (hard) now that we have more competition.
5 Can you check the text of these ads ________________ (carefully) next time?
6 This ad with child actors tested ________________ (well) than the one with adult actors.
7 This new software will allow you to edit film ________________ (quickly).
8 The focus group results came in much ________________ (late) than we wanted.

B Choose the correct option.

1 Paul drives **the most careless** / **the most carelessly** of anyone in my family.
2 Janet sings **the best** / **the better** of anyone in her choir.
3 Greg gave to charity **the more generous** / **the most generously** of everyone in the office.
4 Celia played soccer **the worse** / **the worst** of all our team.
5 Bradley works **the hardest** / **the most hard** of all the engineers in his company.
6 Of all the managers, Francesca stays **the latest** / **the later** in the office.

Macmillan Education
4 Crinan Street
London N1 9XW
A division of Macmillan Education Limited

Companies and representatives throughout the world

Speak Your Mind Level 3 Student's Book ISBN 978-1-380-03141-9
Speak Your Mind Level 3 Student's Book + access to Student's App
ISBN 978-1-380-03134-1
Speak Your Mind Level 3 Student's Book + access to Student's App
and Digital Workbook ISBN 978-1-380-03135-8

Written by Mickey Rogers, Joanne Taylore-Knowles and Steve Taylore-Knowles

The authors have asserted their right to be identified as the authors of this work in accordance with the Copyright, Designs and Patents Act 1988.

First published 2020

Designed by QBS Learning
Illustrated by QBS Learning pp. 13, 19, 41, 112; Judit Tondora (Astound) pp. 92, 125.
Cover design by therestless.co.uk
Cover adaptation by Roberto Martínez
Cover photographs by **Getty Images**/Chatuporn Sornlampoo/EyeEm (background); **Shutterstock**/Aaron Amat (lower body), Shutterstock/REALDEE (window), Shutterstock/ShotPrime Studio (upper body-blazer), Shutterstock/szefei (upper body).
Picture research by Fernanda Rocha/Ikonia LLC

Authors' acknowledgements
Mickey, Jo and Steve would like to thank everyone at Macmillan Education and RedNova Learning who have made this project possible and who have gone the extra mile (literally!) to meet up, work together, and throw around a million ideas, some of which even made their way into the books! Jo and Steve would also like to thank Scout for her patience and understanding and for letting her parents get on with it when they needed to!

The publishers would like to thank all the teachers that piloted and reviewed the series.

The authors and publishers would like to thank the following for permission to reproduce their photographs:
Alamy Stock Photo/Peter Casolino p. 20(dog handler), Alamy Stock Photo/Chronicle p. 58(cbr), Alamy Stock Photo/paul cox p. 74(b), Alamy Stock Photo/Harriet Cummings p. 82(6), Alamy Stock Photo/GL Archive p. 62(d), Alamy Stock Photo/Tetra Images, LLC p. 114(cr), Alamy Stock Photo/Thierry GRUN p. 20(wildlife photographer), Alamy Stock Photo/imageBROKER p. 20(zookeeper), Alamy Stock Photo/Images by Itani p. 52(a), Alamy Stock Photo/Pictorial Press Ltd p. 68(tl), Alamy Stock Photo/Pixsooz p. 76, Alamy Stock Photo/Porky Pies Photography p. 65(tr), Alamy Stock Photo/Alexandra Radu p. 110(1), Alamy Stock Photo/Bulat Silvia p. 45(b), Alamy Stock Photo/Flo Smith p. 114(tl), Alamy Stock Photo/Stocktrek Images, Inc. p. 68(cl), Alamy Stock Photo/Terry Whittaker Wildlife p. 20(zoologist), Alamy Stock Photo/Arman Zhenikeyev p. 20(horse trainer); **Getty Images** p. 95, Getty Images/AFP/Stringer p. 52(b), Getty Images/AFP/ROBIN UTRECHT/Contributor p. 98(?), Getty Images/AzmanJaka p. 22(cr), Getty Images/Ezra Bailey p. 136, Getty Images/ChristopherBernard p. 67, Getty Images/Bettmann/Contributor p. 98(?), Getty Images/ullstein bild/Contributor pp. 12, 62(b), Getty Images/Boston Globe/Contributor p. 8, Getty Images/Busà Photography p. 70(4), Getty Images/Caiaimage/Paul Bradbury p. 58(ctr), Getty Images/Caiaimage/Sam Edwards p. 102, Getty Images/Vitalij Cerepok/EyeEm p80(cl), Getty Images/DjelicS p. 72, Getty Images/martin-dm p. 70(5), Getty Images/elvira boix photography p. 107, Getty Images/Christian Ender/Contributor p. 6, Getty Images/filadendron p. 29, Getty Images/Maciej Frolow p. 60(f), Getty Images/Jure Gasparic/EyeEm p. 60(d), Getty Images/GK Hart/Vikki Hart p. 20(vet/veterinarian), Getty Images/harpazo_hope p. 94(?), Getty Images/Kauko Helavuo p. 134, Getty Images/Heritage Images/Contributor p. 10(l), Getty Images/Hero Images pp. 85(Martin), 94(cr), Getty Images/Tom Hoenig, Red Chopsticks Images p. 91(b), Getty Images/Gary Hofheimer p. 78(A-br), Getty Images/Image by cuppyuppycake p. 17, Getty Images/JackF p. 22(j), Shutterstock/Jet Shopping Media p. 96(br), Getty Images/Thanagon Karaket/EyeEm p. 60(b-notebook), Getty Images/Clodagh Kilcoyne/Contributor p. 62(a), Getty Images/Keith Ladzinski p. 7, Getty Images/Lucy Lambriex p. 114(tr), Getty Images/Josh Liba p. 118, Getty Images/Mikolette p. 39, Getty Images/Tara Moore pp. 28, 88, Getty Images/Harald Nachtmann p. 66, Getty Images/Richard Newstead p. 50, Getty Images/NoDerog p. 94(br),Getty Images/Dennis O'Clair p. 37, Getty Images/Pekic p. 25, Getty Images/PeopleImages pp. 31, 106, Shutterstock/Richard Peterson p. 101, Getty Images/AndreyPopov p. 60(a), Getty Images/MediaProduction p. 110(3), Getty Images/Mondadori Portfolio/Contributor p. 62(c), Getty Images/National Geographic Image Collection/Steve Winter p. 65(tl), Getty Images/Photographer is my life p. 70(2), Getty Images/Popperfoto/Contributor p. 96(cr), Getty Images/Roberto Ricciuti/Contributor p. 10(r), Getty Images/Christina Sarmiento/EyeEm p. 24, Getty Images/sbayram p. 22(c), Getty Images/serts p. 42(tr), Getty Images/shylendrahoode p. 110(5), Getty Images/John S Lander/Contributor p. 52(g), Getty Images/Douglas Sacha p. 82(2), Getty Images/shaifulzamri p. 94(tr), Getty Images/Sovfoto/Contributor p. 63, Getty Images/stevecoleimages p. 70(6), Getty Images/Mark Stevenson/Stocktrek Images p. 78(b-composite), Getty Images/Stocktrek Images p. 78(A-bl), Getty Images/Ibrahim Suha Derbent p. 22(d), Getty Images/Alexander Spatari p. 52(h), Getty Images/Chase Swift p. 21, Getty Images/talevr p. 60(e), Getty Images/Rainer von Brandis p. 20(marine biologist), Getty Images/vovashevchuk p. 110(4), Getty Images/Klaus Vedfelt p. 40, Getty Images/vusta p. 22(e), Getty Images/warrengoldswain p. 108(tr), Getty Images/Westend61 pp. 23, 26, 77, 85(Ari), 128, Getty Images/Wilfred Y Wong p. 52(d), Getty Images/10'000 Hours p. 45(m); **PhotoDisc**/Getty Images pp. 80(cr), 86; **Shutterstock**/New Africa p. 110(2), Shutterstock/Africa Studio pp. 82(4), 15(7), Shutterstock/Edgar Airborne p. 14(b), Shutterstock/Alexxndr p. 137, Shutterstock/Aaron Amat p. 44, Shutterstock/AnnaElizabeth photography p. 73(tl), Shutterstock/Papa Annur p. 52(f), Shutterstock/ArchMan p. 22(g), Shutterstock/baranq pp. 126, 138, Shutterstock/Gyorgy Barna pp. 46, 130,Shutterstock/R.Bordo p. 117(composite), Shutterstock/Bilanol p. 82(5), Shutterstock/Rich Carey p22(f), Shutterstock/Castleski p. 90, Shutterstock/Thomas Cooper p. 78(A-tm), Shutterstock/Steve Cukrov p. 52(e),Shutterstock/dotshock p. 85(Asha), Shutterstock/MikeDotta p. 78(A-tr), Shutterstock/Everett Collection p. 100, Shutterstock/Iakov Filimonov p. 20(breeder), Shutterstock/flower travelin' man pp. 42(1-7), 43(emojis), Shutterstock/fotohunter pp. 64-65(b), Shutterstock/FrameStockFootages p. 104, Shutterstock/Elizaveta Galitckaia p. 124, Shutterstock/Georgejmclittle p. 141, Shutterstock/Herschel Hoffmeyer p. 78(A-bm), Shutterstock/HomeStudio p. 15(3), Shutterstock/ImageFlow p. 60(c-background), Shutterstock/Eric Isselee pp. 22(a, i), Shutterstock/Alexsander Iusupov p. 60(b-background), Shutterstock/Budimir Jevtic p. 82(1), Shutterstock/AlenKadr p. 131, Shutterstock/Anan Kaewkhammul p. 22(h), Shutterstock/KENG MERRY Paper Art pp. 54-55(b), Shutterstock/Klepach p. 54(cl), Shutterstock/plew koonyosying p. 52(c), Shutterstock/Jacob Lund p. 32(cr), Shutterstock/marylooo p. 15(4), Shutterstock/Natee Meepian p. 115, Shutterstock/Mega Pixel pp. 36, 129, Shutterstock/metamorworks p. 82(3), Shutterstock/Microgen p. 132, Shutterstock/MITstudio p. 120(cm), Shutterstock/MK photograp55 p. 78(b-composite), Shutterstock/Nadino p. 85(Susana, Claudia), Shutterstock/Nika Novak p. 91(d), Shutterstock/Camila Paez p. 73(cl), Shutterstock/pbk-pg p. 70(1), Shutterstock/Phonlamai Photo p. 30, Shutterstock/photokirov p. 15(8), Shutterstock/Pixel-Shot p. 94, Shutterstock/pogonici p. 16, Shutterstock/Bob Pool p. 74(cl), Shutterstock/Mike Price p. 22(b), Shutterstock/wattana racha p. 135, Shutterstock/Rawpixel.com p. 45(t), Shutterstock/Valentina Razumova pp. 122(r, l), Shutterstock/restyler p. 15(1), Shutterstock/Michael Rosskothen p. 78(A-tl), Shutterstock/Alex Ruhl p. 117(composite), Shutterstock/Dmitry Rukhlenko p. 64(cr), Shutterstock/RyFlip p. 108(br), Shutterstock/Sensay p. 57, Shutterstock/Sergey85 p. 120(cr), Shutterstock/Yuri Shevtsov p. 105, Shutterstock/Siberian Photographer p. 127, Shutterstock/SmileStudio p. 133, Shutterstock/spacezerocom p. 91(a), Shutterstock/SSokolov p. 47, Shutterstock/Anton Starikov p. 15(5), Shutterstock/Vladyslav Starozhylov p. 91(c), Shutterstock/StockLite p. 38, Shutterstock/takoburito p. 74(background), Shutterstock/Thawornnurak p. 42(tl), Shutterstock/Tortoon p. 125, Shutterstock/Alex Tuzhikov p. 60(c-hammock), Shutterstock/u3d p. 84, Shutterstock/Vagengeim p. 97, Shutterstock/vectorfusionart p. 34, Shutterstock/vetkit p. 125(background), Shutterstock/Vik Y p. 120(cl), Shutterstock/Praiwan Wasanruk p. 32(br), Shutterstock/Waj p. 14(t), Shutterstock/wavebreakmedia p. 56, Shutterstock/Micha Weber p. 140, Shutterstock/White Space Ukraine p. 15(2), Shutterstock/Gayvoronskaya_Yana p. 116, Shutterstock/Yellowj p. 60(b-shower), Shutterstock/Yeti studio p. 15(6), Shutterstock/Monster Ztudio p. 87, Shutterstock/2p2play p. 92; **123RF**/axsimen p. 42(tc), 123RF/Mathee Boonphrom p. 48, 123RF/ferli p. 108(tl), 123RF/iriana88w p. 70(3), 123RF/kampwit p. 20(cr), 123RF/Tyler Olson p. 108(tm), 123RF/sellphoto1 p. 18.

Additional sources:
p. 24, "Abandoned Dogs Roam Detroit in Packs as Humans Dwindle" by Chris Christoff, August 21, 2013, Bloomberg website. p. 28, "Measuring Consumer Information" by Roger Bohn and James E. Short, 2012, *International Journal of Communication*, Vol. 6, pp. 980–1000. p. 40, "Is Nonverbal Communication a Numbers Game?" by Jeff Thompson, September 30, 2011, *Psychology Today* website referencing Mehrabian, A. (1972). *Nonverbal Communication.* New Brunswick: Aldine Transaction. p. 40, "What 'Personal Space' Looks Like around the World" by Amanda Erickson, April 24, 2017, *The Washington Post* website. p. 42, "The Number of Emails Sent per Day in 2019 (and 20+ Other Email Facts)" by Henry Tschabitscher, January 3, 2019, *Lifewire* website. p. 42, "Number of Mobile Phone Users Worldwide from 2015 to 2020" by Statista, November 2016, Statista website. p. 42, Data from Appfigures, Appfigures website, 2018. p. 42, Data from WhatsApp, WhatsApp Blog website, 2018. p. 42, "Number of Daily Active Snapchat Users from 1st Quarter 2014 to 3rd Quarter 2018" by Statista, October 2018, Statista website. p. 46, "Digital Advertising to Surpass Print and TV for the First Time, Report Says" by Hamza Shaban, February 20, 2019, *The Washington Post* website. p. 46, Internet World Stats website, May 9, 2019. p. 48, "IPCC Press Release #2018/24/PR" by Intergovernmental Panel on Climate Change, October 8, 2018, IPCC website. p. 98, "Musical Talent is Rooted in the Genes, Study of Twins Suggests" by Jillian Rose Lim, August 11, 2014, *Huffington Post.* p. 98, "Practice May NOT Make Perfect: Innate Talent is What's Required for Greatness in Areas Such as Games or Music" by Emma Innes, May 21, 2013, *Daily Mail* website. p. 98, Gladwell, Malcolm. (2008). *Outliers: The Story of Success,* Little, Brown and Company. p. 104, "Remembering How Reality TV Talent Shows First Got Started" by Bill Lucey, June 14, 2011, *The Morning Delivery* website. p. 116, "Cramming for Exams? Join the Crowd" by Justin Gerwick, June 4, 2014, *The Hawkeye.*

Printed and bound in Brazil

2024
35